THE NPR INTERVIEWS 1996

THE NPR INTERVIEWS 1996

EDITED AND

WITH AN

INTRODUCTION

BY ROBERT SIEGEL

HOUGHTON MIFFLIN COMPANY

BOSTON • NEW YORK 1996

For information about permission to reproduce
selections from this book, write to
Permissions, Houghton Mifflin Company,
215 Park Avenue South, New York,
New York 10003.

For information about this and other Houghton Mifflin
trade and reference books and multimedia products,
visit The Bookstore at Houghton Mifflin on the
World Wide Web at http://www.hmco.com/trade/.

ISSN 1078-1211
ISBN 0-395-78323-2 (PBK.)

Printed in the United States of America

QUM 10 9 8 7 6 5 4 3 2 1

Book design by Robert Overholtzer

CREDITS

CONTENTS

RELIGION

THE STORY OF THE YEAR: TERRORISM

MUSIC

THE WORLD

ANNIVERSARIES

Sports

Washington

America Talking

Enders

INTRODUCTION

WHY READ RADIO? The sound is gone, the infinite textures of the human voice fade on flat paper. Listen here for the nervous titter of the Dalai Lama, the feline seductiveness of Eartha Kitt, the brisk military manner of Colin Powell, and you will listen in vain. Those traits have all deserted the text, leaving behind only words. And therein lies the value: the words. In the course of preparing *The NPR Interviews* series, I have become an avid reader of radio, savoring these distilled versions of interviews from National Public Radio's News and Information magazine programs: *Morning Edition, All Things Considered,* and *Weekend Edition.* They are a record of what people said and how they said it in the year 1995, and their words are full of truths and surprises.

Reading this real-life dialogue is a reminder of how much we reveal about ourselves in our best stories: not just the confessional interviews with artists or campaigning politicians, but the interpretations of O. J. Simpson's acquittal offered by Harlemites, or the verdicts rendered by Kansas City suburbanites on the debut of the Republican Congress. Such talks with ordinary Americans about the stuff of headlines reveal how we assimilate the world, measure our progress in it, and express ourselves about it.

A World War II veteran and former prisoner of war recounts his escape at the war's end, and his tale is as gripping as a novelist's rendering. A survivor of the Oklahoma City blast describes her escape from the Alfred P. Murrah Federal Office Building, and the terror of the day is palpable. The couple captured by the photographer Alfred Eisenstadt in the century's most famous kiss are reunited fifty years later, and they reflect on that fleeting encounter and exchange news of the real lives that preceded it and ensued. We ask people to tell their stories on NPR, and hearing them the first time can be moving, amusing, or inspiring. Reading them for the first time can be affecting, and reading them again, digesting their recollections, is doubly so.

I am forever struck in assembling these collections by the similarities linking what appear to be disparate conversations. In the "Music" chapter, for example, three women singers all credit a middle school teacher with inspiring them to perform or to pursue their singing in school. That they should be an operatic mezzo-soprano, a folksinger, and a jazz singer seems incidental to the common experience of a talented youth receiving the decisive guidance of a teacher. Equally, two writers interviewed separately in the "Arts and Letters" chapter, Isabel Allende and Delia Ephron, describe the act of writing as a means of coping with the death of a loved one, a daughter in one case, a father in another. To me, there is also a wonderful resonance in a most unlikely pair of interviews, Linda Wertheimer's talk with the writer William Maxwell and mine with the artist Maurice Sendak. Maxwell sensitively describes the accessibility of a lifetime of memories, the freedom of old age to wander mentally through the house of his childhood, inspecting it and taking inventory. Sendak hilariously confesses that the bulbous-nosed creatures of his illustrations are the relatives who promised, threatened, him as a child, "I'm going to eat you up." They have appeared in disguise as the Wild Things, he says, and they now take center stage, unconcealed as the dancing Miami Giants. In the text of that interview, you cannot hear how much Sendak made me laugh, but the words should suffice to inspire laughter anew.

There are some changes in this third annual volume, three new chapters. The music interviews, which in the past I included in the "Arts and Letters" chapter, are now in a category by themselves. These interviews with performers and composers, typically embellished with the music under discussion, are a hallmark feature of NPR programs. The practiced public radio listener can imagine the Joni Mitchell Studio 4A performance that is absent from the transcribed version of Liane Hansen's interview, or the fade-in of a recorded Natalie Merchant vocal at precisely the moment that Linda Wertheimer inquires about it. Such moments are the stuff of vivid radio and impossible to replicate here. But there remain the words, Joni Mitchell recalling her youth in Canada, Merchant explaining her need for self-renewal, and those words make compelling reading, even without musical accompaniment.

"Anniversaries" is the second new chapter, an acknowledgment that NPR marks a great many historic milestones with interviews that are remembrances. This year's collection includes, among others, interviews related to the fiftieth anniversary of the end of the Second World War and a terrific childhood recollection of watching Charles Lindbergh take off from Long Island. The third new chapter is devoted to sports and includes interviews that, in previous volumes, I would have shoehorned into the "America Talking" or "Enders" chapters. I confess to a special fondness for this new chapter, as it includes my favorite interview among those that I conducted throughout the year, with Y. A. Tittle and his daughter, Diane Tittle de Laet. As the Welsh baritone Bryn Terfel says in another context, "I affiliate myself wholly" to this interview, as a football fan, as a proud father of two daughters, and as a man who has lost much of his hair.

"The Story of the Year" is "Terrorism." With the cold war safely over, and no great global conflict threatening to succeed it, our most dangerous enemies became tiny sects, cults, and terror cells often armed with weapons simple to manufacture and deploy against civilians, and capable of enormous destruction. The year 1995 witnessed a nerve gas attack on the Tokyo subway, bombings in Israel, and the truck bombing in Oklahoma City. Interviews about all these events capture the challenge that calculated political violence poses to our security, and our hopes for a peaceful and reasonable world.

In this year's collection, the personnel are all, I hope, familiar. Linda, Noah Adams, and I hosted weekday *All Things Considered*, while Daniel Zwerdling was the weekend host; Jacki Lyden appeared occasionally as his substitute. Scott Simon and Liane Hansen hosted *Weekend Edition Saturday* and *Sunday*, respectively. Susan Stamberg and Neal Conan filled in for Scott. Bob Edwards, with Neal or Alex Chadwick filling in from time to time, remained the host and anchor of *Morning Edition*.

Every interview reprinted here reflects the effort not only of an interviewer, but of a booker, a recording engineer, an editor, a tape cutter, and often a research librarian who compiled a file for it. A simple and elegant result on the air reflects a complex, professional organization behind the scenes with many hands, all of whom deserve credit for this book. The staff of the National Public Radio Program Library made the task especially pleasant this year. My thanks to Denise Chen, Beth Howard, Katherine Plumb, Tom Tuszynski, and Robert Goldstein. In addition, this entire project would be impossible but for the efforts of Peter Jablow of NPR; Gail

Ross of Lichtman, Trister, Singer and Ross; and Wendy Holt and Wendy Strothman of Houghton Mifflin. Jayne Yaffe is, as ever, a thoughtful and meticulous manuscript editor, sensitive to the shortcomings of radio people, for whom spelling and punctuation are exotic skills. Deborah Sosin once again proofread the book with great thoroughness. Above all, I am grateful to Julia Redpath, who returned as research assistant and found time to put so much effort into this collection despite the demands of work on *All Things Considered.*

Finally, the decision to include some interviews and exclude others remains a subjective one, and to the extent that the selection is imperfect, my imperfections alone are responsible.

ARTS AND LETTERS

M AURICE SENDAK, the award-winning illustrator of such books as *Where the Wild Things Are* and *In the Night Kitchen*, claimed that he was warmly received at the NPR New York Bureau because our staff mistook him for the Italian novelist Umberto Eco. But Sendak was being modest about his own accomplishments. At the time, his activities included designing opera sets, drawing pictures for a new edition of a Melville novel, and illustrating a book called *The Miami Giant*. He was at the bureau to talk about a series of animated stories on Nickelodeon, the cable television channel. *Little Bear* is based on a set of children's books that Sendak had illustrated in the 1950s. The Nickelodeon series, like the original books, depicts a place where the wild things decidedly are not, where an infinitely patient and loving mother bear tends to her unfailingly lovable son. There is no hint of terror. Mr. Sendak told Robert Siegel that there was no place for such typical Sendak touches in this piece of Sendak animation. October 31, 1995

Sendak: I'm a careful illustrator, and the *Little Bear* text that Elsa Holmelund Minarik wrote was so exquisitely perfect, and it did not have surreal or dark corners. It was miraculously fresh and sunlit without being tacky or sentimental or foolish. I mean, she's a brilliant, brilliant writer. So it would have been completely inappropriate to have sneaked in surrealistic or dark little corners to a book that begged not to have dark little corners. I can shut those shadows off at will if the work is worth the effort, and *Little Bear* was absolutely worth the effort. I love the entire series. Now I'm very critical of the work I did when I was young. The *Little Bear* books stand on their own.

Siegel: Our highly unscientific market research here on the staff of *All Things Considered* found that two children who were five and seven and a half loved the Nickelodeon shows. A two-year-old and a three-year-old both found they couldn't quite follow it. But the kids five and seven just were delighted by it.

Sendak: Well, I'm glad, but to be blunt, I'm not so interested in that kind of information because it puts children in that awful space of being categorized into what ages will or what ages won't, and I've always defied that. I've always defied that from the beginning of my career. You can't do that to them any more than you can do it to us, and I don't know why we do it to them. I mean, kids have all the complicated and variable tastes that adults do, and often they'll say things because it's expected of them to like this because they're five, and they were put together in that room to watch that thing because they're five. It's fake. It's really fake. I remember a story I've repeated often of a library conference in New York City, and a woman stood up and said, "You know, I read *Where the Wild Things Are* to my daughter, and every time I read it to her, she puts her hand over her ears and screams." I was stunned. And I said, "Well, why are you torturing your child? Do you not like her? Would it not be easy to give her away to somebody who does like her?" And she said, "But it won the Caldecott. She's supposed to like it." There you go. Poor kid. She's probably in some home at this point.

Siegel: If the mother didn't take your suggestion to keep the book and give up the child.

Sendak: Exactly. It's a pretty good book. She obviously had a kid without much feeling.

Siegel: Well, now, talking about defying the expectations of what we like at various ages and how we react, I want to ask you about a book that you have illustrated called *The Miami Giant*, which at first glance appears to be, if you'll pardon the expression, a children's book, but I found here the ideal age for appreciating it seems to be somewhere between forty and fifty.

Sendak: [*laughing*] Well, you see, you're doing the same thing.

Siegel: Yes, I am.

Sendak: It's an inevitable thing. It's like Pavlov's dog. People think there's such a thing as just books for kids and then there are just books for grown-ups, and, in truth, there are in some cases. No kid is going to read *Moby Dick*. But in point of fact, it's a very kind of ambivalent line, an uncertain line, and I've been struggling and fighting against it, and so is Arthur Yorinks, who's a good personal friend of mine and my partner in a children's theater venture. And we have known each other for more than two decades and for various reasons decided not to do a book together, but then it suddenly struck us both — why not? Arthur writes hilariously funny books. I don't. I can't. So why not join forces? And I read *The Miami Giant*, and I fell on the floor. I mean, it's so absurdly funny and clever. And of course, people will say, "Oh, well, but will kids get this?" And they will or they won't. Some will like it, some will not like it. Some will get things that adults will never even see. That I know for a fact from forty years of letters from children. It's amazing what they see. So this cross thing doesn't worry me at all.

Siegel: The story, I should say, is the story of a fictional contemporary of Columbus's who, while setting out to sail to China, instead discovers Miami and the race of giants who live and dance there. Now, there's a character in this book who's one of the dancing giants. I'm looking at him right now. He has a mustache beneath a rather broad, bulbous nose, head somewhat flat, and he's squinting a bit, and he looks a lot like those people in the Night Kitchen, from another of your books. He looks a lot like a face that keeps on recurring in lots of your books. Who is that?

Sendak: Well, it's funny. I hadn't thought about him looking like anybody in *Night Kitchen*, but you're sort of right. Actually, they're all my relatives. The Wild Things were the original disguise of the relatives. I dislike my relatives intensely, and I didn't know until I was ten that I was supposed to love and respect them. It did not come naturally to me at all. And they were crude, and they spoke a foreign language, and they pinched, and all children are very arrogant and snotty about people eating up their food and coming to their house, although they're not supposed to say that about their uncles and aunts. So I took my vengeance on them in *Wild Things*.

Siegel: I see.

Sendak: But, see, they were still living then. Now, in *Miami Giant*, here they are, folks, just as they were. This is what they looked like, and there's even a lineup when Giaweeni, the Columbus, the explorer character, sees them for the first time, and they're sort of doing a conga. It's very much like a lineup in *Where the Wild Things Are*, except here they are in their *originalesche*.

Siegel: And this is the adult's revenge for a thousand pinched cheeks by aunts and uncles?

For forty years, WILLIAM MAXWELL edited other writers' fiction for *The New Yorker* magazine while also writing his own. He has published six novels and three collections of short stories. At age eighty-six, he published *All the Days and Nights*, a collection of short fiction that includes a story from the 1930s and at least one from every decade since. The earlier stories, he told Linda Wertheimer, are simpler. "As you grow older," he said, "you do see things in a more complicated way." In addition to the short stories, there are twenty-one fables at the end of the book, which Maxwell calls "improvisations." February 8, 1995

Maxwell: Actually, they began because my wife liked to have me tell her stories when we were in bed in the dark before falling asleep. And I didn't know where they came from, but I just said whatever came into my head and sometimes I would fall asleep in the middle of a story and she would shake me, and say, "What happened next?" And I would struggle back into consciousness and tell her what happened next. And then I began to write them for occasions, for Christmas and birthdays and things like that. And I would sit down at the typewriter and empty my mind entirely and see what came out on the typewriter, and something always did. And from the first sentence, a story just unfolded.

Wertheimer: Why don't we take turns here and whet the appetite for these little fables because I want to ask you about these first sentences. I'll read one. [*reading*] "There was a man who had no enemies — only friends. He had a gift for friendship. When he met someone for the first time, he would look into the man or woman or child's eyes, and he never afterward mistook them for someone else. He was as kind as the day is long, and no one imposed on his kindness." And then you take the next one.

Maxwell: Yes. [*reading*] "There used to be, until roughly a hundred and fifty years ago, a country where nobody ever grew old and died. The gravestone, with its weathered inscription, the wreath on the door, the black armband, and the friendly reassuring smile of the undertaker were unknown there. This is not as strange as it first seems. You do not have to look very far to find a woman who does not show her age or a man who intends to live forever."

Wertheimer: I like that one a lot. Here, I'll read the next one. [*reading*] "Once upon a time there was a man who took his family to the seashore. They had a cottage on the ocean, and it was everything that a house by the ocean should be — sagging wicker furniture, faded detective stories, blue china, grass rugs, other people's belongings to reflect upon, and other people's pots and pans to cook with." Is the beginning of a story like this the most important thing?

Maxwell: Yes, there would be no story without it, and I am astonished that there always is a story, but first it has to come out of the absolutely empty mind. It's mysterious. I think it invokes the ancient storyteller because storytelling was once a profession, of course. And it is in direct contact with the unconscious mind, and I've never exerted any shaping influence upon it. Sometimes when I was done I would cut unnecessary words, but I never tried to reshape the story or make it into a different story.

Wertheimer: And it's a different process from writing the real short stories?

Maxwell: Yes, it is totally different. With real stories, I feel responsible. I feel that I must shape them to be plausible. I feel that they must have the breath of life, and I work like the devil over them. And these — no work is involved at all. I am really a kind of medium to which they appear.

Wertheimer: In this collection, there are stories that are older than I am. "Young Francis Whitehead" is the oldest story, published in 1939, and you return in the collection several times to the theme of young people separating themselves from their families and their families not understanding what their role is if their children and the young people are gone.

Maxwell: And the young people not really knowing either, but trying to find a way. I think it's part of an inevitable growing up, don't you?

Wertheimer: Mmm-hmm.

Maxwell: And very painful both to the children and to the families, and then fortunately they come back again when they get older, a reconciliation they face sometimes when women have children, sometimes when men go into middle age. Sooner or later, if there was love in the first place, there is reconciliation in the end.

Wertheimer: There's a little tiny story called "Love" that you wrote in 1983, but it was about a much earlier time, about a little boy whose schoolteacher dies of tuberculosis.

Maxwell: It was a very odd experience. It's the only story I ever wrote that wrote itself. I don't mean improvisations, which do write themselves, but a story. It was as if it had already been written in my mind because one sentence followed another and I saw no way of changing or improving it. And I just stood back, and said, "Well, I've had a breakthrough. Now I know how to write and things are going to be easier from now on." But I hadn't had a breakthrough. I didn't know any more about writing than I had before. It was just that that material, because it was way back in my boyhood, had settled itself in my mind into a permanent form and all I had to do was say it.

Wertheimer: You also write a fair amount about age.

Maxwell: I do think being an old man is the most interesting thing that's ever happened to me because of all sorts of strange experiences, and of the opening up of memory (which I expected), and of the enjoyment of life being progressively greater instead of diminished by age. That was a surprise. Memory is perhaps the most remarkable part of all because you live in the past, you live in the present, and you, like everyone, live in the future. Only when you're old, they pass so easily into each other without any effort at all so that the past is quite as real as the present, and the future is, of course, problematical, and that's interesting. But I have enjoyed good health and that has meant that life has continued to be interesting.

And I've also had one amazing experience in the night, in the dark, in bed. I suddenly was able to remember in detail the house I grew up in and left when I was twelve years old. And I went from room to room seeing things that I hadn't remembered for seventy years and more. And being able to look as if I were actually there, as if the house was actually there, I saw that level of the bookcase, I saw pictures, I saw empty rooms, I saw furniture, and could look at it as long as I wanted to. It was as if some shutter had slipped back in my mind and I had absolute, total memory of the past. And when

....

When her daughter lay comatose from what proved to be a fatal illness, ISABEL ALLENDE, the writer and niece of the late Chilean president Salvador Allende, sought the companionship of memories by writing an autobiography. In it, the fantastic characters of her family weave through lives of exile, estrangement, and passion. Critics called *Paula* the most direct, affecting, and powerful of Allende's books. Scott Simon spoke with the author of *The House of Spirits*, *The Infinite Plan*, and other novels about her memoir and about the experience that led her to write it. July 15, 1995

Simon: Let me ask you straight-out: Is it hard to enjoy the lavish critical praise this book has received, given the fact that it was your daughter's illness and death that occasioned it?

Allende: You know, I had a lot of confusion at the beginning. I didn't know if I really wanted to publish this. I wrote this book when Paula was sick. It started as a letter for her because I was convinced that she was going to wake up and maybe, at that point, she would need to know who she was, what had happened, who were all these people around her bed? Six months later, I learned that she would never wake up from the coma; she had severe brain damage. I went on writing, not for her anymore, but because I couldn't stop. After she died, I thought that I was going to die as well. I felt that my life had absolutely no purpose anymore. And my mother and the rest of the family convinced me that the only way that I could go through the mourning and get back on my feet was writing. And because I couldn't write anything else, I rewrote that long letter that I had written for Paula. And that is how this book was born. And I thought it was a sort of legacy for my son and my grandchildren, but not something to be published because I had not changed names or disguised anything. Everything was there. We were all very exposed.

Simon: I found myself laughing out loud so many times.

Allende: Well, but that is what life is about. It's about losses and pain and celebration, and I feel that this is not a sad book, and this is not a sad story. Of course, it's a tragic story of the untimely death of a young woman, but it's also a celebration of family, of relationships, of life. And our life is quite crazy. I come from a very weird family, and that's always great for a writer. I don't need to invent anything.

Simon: I have to ask you about a man who sounds like an extraordinary character, except you, in a funny way, have paid the high compliment of saying that he's so decent and has so much common sense that you never turned him into a character in one of your novels, and that's your stepfather.

Allende: Yes. The ugliest man in his generation. [*laughs*]

Simon: But he sounds like one of the most enjoyable, too.

Allende: Oh, yes. He's a wonderful character, wonderful. But, you know, my mother was a very beautiful woman, and when my father walked out of our lives and she was left a single mother with three kids, she had a lot of suitors. And all of them had something to offer, except the one that later became my stepfather, the one who won her heart. I could never understand why she chose him. Why? I mean, he was so ugly. He was a Catholic with four children in a country where there is no divorce. Can you imagine? And he had no money. There's absolutely no reason why she would marry this — sort of — green frog.

Simon: She loved him.

Allende: And he ended up being the most wonderful father and friend.

Simon: Could I get you to tell the story, in which you talk about him being a great grandfather, too, to Paula and your son, the story about how he had her convinced that he could turn the fountain in Lake Geneva on. He was a diplomat, we should explain.

Allende: He was a diplomat in Geneva, and when we went to visit him, Paula must have been two years old. And he convinced her, first, that he was the owner of Coca-Cola, and if anybody in the whole universe wanted to have a drink of Coke, they had to call him. So she learned to call into the United Nations building in French to ask for a drink of Coke. He also convinced her that the fountain in Lake Geneva was his, and he could order the fountain on or off. You know how Swiss are very precise about time, so he knew the schedule perfectly, and he would tell Paula, "Do you want the fountain right now?" Paula said, "Yeah, yeah." He said,

"No, well, you have to wait five minutes. I will tell you exactly when it will be on." And he would pretend that he was calling on the phone to order his slaves to turn on the fountain and at the precise instant that he would order it, it would come up. He also told her that he was a prince, and that he had descended directly from Jesus Christ. You know that Jesús is a very common name in Spanish, and so in order to prove this, he took Paula to the Catholic cemetery in Santiago where there is the tomb of a man called Jesús Huidobro. Huidobro was his family name. So he said that, "You see, Jesus belonged to my family." And Paula was totally convinced that she descended from Jesus Christ.

Simon: Oh, my. I should explain for our audience that he's also a man of great courage. After the coup that ousted your uncle, he also went into exile.

Allende: Yes. They had to leave with false passports and find refuge in other countries until, finally, they ended up in exile in Venezuela.

Simon: Some of the most revealing portions of the book, to me, are when you describe life in exile in Venezuela. And I must say, you know, over the years, there's that phrase that sometimes gets into people's official résumé — "in exile" — almost as if their life gets suspended. But, as you account for it in your personal story, of course, that's never true. Human lives never get suspended.

Allende: No.

Simon: But to live as an exile is a constant state of anxiety.

Allende: No. It's not. There is the anxiety that you cannot return to your country and that you're always looking back to the past, but if you are smart enough, you adapt and you realize that life continues, and you have to get back on your feet and go on working. However, I did not do that. My former husband did it. My children did it and many other people did it. I didn't. I was always hoping that I would go back. I never quite adapted. I never unpacked. I don't know what happened to me. I was hurting very much. It was a difficult time in my life. I don't know.

Simon: You did have — if you don't mind me asking, since you write about it — what I'll refer to as a romantic encounter with a musician.

Allende: I can't remember his name, gosh.

Simon: You seriously can't? I thought you were just being oblique.

Allende: [*laughs*]

Simon: You cad! You women, I knew it. I knew that was the case. She can't remember any of us.

Allende: [*laughs*] Well, I can't remember any. That's true. I have a very bad memory. On the other hand, it's not that I had that many. Please.

Simon: No, no, no. I didn't mean to say that. I liked the line you used on him to get him interested: "Oh, Che Guevara. He came to dinner at my house."

Allende: Oh, yeah. I always do that.

Simon: And the poor, pathetic fool was putty in your hands after that.

Allende: Yeah. You know there are two things that you can tell a man to have him eating out of the palm of your hand. You can say that Che Guevara had dinner with you, once. Or you can say, "Tell me your story." Get them talking. When they start talking about themselves, they think you're a really smart girl.

Simon: And, plus, you can store away a lot of good material that way, too.

Allende: Yeah. Oh, I married a man for his story.

Simon: Really? The gentleman you're married to now, out in San Francisco?

Allende: Yeah. He thinks I married him for the green card, but actually, that's not true. Because now I have the green card and I'm still married.

Simon: May I ask, when you write about what I'll refer to as that phase in Paula's life when she dies — it's some of the most affecting prose I have ever read, and I can't bring myself to quote from it or even ask you to do it; it's just too wrenching. Does the writing help you stand back from it a little?

Allende: Writing is always a joyful process, even when you're writing about something that is very painful. Just the fact that you stop, you go into a quiet place inside you, and you transform something that may be very painful into words, gives boundary to the pain. It sorts out the confusion. It helps you to understand, and, finally, to accept. So, in a way, writing about this was not so painful. The experience was, but the writing was always joyful. This was my therapy. This was my drug. I could do it because I could write.

The poems of YEHUDA AMICHAI are about love, war, and peace. They are also about the city where he has lived most of his life, Jerusalem. At age seventy-one, Amichai is Israel's most renowned poet. In an interview with Robert Siegel, he read his poem "God Takes Pity on Kindergarten Children," which Prime Minister Yitzhak Rabin recited in English translation as he accepted the Nobel Peace Prize. October 24, 1995

Amichai: [*reading*]

> God takes pity on kindergarten children,
> Less on schoolchildren.
> On grownups, He won't take pity anymore.
> He leaves them alone.
> Sometimes they have to crawl on all fours
> In the blazing sand,
> To get to the first aid station
> Dripping blood.
>
> Maybe He will take pity and cast His shadow
> On those who truly love
> As a tree on someone sleeping on the bench
> On a boulevard.
>
> Maybe we too will spend on them
> The last coins of favor
> Mother bequeathed us,
> So their bliss will protect us
> Now and in other days.

Siegel: In that poem that you just read, there is a line in the middle about how sometimes grown-ups must crawl through the blazing sand to the first-aid station. That seems to be a very Israeli moment in a poem, a moment saying "we have all been in war and we have all bled."

Amichai: Yes, and it also says something about God and human beings, that we all have pity on the small child. And the bigger they grow, the less we need to have pity. But certainly a grown-up man, a soldier at his full power, full strength, he needs more help than all the babies together.

Siegel: And a situation that a great many Israeli men have experienced.

Amichai: Oh yes, yes. I went through four wars, yes.

Siegel: How important is Jerusalem to you?

Amichai: Well, it's the place where I have lived about sixty years of my life. That's quite a lot. But it's a city filled with trouble and history and people killed for holy places, and I have a lot of things to grieve about that.

Siegel: You have written so many poems about Jerusalem, I'm wondering if you could read to us from some of them.

Amichai: I would like to read maybe one poem which has to do with Jerusalem being a tourist city. I actually use tourists to make my point that as much as I've been in wars and in quite tough units all the time, I still believe that the holiest of places is not worth the life of one man. "Tourists."

1

So condolence visits is what they're here for,
Sitting around at the Holocaust Memorial,
Putting on a serious face at the Wailing Wall
Laughing behind heavy curtains
In hotel rooms.
They get themselves photographed
With the important dead
At Rachel's tomb and Herzl's tomb
And up on Ammunition Hill.
They weep at the beautiful prowess of our boys,
Lust after our tough girls
And hang up their underwear
To dry quickly
In cool blue bathrooms.

2

Once I was sitting on the steps near the gate of David's Citadel, and I put down my two heavy baskets beside me. A group of tourists stood there around their guide, and I became their point of reference. "You see that man over there with the baskets? A little to the right of his head there's an arch from the Roman period. A little to the right of his head." "But he's moving, he's moving!" I said to myself: Redemption will come only when they are told, "Do you see that arch over there from the Roman period? It doesn't matter, but near it, a little to the left and then down a bit, there's a man who has just bought food and vegetables for his family."

Siegel: You said, just before you read "Tourists," that this poem expresses your conviction that, although you have been in wars and tough units, you don't believe that any sites are worth dying for. How do your countrymen feel about that nowadays? Is Israel willing to part with control over great Jewish historic sites over the next couple of years?

Amichai: Well, first of all, I think that's what we are doing now and I think it's very good that we are doing it. We didn't conquer the West Bank because we wanted to conquer them, but we were attacked from there three times. But I think that now we should come to some accord. We have come to it with Jordan, with Egypt, and even if there is no love yet, love and peace will come later. But first of all, no war.

Siegel: The poem that you read at the outset was read by Yitzhak Rabin in his speech accepting the Nobel Peace Prize. How did you feel about that, being quoted at that point?

Amichai: Well, I was very happy and proud of it, of course. And first of all, I'm happy that our statesmen and also Mr. Peres sometimes use literature and the Bible, of course, in their speeches. In Israel, poets and writers are involved whether they want or not, so we don't have to look to be involved. We are because we all go to the army and we all have the same problems, so in a way you don't have to look for some cause to be involved with. It's just part of our lives. And everything is a question of life and death, so I don't think I've written quite a lot of love poems, but there's almost no love poem in which war, politics, or other things don't come in because it has all to be together.

Siegel: And has that created something special about Israeli letters or poetry, the fact that everyone has been part of the army all this time?

Amichai: Well, I think it has. That's why I think poetry is still the mainstream of literature in Israel because of this tradition from the Bible through prayers, so it's still the mainstream and, of course, everyone needs poetry. And let's give you an example. If you go to war, actually the natural thing should be to take Tolstoy's

War and Peace with you, which is a large thing — eight hundred pages long.

Siegel: That's if you are counting on a long war.

Amichai: Yeah, yeah, a long war. But you have to carry it, so you have to take less ammunition with you, which is bad. So a poem, you can take it in your head, certain lines, whether it's a prayer or it's a piece from the Bible. Because every poem is a kind of life and death and every poem is a prayer and every prayer is a poem.

Siegel: Can you read to us another poem?

Amichai: Maybe I'll read you one which really maybe points out this last thing I said about every poem being a prayer. And it's called "Gods Come and Go, Prayers Remain Forever."

I saw in the street on a summer evening
I saw a woman writing words
On a paper spread on a locked wooden door,
She folded it and slipped it between the door and the doorpost
And went off.

I didn't see her face or the face of the man
Who will read the writing and not the words.

On my desk lies a rock with the inscription "Amen,"
Piece of a tombstone, remnant of a Jewish graveyard
Ruined a thousand years ago in the city of my birth.

One word, "Amen," carved deep in the stone,
Hard and final, Amen to all that was and will not return,
Soft Amen, chanting like a prayer,
Amen, Amen, may it be His will.

Tombstones crumble, words come and go, words are forgotten,
The lips that uttered them turned to dust,
Tongues die like people, other tongues come to life,
Gods in the sky change, gods come and go.
Prayers remain forever.

During World War II, the U.S. Army censored press reports from the front, but, censorship notwithstanding, soldiers and the American public got an accurate view of the war in the cartoons of BILL MAULDIN. Mauldin spent three years in the Forty-fifth Division and began drawing cartoons while fighting in Italy. His cartoons first were published in his division newspaper and later picked up by *Stars and Stripes*. Mauldin's two main characters, Willy and Joe, were baggy-eyed, unshaven infantry riflemen from Oklahoma and were modeled on men in his own unit. His drawings showed the misery, boredom, and numbing exhaustion of life at the front. After the war, Mauldin won two Pulitzer Prizes as an editorial cartoonist for the *St. Louis Post-Dispatch* and the *Chicago Sun-Times*. When his collection of World War II cartoons, *Up Front*, was reissued for the fiftieth anniversary of V-E Day, he told Bob Edwards that he thought the material had not dated. May 4, 1995

Mauldin: There was Korea and there was the Six Day War in the Middle East and there was Vietnam. You know, I covered all those wars and the basic life of a combat soldier is still the same. It's very uncomfortable.

Edwards: You said, "I've seen too much of the war to be funny about first sergeants and corporals, and I've seen too much of the war to be cute and fill it with funny characters."

Mauldin: Did I say that?

Edwards: Yes, you did.

Mauldin: That's pretty profound. It reminds me of Adlai Stevenson's immortal comment when he lost his first presidential bid in 1952. He said, "I'm going to quote Lincoln: 'It hurts too much to laugh and I'm too old to cry.'" So that sort of summed it up.

Edwards: You spared no one with these cartoons: the Army Air Corps, quartermasters, chaplains, medics, MPs, the British, the French, and of course anyone in the rear echelon.

Mauldin: Yeah, they were all fair game, I think. I pitched entirely to the infantry soldier and the combat engineers and the combat medics, of course, too. In other words, anybody who got shot at a lot. And I didn't give a hoot what the rest of the army thought about what I did. I was not looking for popularity there. I was pitching to these guys because all they had really was that little military newspaper — the division newspaper and later on, the *Stars and Stripes.*

Edwards: The one that gets reprinted the most, I guess, is the one in which the old cavalryman shoots the jeep with the broken axle.

Mauldin: Yep.

Edwards: He's come from the old cavalry, where if a horse breaks a leg that's what you do.

Mauldin: That was in many ways my favorite one because it didn't need any words. It had a lot of history in it. It had a lot of tradition in it. And I was always very proud of it as a piece of work. I first drew it in 1941 during maneuvers in Louisiana. And then I redrew it from time to time because I didn't think it got appreciated enough. I don't know if you remember a cartoon panel called "Out Our Way," by J. R. Williams, but he had this little habit. If he had a hangover on a Monday morning, for example, and a deadline coming up, he would recycle an old cartoon. And then he would put "redrawn by request" up in the corner of it. So that's what I did with that and I kept redrawing it "by request" until I had done it about five or six times. And it worked. People began saying, "Hey, that must have been a hell of a cartoon, Mauldin." So anyway, I did it in bronze, actually. I've got a five-hundred-pound reenactment of that cartoon sitting in my front yard right now.

Edwards: But my favorite is the one in which an officer is watching a sunset.

Mauldin: Oh, yeah.

Edwards: And he says to his aide, "Beautiful view. Is there one for the enlisted men?"

Mauldin: Well, that was one of my favorites, too. That summed up a lot of feelings about the military.

Edwards: The subject of booze came up a time or two.

Mauldin: Yes. One of my crusades in the military was always for a liquor ration for enlisted men.

Edwards: The officers had one.

Mauldin: Yes, the officers had one, and I always thought enlisted men should have one, too. The British were way ahead of us on that.

Edwards: You did a cartoon about that, and someone wondered if maybe you'd been drinking too much. There were three guys in the picture and there were seven hands.

Mauldin: Yes, that was drawn when I was drinking too much. You're right. I couldn't believe it when I saw it in print. I hadn't realized what I had done until I saw it.

Edwards: You actually considered killing off Willy and Joe on the last day of the war.

Mauldin: Well, in many ways, I am still sorry I didn't do it. I thought it would have been a good grandstand play because their counterparts in real life were all dead by then. They were. There were no survivors, to speak of, of the old line infantry. So they would have been dead, realistically speaking. And I thought this would bring that fact home to people in a very dramatic sort of way to go ahead and have these guys killed on the last day of the war. The one thing every infantry soldier dreads the most is getting killed on that last day. So I thought about it. And in many ways, I wish I had done it. The *Stars and Stripes* told me, "This'll be the one cartoon you ever did for us that we wouldn't print." So I realized they had me stopped there. So I never did it.

Edwards: On many a Veterans Day, Charles Schulz has had Snoopy announce he's going to go to your house for some root beers.

Mauldin: Yeah. It's funny. Schulz has been doing that for many years, and he generally sent me the originals of these things. So I have a large collection of them. But I ran into him in California one time and met him for the first time. I had never met him before. And I said, "Why the hell are you doing this? You know, I appreciate it. I mean, you're sort of keeping me alive. It's the most popular comic strip in the country. But why are you doing it?" And he had this wonderful answer. He said, "I was a machine gunner in France during World War II." And I thought that was very eloquent and wonderful.

The Washington Shakespeare Theatre production of *Macbeth* featured mists generated by dry ice, weird sisters who ascended and descended a stylized tree, and the actor STACY KEACH in the title role. Macbeth, the general inspired by ambition, prophecy, and a gorgeous wife to murder his way to the throne of Scotland, is a role that requires a great performance. It is also a role that Keach, who had already played Richard III, Hamlet, and Coriolanus, told Robert Siegel he had long avoided. September 20, 1995

Keach: When I first started in this business years ago, I did a satire of *Macbeth* called *Macbird.* Lyndon Johnson was Macbeth, you know, as Macbird. It was a sort of coffeehouse satirical account of the assassination of John F. Kennedy. And everybody thought I was fifty years old and could only do Lyndon Johnson imitations in those days. So it was very difficult for me to get beyond that. And I had such a good time with it. I kept going back to *Macbeth* and looking at the original play. And I think of all the major tragic roles in the canon, it's probably the most difficult. I think it's more difficult than Hamlet and certainly Coriolanus or Othello or Lear, even. I mean, I think Lear is the pinnacle, sort of, for an actor and one day I hope to do that, to climb that mountain. But *Macbeth* I have always avoided because, first of all, he does all the work, and she gets all the glory.

Siegel: But the question about Macbeth that I always have is what, if you're playing him, do you find appealing about the guy? I mean, here he is, you meet him first slashing at people on the battlefield and in a moment he's setting out to murder his way to the top.

Keach: From a moral point of view, there's not much appealing about him at all. In terms of his imagination, what Shakespeare has given him in terms of his ability to put things in certain forms of poetry and also philosophy — extraordinary insights into the human condition. He has also got a moral blindness, a blind spot in his character, that is very interesting for an actor to pursue. And the pursuit of madness and paranoia is always interesting, I think, to try to attach behavior to and for an actor to get into.

Siegel: Macbeth is a character, who upon being told by three weird sisters that he's going to be king almost instantly can't bear the fact that Banquo, the guy he's with, is told, "And you're going to be the father of kings."

Keach: Right.

Siegel: This is at some level a very insecure fellow.

Keach: Very insecure, very insecure. And it also suggests that this is something that has been on his mind previous to this first encounter with these witches. It's also suggested in the letter to Lady Macbeth that they have talked about this before. This is not something that just happens on the spot. But this is something that has been bubbling in their consciousness for some time.

Siegel: So the way that you see *Macbeth* is that these witches, these spirits who appear, assist them, and it's all inspiring them further along lines they've already been thinking?

Keach: Right. Well, the witches are sort of the prophets. I mean, they are the ones who say this is going to happen to you. And I think he has some doubt about it. Certainly Banquo does. But almost within two minutes, Rosse comes on stage and says that Macbeth has been given, that he's been granted, the thane of Cawdorship.

Siegel: The thaneship.

Keach: Yeah. So already he says, "Glamis, and Thane of Cawdor: The greatest is behind." Now, "the greatest is behind" means "is next" in Shakespearean language. The greatest is yet to come, it really means. It's really hard to communicate that. But nevertheless, that's what's on his mind. And then he begins to deliberate about whether this is a good idea or bad idea. And, finally, he frankly very objectively sees the real possibilities that this is not a good idea. He says, "Present fears are less than horrible imaginings. My thought, whose murder yet is but fantastical, shakes so my single state of man, that function is smothered in surmise. And nothing is, but what is not," which means to me that what Shakespeare was saying is that this has been on his mind, and he's already had thoughts of the possibility of taking over that kingship.

Siegel: It appears, watching you play Macbeth between the battles and going nuts and committing murders — it looks exhausting.

Keach: Right. It is exhausting. It is. You get a break in the second act, but the first act is pretty much nonstop right up through the banquet scene. Yeah, it's an exhausting role, not as exhausting as Hamlet or Richard III. *Richard III* is an hour longer, for one thing, and he's on stage even more. But, yeah, it's exhausting. You have to be in pretty good shape.

Siegel: A workout.

Keach: It is a workout. The nice thing about that is, of course, I can go out after the show and I can eat whatever I want to and not worry about gaining weight.

Siegel: How much weight do you think you lose in a performance?

Keach: Well, I must lose a couple, three pounds in water weight every night, you know. And I know since I've started this last week, about six pounds. I will probably lose ten more pounds between now and the first of November.

Siegel: Really? It's that demanding to do?

Keach: Yeah.

Siegel: This production, like every production of *Macbeth*, has to figure out what to do with witches and demons and supernatural things, and I think it really does it very well in that it plays it to the hilt. There's a lot of mystery going on there on stage.

Keach: Yeah, you know, it's difficult, I think, for a contemporary audience to come to believe in witches. I mean, in Shakespeare's day, they were accepted. Ghosts and witches were part of everyday life. But today it's a little more difficult. So, Joe Dowling, our director, and I discussed this at great length, and we thought that, Well, who are these witches, really, I mean? At least initially, who are they? And we came to the conclusion that they were really the voices of the dead, that the voices of the dead seem to be the voices that seem to speak to all of us in terms of how we conduct ourselves in terms of what we do in Bosnia, Ireland, Africa, in the places where there are wars. It's like our family members who have died seemed to be talking to us, and saying, "Get them." It's revenge. So we decided that we would start the show with a battle. And then out of the dead bodies of the soldiers, the witches would sort of morph into view.

Siegel: Tell me about Lady Macbeth. And in this case, the actress is Helen Carey.

Keach: Wonderful actress, and she's doing a great job with it. I think that the interesting thing that happens with that relationship is that Macbeth really needs Lady Macbeth to sort of be his spur. And then once he murders Duncan and realizes the horror of what he's done, he then holds her responsible, I think, in his mind, and she's accountable then. And then he turns on her, he turns on her completely. He doesn't want to have anything to do with her anymore, wants to separate himself from her. And then goes off and begins to kill people on his own. So he cuts her off, and I think that's one of the reasons that she goes crazy is that she's sort of discarded and cast aside.

Siegel: Well, toward the end of *Macbeth*, after she has already gone crazy, there are some noises heard from offstage. Macbeth delivers a great soliloquy. Now I'm going to feed you a line.

Keach: Uh-huh.

Siegel: This is my big line.

Keach: Go ahead.

Siegel: Seyton, who is Macbeth's servant?

Keach: He's a servant, but in this production he's sort of my surrogate child.

Siegel: He arrives and tells you, Macbeth, "The Queen, my Lord, is dead."

Keach: [*reciting*]

> "She should have died hereafter;
> There would have been a time for such a word.
> Tomorrow, and tomorrow, and tomorrow,
> Creeps in this petty pace from day to day,
> To the last syllable of recorded time;
> And all our yesterdays have lighted fools
> The way to dusty death. Out, out, brief candle!
> Life's but a walking shadow; a poor player
> That struts and frets his hour upon the stage,
> And then is heard no more: it is a tale
> Told by an idiot, full of sound and fury,
> Signifying nothing."

O RHAN PAMUK says that twenty years ago, when he was an architecture student in Istanbul, he had a screw loose; he couldn't stop reading novels. So he decided to write novels instead, books that grapple with problems of cultural and spiritual identity. His novel *The White Castle* was about East and West, about a seventeenth-century Turk and his look-alike Venetian slave. A second novel translated from Turkish into English (by Guneli Gun) is *The Black Book*, a contemporary story about an Istanbul lawyer named Galip whose wife disappears along with her half brother, a celebrated Turkish newspaper columnist named Galal. Galip searches for the two of them, and the search takes him through Turkish history, Sufi Islam, philosophical puzzles, jokes, and above all, through the city of Istanbul. Orhan Pamuk told Robert Siegel that until he started writing, nobody had written a Turkish novel about Istanbul. January 30, 1995

Pamuk: The main body of Turkish fiction before me, let's say, was village novels about the poor peasants. And urbanization in Turkey compared to Western countries developed a bit late. So, in a way, the city was not written about. I also had this privilege of seeing in forty-two years of my life a city grow from a million to twelve million, and I thought that this was a unique experience, even in the history of mankind, that I had witnessed. So, in a way, Istanbul is one of the main characters of *The Black Book*.

Siegel: Your character, your columnist, Galal, disappears with the wife of the protagonist of the book, Galip, setting up a mystery for Galip. Where did his wife go with her half brother, Galal? Are you writing a kind of detective story here?

Pamuk: Yes, *The Black Book* is a detective story. It is perhaps a detective story with a metaphysical bent. It is not only a search for the lost wife, but it's a search for the meaning of life in Istanbul, the

identity of Istanbul, and both characters, and also about life in
Turkey, about Middle Eastern culture, about the identity of Islam.
So while on one hand I had this hero walking in the streets of
Istanbul, on the other hand I tried to organize the narrative around
some certain problems. I tried to pull into the novel the old Sufi
anecdotes, the Islamic tales, tales from Arabian knights and the
little, strange, bizarre, grotesque stories that I compiled from old
newspapers, giving a sense of the richness of the life in Istanbul and
in this part of the world.

Siegel: I'd like to ask you about one story in the book, and
whether it's drawn from older tales or one of your own devising,
which is about a competition of artists, as you place it, in an Istanbul bordello.

Pamuk: Oh! That comes from Ghazālī, the twelfth-century Islamic philosopher, and then Mawlana Jalal al-Din Rumi, a thir-
teenth-century mystic writer, had grabbed and rewritten that story.
And all the other mystics in their own way interpreted and changed
and rewrote that story. And placing it in that bordello is my way of
rewriting that story, the story about the competition between two
painters.

Siegel: The story is that two painters compete on opposite walls,
curtained off from one another's sight, each to make the most wonderful decoration of the wall. And when the curtains are finally
removed, one has painted a huge panorama of Istanbul, and the
other has put up a mirror which reflects the other wall. Everybody
finds the reflection superior to the painting itself. Now, would a
Turkish reader know that story, or is it an obscure story?

Pamuk: A regular Turkish reader wouldn't notice that it comes
from a twelfth-century Sufi tale. What I like about all these details,
those stories, is that you don't have to know those stories before in
order to understand the book, enjoy the book. The book was very
popular in Turkey, and most of the readers missed the fact that all
the stories are actually rewritten by me.

Siegel: In another story, this one from the waning days of the Ot-
toman Empire, a man makes the first Turkish mannequins. They
are rejected first by the Ottomans for violating the Islamic injunc-
tion against graven images. Then, after westernization, they are
rejected again for looking too Turkish, too authentic. Who are these
Turks of Istanbul who prefer mannequins that look more Western

than they do? Can one ever be one's self? Those questions recur often in your novel.

Pamuk: This is an obsession which I have received from the Turkish culture. Turks are very much concerned — not only Turks, in fact, but all Middle Easterners or people who live in the peripheries of the world — are much concerned about their identities. Who are we? Are we Westerners? Are we Easterners? What is our identity? Are we, first of all, Turks or Muslims? These are the basic questions that are being asked in Turkey for the last two hundred years because there is a major civilization change that's going on here. So, when beginning a book, if I have any, let's say, intellectual problems, philosophical problems, the problem of identity is a crucial one.

Siegel: I'm intrigued by what you say about the "problem of identity" for people who live, as you say, "on the periphery," because you do seem to be writing from a place — along with others who come to mind like Salman Rushdie, for example, who may not occupy the same geographic place — but some place on the border between the West and the East. And so you're writing as a kind of an inside outsider from that perspective. Do you feel that way?

Pamuk: I agree. You know, borders are changing, but I feel that I'm now, along with people like Kazuo Ishiguro or Salman Rushdie, coming from a place in which those borders are the very real, essential places from which one can develop radical fiction, from which one can go back and forth to the periphery, producing something vital, something which has energy, and producing new fiction, words that have not been said before.

Siegel: And when you speak of the center and the periphery, what is the center and what is the periphery?

Pamuk: Actually, it sometimes seems to be so simple to me. It seems that the fate of mankind is being decided at what we call "the center" — New York, London, Paris — or the center cities of Western civilization, while people like us, the ones who live in the peripheries, are trying to reach the essence of things. This also reflects the cultural relationships between center and periphery. And the art of the novel has been produced by Western societies; again, by the same capitals. And now we're trying to grab that from their hands and produce something new, something different, new stories.

Siegel: "Grab that" suggests an act of aggression or of theft.

Pamuk: Yes.

Siegel: Do you intend that?

Pamuk: Not of aggression but a bit of ambition, and an ambition to write a total novel, ambition to write something that had not been written before, and show it to the rest of the world. I think if you lived in these parts of the world, you would sympathize with this ambition.

T he generation caught between raising its own children and caring for its aging parents is sometimes called the "sandwich generation." DELIA EPHRON writes of this group and is a member of it. In her first novel, *Hanging Up*, a father who was always impossible begins to lose his mental capacities, and his three daughters are charged with caring for him. Ephron's fictional sisters compete with one another for their father's attention and affection, even as he drives them up the wall. As Ephron readily conceded to Susan Stamberg, her fiction is not far off from the facts of her own family. August 12, 1995

Stamberg: You dedicate this book, *Hanging Up*, to your father, Henry Ephron, and you give his dates, 1911 to 1992. Like the father in your book, Lou Mozell, your dad was a writer. He was a screenwriter. Lou Mozell lived in Los Angeles. He had three daughters. Your father had four: you and your sisters Hallie, Amy, and Nora. What's my first question, Delia?

Ephron: Oh, maybe, is this based, a little bit, on my life?

Stamberg: Uh-huh.

Ephron: Yes, of course. I tell you, I had this book contract just before my father got sick. I was going to write about something else, and suddenly, these events just took me over, and I'm so embarrassed about this, but I actually started making notes while he was sick because I was so overwhelmed. And I thought, This is terrible that you're taking notes.

Stamberg: But it's what happens.

Ephron: Yes, it was a way of dealing with it, I hope, I think. He had been such a difficult figure in my life.

Stamberg: These girls that you create — the Mozell sisters — let's talk about them a little. Georgia — she's the eldest. She's an enormous success. She has her own magazine. She bosses everybody else around. Eva's the narrator. The third sister is Maddy. She's kind of ditzy. She's the baby of the family. She's an actress on a TV soap. And you're writing about a lot of things. You write about their relationship to one another, also, the way they compete for the father's attention and affection, even though he is a royal pain.

Ephron: Now, I have to tell you, my father tortured us by phone. I mean, one reason why my book is about the telephone as well as about sisters is that my father used to phone us up, one after another, trying to work us all into a frenzy about the others' accomplishments. So he would call up, and he would say, "Oh, your sister's going to be president," something, like, completely insane like that. Or he would say, "Are you jealous of Nora?" phoning one after another, over and over. He was in ecstasy.

Stamberg: This whole notion of competition between sisters could turn you into a truly bitter person, couldn't it?

Ephron: I guess it could. The other day I said to someone that Nora had a slightly higher math aptitude than I did, and I realized that there is not a thing about my sisters about which I don't know the difference. I know who has cuter knees, who has cuter thighs. I know who has a higher math aptitude. There is not a detail of our lives that I cannot tell you.

Stamberg: That's incredible, because that's another piece of you, right? She completes who you are, and vice versa?

Ephron: Yes. I am the only one with naturally curly hair, but, I have to tell you, I had this very glamorous jacket photo taken with about five pounds of makeup on my face and I was thrilled to death and I called up all my friends and I showed them the photo, and I was just bouncing around. And they all said, "Oh, you look so great. You look so great." And then I showed it to two of my three sisters, and they said, both said, "That doesn't look like you." I swear. Siblings.

Stamberg: The title is *Hanging Up* because they spend their lives on the telephone and, in a way, that intrigued me so much because I'm an only child, Delia. And I wonder, is it really how it is with sisters, that you keep listening to what's on the tom-tom?

Ephron: Not only that, but if one of them tells you something really dumb, you immediately call up the other, and say, "Do you believe what" — I won't say which one — "said?" And then you laugh about it together. I mean, there's this whole thing of conversations going back and forth, and my father was causing a lot of trouble. We'd say, "Did you talk to Dad today?" You know, those calls would go on. And also I was amazed because I think that older parents really can torture their children by phone. The last thing my father forgot was my phone number. He couldn't recognize his own pants, and he could punch out a seven-digit number plus an area code and get me, never a wrong number.

Stamberg: How did he die? Was it Alzheimer's?

Ephron: It wasn't Alzheimer's. He just started to fade. Then they put him in a geriatric-psychiatric ward, and the doctors there assured me he would live two more years, and I said, "No. No, no." I could see it. You know, it's the strangest thing when doctors tell you things and, yet, right in front of your eyes, you know better.

Stamberg: Yeah.

Ephron: It's very confusing.

Stamberg: But you know the individual.

Ephron: You know from your heart.

Stamberg: But that's another extraordinary thing that happens in our lives as well as in the pages of your book, where death begins to look like the best solution.

Ephron: Yes. I think, from the child's point of view, that's true. And I know from having a very difficult father, or a father who has caused you a lot of pain, you have, in times in your life, thought, My life would be so much easier if you were dead. And I really wanted to write about how complicated those things get when they actually do start to die. Because I was thrown right back into childhood with my father when he started to get very sick. I became his confidante again, which was the role I had played as a child, and I had thought I wanted this man out of my life. And while I did, at the same time, I was really grief-stricken.

Stamberg: You, in the book, write about this notion of being the sandwich generation; we are dealing with parents who are aging and who are dying — and yet you are able to find humor in this. Page after page had me laughing out loud.

Ephron: It's the curse of being an Ephron, I guess. I don't know. You know, parents also, they differentiate you by the "You're the this one. You're the that." I mean, Nora was the smart one. I was the witty one. Those were our roles in life, and I think I just always grew up dealing with pain by finding ways to laugh about it. And I remember there was a point where my father was put in the New

York Psychiatric Hospital, which happens to be on Bloomingdale's Road and so its nickname is Bloomingdale's. And I cannot tell you how many jokes we got out of the fact that my father was out shopping for three months, you know, enforced shopping. But, as sisters, we always found a way to laugh at pain. I mean, I can remember, as a child, sitting down with them to regale them with stories, and we would be falling off our chairs, and, yet, at the same time, it was very difficult.

Stamberg: I'd like you to read a passage for us now. It's not a particularly funny passage. The father, Lou Mozell, is dying.

Ephron: [*reading*] "So now it's just me, Dad, and death, hanging out together. I try to feel its presence. I imagine it floating above the bed, a shadow of my father, all negative image, until, boom, it drops. But I feel nothing. I have heard and read of inspiring death-room scenes, family clasping hands around a bed, providing a hammock of comfort that allows the dying person to let go, if the person wants to, which is something I can't grasp. Death and peace. How can you feel peaceful if you don't feel anything? The idea that peace comes with death is one more false comfort for the living. No, there is no spiritual feeling in this room. I look at my father closely, aware that for most of my adult life I have tried not to. He has a mustache suddenly. I suppose the nurse couldn't manage to shave the hairs beneath his nose and left them. Or maybe she amuses herself by putting mustaches on dying men, the way kids draw mustaches and beards on people in magazine photographs.

"'Dad?' I throw the word out into the air. It feels ridiculous, like throwing a pass with no receiver."

Stamberg: This is your first novel. And you've done a number of books either for or about children — *How to Eat Like a Child, The Girl Who Changed the World.* And you've also done screenplays with your sister Nora Ephron, *Sleepless in Seattle, This Is My Life.* And you're shooting the next one, *Michael,* about the existence of angels. What do you find to be more difficult — a screenplay or a novel?

Ephron: A novel. There is no question. Well, first of all, I have to tell you I collaborated on both my screenplays, so if I can't solve something, I just say to Nora, "I have a problem. You work on it."

Stamberg: You can't collaborate on a novel, right?

Ephron: Not really, no. It is so personal. I feel that everything I

When the software magnate Bill Gates purchased the Bettmann Archive, one of the world's largest collections of photographs and visual images, he assured the survival of Dr. OTTO BETTMANN's remarkable project. The Bettmann Archive includes some of America's most widely recognized photographs of everything and everyone from Civil War battlefields to Marilyn Monroe. Gates bought the collection of sixteen million pictures with plans to digitize them and make them available through computer networks. The founder had previously sold the archive to the Kraus Organization, which in turn sold it to Gates. Otto Bettmann, the self-styled "picture man," started it in the 1930s after fleeing Nazi Germany and coming to the United States with a trunk full of old photographs. In retirement at age ninety-two, Bettmann published a book about his other passion, the music of Johann Sebastian Bach, and he told Robert Siegel that he was happy that the archive bearing his name would make the transition to the computer age. October 11, 1995

Bettmann: I am quite delighted that my archive that always conjures a picture of oldness, of archaeology, has now made the step into the twenty-first century.

Siegel: Could you take us back to the 1930s and how the idea of the Bettmann Photo Archive came to be?

Bettmann: I started really in Berlin when I was fired from the museum in Berlin, the Kaiser Friedrich. I was looking for a livelihood, and I had a small collection of subject pictures which I expanded, and I arrived in New York in 1935 with two big steamers full of pictures. And I hardly thought I could make a living from this material. It was more of an avocation, but I found ready help among advertising agencies, publishers, textbook people. It was the beginning of the visual age. *Time* started, *Life, Look* magazine, were in the offing, and they were very hospitably welcomed.

Siegel: Are there a few photographs among the millions that come to mind right away that are favorites?

Bettmann: Well, one of my favorite pictures is a picture of the first radio station which really put me into business. It was designed by the seventeenth-century monk by the name of Athanasius Kircher. That really put me in business for CBS. The then-president, Dr. Stanton, saw this picture, and he made a big spread in *Fortune* magazine out of it and gave the Bettmann Archive credit.

Siegel: Now, wait a minute. Did you say that the first radio station was designed by a seventeenth-century monk?

Bettmann: By a seventeenth-century monk, yes. It was, of course, a prediction, simply an idea how sound transmission would work in the future. And other people came to me — "Well, tell me the beginning of shaving. Tell me the beginning of fashions. Tell me the beginning of medical things."

Siegel: When someone would ask you, "Now that we've seen a picture of the very origin of the idea of radio from the seventeenth century, could you find the origins of shaving?" how would you go about finding images of that? How would you know everywhere to find a picture that told us something about shaving?

Bettmann: Well, I go to hundreds of books. When you are a picture searcher, you develop some sort of a sixth sense where to go. Americans, who are really people of the future, have a great interest in how things came about. Once a pharmaceutical manufacturer asked me what I had on the history of sleeping, and we have a whole file of pictures of how people were put asleep, perhaps hit over the head, or there's a very touching picture that shows a famous prince hiring a violinist, and he simply puts him to sleep. As a matter of fact, Bach's Goldberg variations were ordered from Bach by a certain Count Kayserling so that his servant and court musician, Mr. Goldberg, could play these melodies when his lord could not sleep.

Siegel: Well, I'm glad that you've brought Bach into this because I wanted to ask you just to conclude if there's any particular work of Bach that comes to mind on the occasion of the sale of the Bettmann Archive that we might play at this moment and would be appropriate.

Bettmann: Well, I think Bach has created super-Bach, Bach, and sub-Bach. Not everything that Bach wrote was so eminently useful.

I n DANIEL PINKWATER's version of the hereafter, thin people have a separate heaven from the one reserved for those who once were larger than life. *The Afterlife Diet* was Pinkwater's fictional treatment of a theme that he has returned to over the years as an *All Things Considered* commentator: excessive weight. The novel is set in an afterworld where the extralarge have passed on to a kind of Catskill Mountains resort in the sky. As one character puts it, "We make them uncomfortable. You know how most people are. They'd rather be dead than fat." Pinkwater, a successful author of children's books, talked about *The Afterlife Diet* with Scott Simon. May 13, 1995

Pinkwater: I knew that I wanted to have my main character dead in the first sentence. It was just something I thought would be stylish and always wanted to do. And also I had come to a point where I needed to say something in a big way about being big. This has been working in me for years and years. I'll tell you what preceded the book immediately. I required an emergency operation. I'm hurried down to the local chop shop and the guys come in with the equipment —

Simon: Daniel, I should explain: chop shop is what some people would call a hospital?

Pinkwater: I guess so, yes. The local facility.

Simon: Sure, OK.

Pinkwater: And they whiz in with the various instruments to check my pulse, my blood pressure, my respiration, my general state of health, and I come out to be in great shape. The anesthesiologist says, "What is this, big fat guy? You're healthier than me." Off they wheel me to the O.R., and there's my wife, of course scared, in the hallway nine o'clock at night in this little hospital. And here comes the surgeon who's going to do the operation, and he says to her, "You know, I'm going to lose him. He's going to die." "What, what?" she says. "What, but he's so healthy. He's in such a good mood." "No, no, going to die. He's going to die. I'll try to save him, but he's going to die." Two hours later they wheel me out. I don't remember this, but I'm told I gave her a little sort of Oliver Hardy wave from the gurney. I was feeling good. And here comes the surgeon again. "Well, I pulled him through, but he's going to die and he's going to die and it's going to be your fault, and he's going to die because he's fat and it will be your fault because you let him be fat, so it's your fault." I heard nothing about this for a couple of weeks because I was busy recuperating, but when she told me the story, I said, "All right. That's it. This goes too far. I have a lot to say about fat prejudice. I'm a fat guy. I have the right." And we have the book with the character dying on the operating table. And then the great rule of fiction writing: there's only one "what if?" Well, what if when you die, you go someplace?

Simon: Mm-hmm.

Pinkwater: Catskills resort. I just spent forty-five minutes at an old and funky one having a cup of coffee with someone. It was a delight. I put it in the book.

Simon: You, of course, have people — I don't want, I can't say "fat," OK — but people —

Pinkwater: Why can't you say "fat," Scott?

Simon: Because I don't feel right saying "fat."

Pinkwater: Why don't you feel right saying "fat"? It's an English word.

Simon: Because I guess it's a word I would avoid because I might be afraid of offending people.

Pinkwater: Because they're fat?

Simon: Or if they think —

Pinkwater: You mean you think they didn't know it?

Simon: Oh God, I am — you know, my job interview at NPR, years and years ago was with a large man, and in any event —

Pinkwater: But not fat.

Simon: I remember sitting there. I was not prepared for how large he was. He rounded the corner, you know, and it took several minutes for him to round the corner, as they say. And he came and I looked up and I guess I had a startled look on my face, and he said, "You weren't expecting me to be so fat, were you?"

Pinkwater: A good man.

Simon: I said, "You're not fat." And he said, "What the hell kind of reporter are you? You can't recognize that I'm fat?" I'm surprised I was hired, much less managed to keep some sort of job. But in any event, I don't know, I just don't feel right using it.

Pinkwater: As you wish. Scott, you can say "circumferentially challenged."

Simon: I'm not sure I feel better about that.

Pinkwater: OK. You can say "diametrically disadvantaged."

Simon: All right. Well, let me try that one. The point of that being you have diametrically disadvantaged people occupying a heaven separate from people who are — who are more slender.

Pinkwater: Just in the beginning of the book we established that they're ghettoized.

Simon: Yeah. You have a copy of your book there, Daniel?

Pinkwater: I happen to have a copy.

Simon: There's a lounge act that you have a comedian launch into.

Pinkwater: Yes.

Simon: And could I get you to read a little of that?

Pinkwater: Why not? [*reading*]

"Hey, good evening, ladies and ghosts! Welcome, welcome to the casino! I'm Charlie, your master of cemeteries, uh, ceremonies. We have a wonderful evening planned for your entertainment, so look alive, everybody . . . or, if you can't manage it, look dead in a pleasant way.

"This fat lady comes up to me and says, 'I'm too heavy, and my hair looks terrible.'

"'So diet,' I tell her.

"'I'm going to, but I can't decide what color.'

"Hey!

"I know a guy who was so fat . . ."

"How fat is he?" the audience shouted.

". . . he had the mumps two weeks before he knew it."

"Ba-dam!

"He was so fat he was arrested for jaywalking, and all the time, he was waiting on the corner for the light to change.

"Zetz!

"I know a woman who's so fat, every time she falls down, she rocks herself to sleep.

"She had to give up golf, because when she puts the ball where she can see it, she can't hit it . . ."

"And when she puts the ball where she can hit it, she can't see it!"
someone in the audience shouted.
. . .
"Hey!
"Zetz!
"Are we having fun, or what!"
Incredibly to Milton, the others *were* having fun. He wasn't. His
jaw had dropped several stale gags earlier, and remained so.
"No, no. You know I love you all," Charlie was saying. "I insult
you, and call you fat pigs, and chubby, gross, disgusting, obese glut-
tons and tubs of lard — but I do it with love."
There was a round of applause, and Charlie dabbed at his eyes with
a handkerchief.
"Thank you, thank you, ladies and elephants."

Simon: Now, you laugh at the beginning, but by the end, I found
myself squirming.
Pinkwater: Oh, that's just the beginning of the beginning. The
book catalogues lots of abuse I did not know that I had retained.
You know, I've been a fat guy all my life. I was a fat kid. Except for
one period where I lost a hundred pounds and felt very strange and
uncomfortable for a couple of years 'til I got fat again. And you tune
out the jokes and the abuse. And, in fact, I was just going to kind of
take this fat theme — I had some things in mind that I thought
might be humorous. And as I wrote it, a lot of stuff came back to
me. And also I was researching as I wrote. I was questioning people.
I did a lot Internet surfing, where I found lots of fat people happy to
tell their story.

One of the things that was interesting that I hadn't known about
and one of the things that I was doing on-line was trying to make
sure I got the woman's perspective of this because I was aware and
am more aware now that it's a different question if you're female. I
believe there is not a fat woman in this society, not one, who is
significantly fat, who has not repeatedly had the experience of people in public, total strangers, saying the most incredibly vile and
vulgar and abusive things to her regularly. Things I couldn't begin
to clean up for the radio.

Now, I myself have had the experience more than once of some
maniac approaching me in a restaurant, and saying, "How did you
let yourself get that way? Aren't you ashamed?" To which I usually

respond now, "Get away from me, loony, or I'll eat you." Now, I apologize to mentally infirm persons who may hear this, but understand it's important to me to be given peace to enjoy my taco platter.

Simon: Uh, "mentally challenged Americans" I think is what you meant, Dan.

Pinkwater: Yes, I'm sorry. Excuse me.

Simon: I have been told some of your personal friends find themselves a little uncomfortable with this book.

Pinkwater: Some liked it, some disliked it and were vigorous in their dislike. Some of them quit speaking to me and haven't spoken to me since. And one, I guess my oldest friend, sent me a very strong letter saying, "Stop fooling around and write a serious book, will you?" I thought it was a serious book, although funny. Another friend of mind who was a psychiatrist by trade said that in this society we hate and fear fat people for the same reason we hate homosexual men. We are afraid that if we were to somehow let ourselves go, this would happen to us.

Simon: When you describe the great Chicago hot dog with peppers and celery salt and all that, I'm reminded of a place called the Trolley Car, used to be right off the corner of Broadway and Irving.

Pinkwater: Yes.

Simon: And there was a time in my life when I probably wouldn't let a day go by without stopping at the Trolley Car.

Pinkwater: Which probably accounts for the robust health you enjoy today.

Simon: But the fact is, I no longer eat that way.

Pinkwater: Neither do I, as a matter of fact. In my new role as fat guru, which is temporary, because of the nature of this book, somehow I've been thrust into conversation after conversation not unlike this one. I want to make it clear I'm not saying nobody should try to modify what they eat. I'm not saying that I'm an advocate of unbridled gluttony. My real point is simply this: the presence of people of different shapes in this society is a fact and is not really that important a fact except that it's made so. I have a lot of things which define me. I'm bald, I'm a writer, I wear glasses, I'm real handsome, I'm fat. Fat's just one of those things.

Simon: Some of the most heartbreaking passages of your book have to do with Milton, one of your characters who, as a child, is ridiculed by the family doctor. And I'm wondering now that I know the story, is that in some ways inspired by your experience with the doctor?

Pinkwater: Oh, that's inspired by any number of experiences. All through my childhood and young adult life, I had various people blaming it on me. Time after time, I was subjected to visits to the pediatrician, where I'd be given a lecture about willpower and moral rectitude. Attributed to fat people are the following qualities: sloth, will-lessness, sneakiness, dirtiness, dishonesty, laziness, and, on the good side, jolliness. And these are more or less the same things that people said about black people when I was a little boy in Memphis, Tennessee.

Any time you have a group that is a safe subject of prejudice, they get the whole pitch. And fat abuse, which can be very funny — it's safe. If a TV comedian did a gay joke or a race joke similar to the fat jokes you'll hear every night, there'd be some kind of hoo-ha. There'd be some kind of public retractions and apologies and contracts canceled and endorsements lost. But it's safe to abuse fat people. It's safe to walk up to a fat woman in the street and say awful things to her because she's just going to take it. She's going to think, Of course, it's my own fault I'm this way.

Simon: What did writing this book represent to you?

Pinkwater: It was a tremendous catharsis, which I didn't think it would be. Interestingly enough, I lost a lot of weight while I wrote the book, too. I lost about a fifth of my total mass.

Simon: Oh, my gosh, the personal-anguish diet? What was the occasion for that, I wonder?

Pinkwater: You know, not a lot is known about these behaviors and what really goes into it. I'd only be guessing and willing to guess in public, part of my eating patterns might have included a kind of eating out of defiance. Like "Don't tell me I can't have the whole thing." You know, I'm already wise that nothing I do is going to make a difference, so leave me be. And in writing the book and sort of sticking it to all of the insensitive people and all of the various quack doctors who have taken my money and all of the various books I've read — I've been this route and done all these things — I may have just somehow diffused all of that anger and defiance so that particular kind of eating I don't have to do any more. So, hey, if you read my book, you might lose weight.

I once did a piece for *All Things Considered* that didn't happen to get aired. I thought it was terribly funny. There was a difference of opinion, but now I get to describe it anyway. I took the microphone into the Big Book Store and simply read the titles of diet books, one after another, getting up to about fifty or seventy. And I remember one sequence was *The Last Diet Book You'll Ever Need*. And by the same author, *The Very Last Diet Book You'll Ever Need*. And by the same author, *This Is Really, No Kidding, the Ultimate Last Diet Book You'll Ever Need*. And then at the end of the piece I just drifted over to the next set of shelves and began reading the titles of dessert cookbooks, which were thoughtfully shelved right next to the diet books.

Simon: Well, Daniel, if you were telling the people at bookstores where to put your book, would it be in the diet section or the dessert section?

Pinkwater: I kind of like the idea that copies, because of the title, may find their way into the diet section and save a soul.

TELEVISION, RADIO, AND FILM

One measure of DAVID BRINKLEY's sixty years in journalism is contained in the subtitle of his memoir: *11 Presidents, 4 Wars, 22 Political Conventions, 1 Moon Landing, 3 Assassinations*. Brinkley joined NBC Radio News during World War II. After the war, when television was still young, he sometimes substituted for John Cameron Swayze on the *Camel News Caravan*, NBC Television's nightly news broadcast. He became one of the most popular figures on television when he was teamed with fellow NBC reporter and coanchor Chet Huntley on the award-winning *Huntley-Brinkley Report*. But his talent for the trade was evident a lot earlier than that. He told Bob Edwards about his first news assignment as a high school intern on his hometown newspaper in Wilmington, North Carolina. November 1 and 2, 1995

Brinkley: The managing editor said, "David, over on North Fifth Street, a woman has a century plant on her front porch, and she says it will bloom Tuesday night at ten o'clock," and I was dumb enough to believe it. And of course, I did a lot of research. I went to the dictionary and read up the one line it said about the century plant, and it said it's a Mexican a-g-a-d-e. I've never really been sure how to pronounce it: Agade or agada or something like that. It said, "Erroneously believed to bloom once in a century." Well, already, my story was gone. "Erroneously believed." I wondered, What the hell can I do with that? I went to North Fifth Street and talked to the woman and she did have what looked like a cactus on her front porch. It was quite an ugly piece of greenery, so I stayed around and looked at the crowd gathering in the streets to see this marvel of nature about to unfold itself. The fire department brought in floodlights. People gathered, brought their children, all of them eating Popsicles and so on. Finally it became clear there wasn't going to be any blooming. The kids began to cry, the fire department complained about having rolled out the floodlights for nothing, and an old guy I stopped to talk to (I can't use his language on the air; I don't know what the rules are here at NPR), he said, "Why do we have to pay for all this nonsense? What's it going to cost to clean up the broken glass and Popsicle sticks and so on?" So I went back and wrote a little story telling exactly what happened, and it turned out to be rather funny, and somehow it got on to the AP wire and was carried across the country, and we found out the next day it had got about five inches in the *Los Angeles Times*. In Wilmington, North Carolina, in whatever that year was, that was big stuff. They were very impressed, and so they offered me a regular, paid job.

Edwards: Well, that's good experience for the job you had at United Press, when the fellow calls you up at three A.M. and wants you to cover the Mexican hat dancers.

Brinkley: The phone rang beside my bed at three A.M. I struggled up, got the phone. It was the New York desk of the UP, and they said a client, a newspaper client in Mexico, wants a story on Mexican hat dancers, that they had performed in Charlotte that night. I said, "They did? Where?" And he said he didn't know any more. So I didn't know where to find them. At three A.M. I didn't feel like calling people and waking them up to find out about a story as trivial as this. I went through the newspapers, looking for some mention of the Mexican hat dancers. I had heard of them, but only heard of them. I knew nothing about them. I couldn't find anything. And while I was pondering what on earth to do, the New York desk called back again and said the client is impatient, they're waiting for the story, and I said, "I'll give it to them in five minutes." So I made up a story, and I said the Mexican hat dancers performed tonight in a Charlotte auditorium wearing their traditional costumes and dances and were frequently interrupted by applause and blah, blah, blah, that kind of nothing, and sent it to them and they liked it and that was fine. I'm still a little ashamed of it.

Edwards: Ultimately, you did stories for the *Camel News Caravan.*

Brinkley: Yes, that was the first regular television news program. It was really pretty bad, but in fact, everything on television was pretty bad at that time because we did not yet know how to do it. I remember once in a while, when we would do a little something on the air, we would get a phone call, and somebody would say, "Mr.

Brinkley, I just want to tell you we're getting very good picture out here in Bethesda."

Edwards: Well, for the younger folk, who only remember the late John Cameron Swayze from Timex, this is a fellow who went on every night with a fresh carnation.

Brinkley: That was part of his deal. He had a fresh carnation every night, and I tell you why he was there. He wasn't there because he had any great record in journalism. They hired Swayze because he had an unusual talent, essentially useless except in this particular environment. The talent was that he could read a page of copy and then recite it back, word for word, letter perfect.

Edwards: You once said he would recite it back, mistakes and all.

Brinkley: He recited what it said on the page.

Edwards: And he would hold up a carton of cigarettes.

Brinkley: That was a requirement of the advertiser, which was R. J. Reynolds. They demanded several things. They asked that there always be a cigarette burning and smoking in the ashtray on Swayze's desk. They required us never to have in our pictures a NO SMOKING sign. Never allowed that. And they never wanted anybody smoking a cigar to be on air. They made one exception, and it was Winston Churchill, and they also, at the end of the program, they asked Swayze to hold up a carton of Camel cigarettes, and say, "We're happy to say that this week" — the war was still going on — "happy to say that we have sent eight thousand cartons of Camel cigarettes to our boys around the world," meaning the boys in uniform and stationed around the world, and that was another requirement, and I did the program once in a while when he was on vacation, and when it came to holding up the carton of Camels, I held it up, but I had it upside down. They were furious, just furious.

Edwards: Tell the story of how later, during your coverage of the civil rights movement, you unwittingly launched the career of a national political figure.

Brinkley: In the course of reporting all this activity in the South, I managed to antagonize great numbers of Southern whites who were opposed to integration, and they hated what I was saying on the air. I was offering no opinions; I was just telling what was happening. And one of our stations in the South so hated me, so despised me because the owner of the station hated what I was putting on the air every night, the news about civil rights. He hired a local tinhorn to come on the air each night after me and he was given the assignment to "answer Brinkley's lies." And he became a famous figure. On the strength of his fame from answering my lies, he ran for the U.S. Senate and was elected and he's there today. His name is Jesse Helms.

Edwards: Well, meanwhile NBC was out looking for its Edward R. Murrow and it found Chet Huntley.

Brinkley: It did. They did it in a way unique to local television, or to television. They sent people around the country anonymously, not telling our affiliated stations they were in town. They checked into hotels or motels and turned on the television and watched the news, looking for somebody they thought was good enough to hire and to bring to New York to replace Ed Murrow. And in California, Los Angeles, I believe, they found one named Chet Huntley, liked him a lot, hired him, brought him to New York, and it wasn't put this way, but they thought he was going to be the new Ed Murrow. He might have been. He was very good. But before he could be established as an Ed Murrow, they assigned him and me to cover a political convention and — very advantageous for me because having lived in Washington I knew it very thoroughly, and Chet having come from California didn't know much about it. But we did it and it got to be done very well and they decided to put the two of us on doing the news and we did and we made a little television history, I guess.

Edwards: That was the 1956 convention. The critics loved it, from 1956 on.

Brinkley: They did. We got some really very nice flattering reviews because we had all grown up, and the critics had all grown up, with news broadcasters who pretended or thought they were the voice of doom. I mean, very heavy and very oppressive, and they delivered the news as if they were delivering the world's obituaries. And we did not. We both talked as we had always talked, as we are talking right now — not really stuffy. It went over very well because it was new and nobody had done it before and they thought it was really something tremendous.

Edwards: You and Huntley had a good long run.

Brinkley: We did. About fifteen years. Huntley was in New York, and I was in Washington all that time. Huntley was in New York but not of it. He was a cowboy. He came from Montana. His life's ambition was to go back to Montana to buy a ranch with maybe twenty or thirty square miles, sit on the front porch of a ranch house with his feet on the rail, cowboy clothes, and watch his cattle out on the field half a mile away and all of the land between him and the cattle was his. Land was very cheap out there. He did achieve that. He bought a ranch. He was so nice that when he had to live in New York he did not fit. For one thing that New Yorkers will understand and maybe others will not, he refused to take his name out of the telephone book. He left it in because he said, "Well, if people are nice enough to look at our program, I should be nice enough to talk to them on the phone." Well, that's an impeccable sentiment. But as a practical matter, it doesn't work. They wake you up at three A.M. to argue about something you said on the air. You can't do that. So anyway, my wife and I were visiting the Huntleys one Sunday afternoon when we were in New York for something, and the phone rang. He answered it himself. It was somebody from Arkansas named Judge Smithers who said, "Mr. Huntley, my wife, Pearl, and I are in New York and we'd like to ask you to have dinner with us. We don't know anybody here except you. Would you come and have dinner with us?" He said yes. And I said, "Huntley, you're crazy. You will run out of conversation before you finish your shrimp cocktail." And that's exactly what happened. Neither of them had anything to say to the other, but he was very nice and he went and played the role and came home. But he did that.

Edwards: Probably people are still asking you, "Aren't you Chet Huntley?"

Brinkley: That's a lovely little story. I was going somewhere, in an airport I think, and a woman, a nice gray-haired lady, stopped me, and said, "Aren't you Chet Huntley?" And I said yes, partly because it would save a lot of conversation. If I'd said, "No, I'm Brinkley," she would have felt she had to apologize and she didn't need to at all. Anyway, I said yes. And she said, "I think you're pretty good, but I can't stand that idiot Brinkley."

Edwards: And people still tell you, "Good night, David."

Brinkley: I do hear it once in a while. People shout it in the streets and then they laugh. I don't mind it a bit. It's rather nice.

The two autobiographies of LEONARD NIMOY suggest some ambivalence on the part of the actor-director toward the television role that made him famous. The first book was called *I Am Not Spock*, referring to the emotionless, pointy-eared Vulcan of *Star Trek*. His second memoir, entitled *I Am Spock*, was an attempt to dispel suspicions that he dislikes or denies a connection with the character. Linda Wertheimer spoke with Nimoy about his relationship to Spock. In the book, he and the television character have conversations, dialogues spelling out their differences and similarities, and Nimoy writes about listening for Spock to become clear to him as a character. October 16, 1995

Nimoy: It came one day to light very early on. We were on the bridge of the *Enterprise* playing the scene that we would play many, many times. We are confronted by some strange and mysterious and powerful object. And everybody is rushing about doing their business, trying to figure out what it is and what to do about it and everybody being very vocal and very energized and I had one word to say. And the word was "Fascinating." And I started out by saying "Fascinating." You know? And the director said, "Let's dry it out. Just be curious and be a scientist." And when I finally grasped what he meant and I looked curiously and simply said "Fascinating," the character appeared.

Wertheimer: It gives us all a cheer to hear you say that. Say it again.

Nimoy: Fascinating.

Wertheimer: I love that.

Nimoy: Oh, good.

Wertheimer: You separate these little plays that were the early *Star Trek*s by author and you say one of your very favorite ones was written by a science fiction author of considerable fame, Theodore Sturgeon. Did the writing, do you think, make a big difference?

Nimoy: Enormous. Enormous difference. That particular episode that I think you're referring to, an episode called "Amock Time," has become a classic favorite. It was terribly important to the Spock character because it was the first time in *Star Trek* that we were going to see other Vulcans and visit the Vulcan planet. Sturgeon gave us a beautiful, poetic script, a great story. Spock had been betrothed as a child and had to go home to fulfill this wedding betrothal. And Spock and the lady, matriarch of the planet, T'Pau, Celia Lovsky, a wonderful actress, are to greet. And Sturgeon had written the words "Live long and prosper" that were spoken for the first time in that episode. The words written by Ted Sturgeon.

In any case, I was looking for something that they would exchange in a way of a physical greeting that might give us a Vulcan touch. I said to the director, "Humans shake hands or they wave at each other and Asians bow to each other. Various cultures have various ways of physicalizing a greeting." He asked what I had in mind. So I introduced the Vulcan hand symbol.

Wertheimer: And that's the famous thing where you separate the second and third finger — second and fourth fingers?

Nimoy: That's right. And the thumb separate as well. So you get two V's shaped by the fingers.

Wertheimer: You say in the book that you and William Shatner and DeForest Kelley had to be the keepers of the flame for your characters. And you seem to feel particularly strongly about Spock in that way?

Nimoy: Well, I do particularly about Spock because I had never played a character over a long period of time that way. But I do feel very strongly about that particularly where actors are involved in acting in a television series. And very often it is the actor who has to remind new writers, new directors, new producers, about precedents that have been set with the character previously. You'll sometimes come on with a writer who has a great imagination and writes a scene for the Spock character with Lieutenant Uhura, for example, where she says, "Let's go out and spend some time under the Vulcan moon, Spock." Spock's response appropriately is "Vulcan has no moon, Uhura." Because Spock said that three episodes back, you see? The writer in this particular episode has to be reminded of that. It's the actor who is portraying the character who has the best memory of that.

Wertheimer: You, in directing *Star Trek IV*, you talk about how even though you were theoretically in charge of this whole thing and you were able to do something you had wanted to do, which was to sort of change the tone of the *Star Trek* movies and lighten up the whole thing, you got into a big fight about a very important moment in the movie and almost lost it. The fight about whether the whales would be understood when they sing?

Nimoy: Yes.

Wertheimer: What would you have done if you'd lost?

Nimoy: I felt extremely, extremely strongly about that issue, and in *Star Trek IV* when this probe is communicating with the whales it's not necessary for us to understand what they're saying to each other. It's not important. I think the magic is that they are communicating with each other, and we must understand that not all things are given to us to understand or is it necessary. There were people in the studio who wanted to put titles on the screen that would say, "Where are you? Why have we lost contact with you? Are you all right?" That sort of thing. And I refused to do it.

Wertheimer: It was then, I guess, a more natural thing than critics and writers seem to feel for you to move from there to *Three Men and a Baby*?

Nimoy: That's an interesting point. A lot of people were surprised. But there was humor in *Star Trek,* particularly humor in *Star Trek IV.* Michael Eisner and Jeff Katzenberg, recognizing that, asked me to do *Three Men and a Baby.* I remember being so satisfied with, I believe it was the *New York Times* review, which said, "One wouldn't think from his past work that Mr. Nimoy has the appropriate humor necessary to do this job." You know? "Fortunately, he does," said the writer, and gave me a decent review for my work on *Three Men and a Baby.* But I had been working in comedy for many, many years, in and out of *Star Trek* and other projects as well.

Wertheimer: The photograph that's on the cover of the book is a very Spock-like photograph, it seems to me, very somber and with that eyebrow climbing up your head. It made me think that it would be interesting to think about Spock as much older and what possibilities that might create. Do you think at all about the possibility that he'll come back again?

Nimoy: I have entertained that thought. I think it might be interesting. The last time we saw Spock in *Star Trek* was in an episode of

The Next Generation called "Reunification," in which we discover that Spock was working as an ambassador under deep cover on a secret mission in the Romulan Empire, trying to bring about a detente with the Romulans. And I thought the episode played quite well. There was a tremendous amount of audience interest in it. And we left Spock there. I wonder if somebody in the current *Star Trek* production world has had any thought about getting in touch with him and finding out if he's willing to tell us the story about what's going on there deep in Romulus.

As a comic actress on television sitcoms, MARY TYLER MOORE was irresistible. First on *The Dick Van Dyke Show* and, later, *The Mary Tyler Moore Show*, she was a prime-time fixture for years. Her characters, Laura Petrie and Mary Richards, were as vulnerable and insecure as they were stunning. The real-life trials of Mary Tyler Moore were far darker than those of the nervous and charmingly flappable TV counterparts. In her book, *After All*, she wrote about her three marriages, her emotionally ungiving parents, her feelings of guilt about neglecting her son, and her alcoholism. She talked about her life and her book with Daniel Zwerdling. December 2, 1995

Moore: I'm so proud of this book because I wrote it myself. It is not an "as told to," as are so many of the books on the market today, and I want to make sure the people understand that what they read is not a professional's idea of what aspects of my life are worthy of being in print, but rather my own.

Zwerdling: When friends read the book, what surprised them? Have friends come up to you, and said, "I never realized that about you"?

Moore: Several of them have said they love the book and I guess what they're surprised about is not the stories of my life so much as the ability to tell the stories, the ability to relate it in an intelligent, cogent, and interesting way.

Zwerdling: They're surprised you're a good writer. Because you are a good writer.

Moore: Thank you. Yes, I guess they are, as I am.

Zwerdling: Is there something you can think of that you wrote in the book that you're actually now surprised to have revealed?

Moore: Yes, and there's nothing specific. There is not a paragraph or two, or even a whole chapter — although contained within chapters are revelations that amazed me, feelings that I no longer have or feelings that have emerged that I didn't realize I possess. I tried not to write a book of resentments about my parents because I no longer feel that. I recognize through my own abilities and lack of abilities that everybody in my life did the best they could at the time, and I think the more we are able to come to that acknowledgment, the healthier and happier we will be. But that really did surprise me.

Zwerdling: Could I tell you a few things that surprised me, reading the book?

Moore: Yes, please do.

Zwerdling: We have heard before, because you have spoken very honestly in the past about your struggle with alcohol, your going to the Betty Ford Clinic, your struggle with your feelings about your son's death, so I'm not going to ask about those. But there were a couple of other things that really surprised me. At one point you were talking about how you never went to college, and you said, "To this day I'll do anything to avoid revealing a lack of knowledge, especially that of poetry, classical music, or philosophy." What do you mean by that?

Moore: Well, I mean I don't have a formal education, and my ability to carry on a conversation is due to the books that I have read on my own throughout the years. I'm still happy with the life that I've chosen for myself. But I wonder how much broader a scope I would have had had I gone to college, had I immersed myself in the classics, in music, in Shakespeare, in Ibsen and Chekhov. Would I not be a much more varied actor in my ability to add color to characters, or perhaps I would have ended up teaching English, in which case I would be retired right now and probably not being interviewed by you.

Zwerdling: But reading this, I have this fantasy, maybe it's the wrong fantasy, of you sitting with a bunch of friends over dinner and getting nervous when a certain topic comes up that you think will reveal that you don't know as much as people maybe think you do. Does that happen?

Moore: Yes, it does, but I've learned a trick, and I learned it long ago. Ask questions and don't be afraid to ask questions. And people who are knowledgeable are delighted to be able to share their knowledge with you.

Zwerdling: Well, give me an example, if you can, of the sort of situation where you get a little knot in your stomach thinking, Uh-oh, here comes that subject.

Moore: Well, I think you just did.

Zwerdling: Well, you give me an example of the thing that makes you the most nervous when you're with friends, when you feel like you're going to be revealed as not as intelligent as they think you are.

Moore: You're like the analyst from hell, aren't you? No, I really don't want to. Let's go on.

Zwerdling: Let me just get the book because I remember it right near the beginning. In the book you write, very movingly, about your father, a very cold, emotionally cold man. In fact, there's one anecdote you tell about how you tried to make a perfect Christmas tree as a young adult because he used to make perfect Christmas trees.

Moore: Well, my father used to do the Christmas tree and he really didn't want any of us to handle it because he was a perfectionist and he knew just how he wanted the tinsel to hang, free from touching any other branches so that it would be absolutely perpendicular to the floor. And I, too, tried to make the perfect Christmas every year as a young adult. In fact, everything had to be so perfect and so warm and gracious and charming and wonderful that Christmas became a grim affair in our house because it needed to be perfect. I even went my father one step further and I created snow on the tree by taking Ivory flakes and putting it in a mixing bowl and blending it with a machine and then dolloping this frothy, white stuff on the branches on top of the perfectly straight hanging tinsel and it would form a thin crust and look like snow. But my father said to me, "Mary, it looks like a snowman threw up on the tree."

Zwerdling: It is sort of funny, but it's really awful.

Moore: Well, yes, it's sad, but you know, good God, who of us in this life hasn't had sadness?

Zwerdling: You write in the book quite a bit about the men in your life, and although you write a little bit about this, you don't write as much, I think, about the women in your life and I would love to hear a little bit about the women in your life, your mother, for instance. You do write a little bit about her.

Moore: Well, I write a lot about my mother but perhaps you have a feeling that I didn't write about her because her inability to take joy in her motherhood absented her from my life to a great degree. She was a warm and loving and bright and funny human being, but she didn't have the gift, as I feel I did not have at age nineteen, for motherhood. I think I write about her to quite an extent, perhaps not in the total number of words laid down on the page, but certainly in terms of my feelings and my later empathy for her.

Zwerdling: You mention at one point that, to you anyway, she seemed to have more fun with her friends than she did with you.

Moore: Yes, just as I'm sure I seemed to my son to have more commitment to my work, which at that time was *The Dick Van Dyke Show,* than I did to him. In writing the book, I think I've come quite a distance from the position I held maybe ten years ago about women and working and motherhood. I understand that, as I say this, there are many women who don't have very much of a choice in the matter: they have to work. But I think, as I didn't think some years ago, that there is a price to be paid for making a commitment to work and career if you have children, and you had best be prepared for it.

Zwerdling: So if a woman, just starting out in her young twenties, comes to you, and says, "I'm wrestling with, you know, what to do about this career possibility, but on the other hand I have children. Can I balance them?" What do you say to her?

Moore: I would like to talk to her before the issue became critical. I'd like to talk to her before she has the children, and say, "If the career is important to you, if you really love it, if you have a passion about it, then follow it, and find a time — because it will come later down the line — where in later life you can have a child and you will have worked through some of the creative drive and you can then address yourself to motherhood." But we're not all that lucky. Some of us have to work and some of us have to make the balance, but I really don't think that child care centers give children what a mother can give a child. I don't think fathers can give what a mother can give. I think they are an important part of child rearing, and I'm so glad to see them becoming more and more involved, but a child needs that person to whom it was connected in the womb.

Zwerdling: When you read back over the book, do you like the person you meet in this book, Mary Tyler Moore? In the beginning of the book, you have a dialogue, and you, Mary Tyler Moore, are saying to Mary, the TV character, "Look, they love you. People identify with your persona. You've been their best friend and now

....

Bob Edwards received instruction on how to serve a fried egg and still impress company from no less than JULIA CHILD, the French Chef. He also got her to discuss her preferences in fast food. For three decades, her voice has been synonymous with fine cooking and public television. At age eighty-three, she returned with a new series, *In Julia's Kitchen with Master Chefs*. May 5, 1995

Child: My role is to represent the audience. "Now, is that four tablespoons? And what was that oven at, 325?" So I'm sort of acting as the audience asking, not stupid questions, but just questions, so we'll know what's going on.

Edwards: This is really your house?

Child: This is my house. Well, it — the downstairs — didn't look much like my house 'cause they took over the kitchen, which is a nice big room, and they moved the kitchen table up into the attic, and then they put a big aisle in, right in the center of the floor. Then we had three cameras that were all in there, and the chef and me. Then the dining room was the control center with all the machines and the director and the producer and so forth.

Edwards: It's bad enough having someone in your kitchen, but you've got camera crews.

Child: Well, I've been in the TV business for over thirty years now, and I was just delighted to have it in my house because then I didn't have to move around.

Edwards: Near as I can determine, you are Public Television's first big star.

Child: I'm the first cook. I think what had happened, it was called educational television, and it was mostly talking heads. I think the people, in Boston anyway, felt they'd like to enlarge their audience, and I had just done a cooking book review on their channel, and they got quite a number of calls saying let's have some cooking. So that's how I got on.

Edwards: Have we changed in our tastes in food now?

Child: Well, from those very early days when our food was very meat and potatoes. And then we've gotten very sophisticated. I think certainly the seventies were very good. I think people were thoroughly enjoying their food. A great many people have become afraid of their food now, which seems ironic because here we've got these wonderful ingredients now — wonderful meats and poultry and fruit and vegetables in the supermarkets. And now we have people that are afraid to eat. People seem to be awfully gullible. They'll believe anything — the scare of the week. I've been having fun promoting our new series, talking to radio hosts, and our scare of the week is of people who don't eat any fat at all. I had a friend who was out in one of those fat farms and there were two lady nutritionists and they were so thin. They looked as though they were just skin over their bones. Kind of pale with kind of flaky skin. Then I was talking to a radio host who said he was interviewing one of these no-fat people who was just that thin, and he was covered with dandruff. So that's our scare of the week.

Edwards: Well, what do you make of all the stories about cholesterol and fat and the richness of food?

Child: Well, I think that for a normal, healthy person, the idea is moderation and small helpings and a great variety of food, and then moderate exercise and weight watching and have a good time. That seems to be left out by these contemporary nutritionists, I think.

Edwards: I feel like such a fraud talking to you. I mean, it would be wonderful to compare basting techniques with you, but frying an egg is a challenge for me.

Child: Well, you should take a few cooking lessons or look at some of our cooking shows. Look at some of my shows if you really want to cook. You've got the opportunity to learn.

Edwards: Do you intimidate people? Are people reluctant to have you over for dinner?

Child: If they don't know me, I always like to get them over for dinner first. Then they'll see that we're a nest of simple folk.

Edwards: But wouldn't people be reluctant to cook for you?

Child: Well, not if they know me.

Edwards: Wouldn't they think you would be judging their food and the preparation and the presentation and the whole deal?

Child: Well, the thing, as I always tell people, is never apologize, because if you cook something and then you say, "Oh, this didn't turn out well," then I, as a guest, would say, "Well, it isn't very good, is it?" But if you cook it and serve it and keep up an animated conversation, everybody's happy. Never apologize. And then serve your fried egg.

Edwards: When you cook, it looks like it could serve a dozen. Do you ever cook for yourself alone?

Child: Oh, yes. If I'm alone. But I get very depressed if I don't eat nicely. But once you learn how to cook, it isn't very difficult and I hope you will take it up.

Edwards: Did you ever have a Big Mac?

Child: I mean, if you're traveling around, what are you going to have? I prefer the Quarter Pounder, though, to the Big Mac.

ROGER EBERT goes to see a lot of movies so that we don't have to. As a critic who separates the cinematic wheat from the chaff, he has acquired an encyclopedic knowledge of chaff. After he wrote a column on film clichés, several of Ebert's readers on the electronic service Compu-Serve began to contribute their own, which he compiled in a book, *Ebert's Little Movie Glossary*. Entries include the "turn-it-off rule: Immediately after the radio or television reports something important to the plot, someone must always reach over and turn it off." Another cliché that Ebert shared with Robert Siegel is the character who carries a bag of groceries, always displaying the proverbial baguette. February 10, 1995

Ebert: This is the baguette-envy entry, and the baguette invariably sticks up exactly six inches off the top of the bag. But there's another entry that carries that, too. Under "H," you'll find "Hollywood grocery bag": whenever a scared, cynical woman who wants to fall in love again is pursued by an ardent suitor who wants to tear down her wall of loneliness, she will go grocery shopping. The bag will break, and it either symbolizes the mess her life is in, which is if it's a sad ending, or, if it's a happy ending, her would-be suitor could help her pick up the pieces of her life and her oranges.

Siegel: One of my favorite sections in the book, under the "L's," are some of the laws that you and other contributors have derived about movies. The "law of economy of instruction."

Ebert: If anyone is ever taught anything in a movie at the beginning of the film, by the end of the film they will be required to know how to do that. Or if they find out anything, they'll later on have to use what they found out.

Siegel: Whatever Obi-Wan Kenobi tells Luke Skywalker, he's going to need that in an hour or so. Jeff Levin of Rochester, New York, has derived for you the "law of inverse wariness."

Ebert: The more dangerous the prisoner, the more lax the security precautions. This cross-references with the "law of the talking killer," which is when the villain has his prisoner in his sights and all he has to do is pull the trigger to kill him, inevitably he talks to him instead of killing him. That gives the victim time to figure a way out of the dilemma. Now, if you cross the "law of the talking killer" with the "law of inverse wariness," you get a James Bond movie because inevitably Bond stumbles into the world headquarters of this megalomaniac who, instead of killing him, talks to him, invites him to dinner, dresses up in a tuxedo, introduces him to his mistress. Then of course by morning James Bond has become the lover of the mistress who is helping him to destroy this man's evil empire.

Siegel: Now, there was another rule that you mentioned. I'm not sure if this is a rule or a law, but it's how one must present a bartender upon first being seen in a movie.

Ebert: The first time you see a bartender, he must be cleaning a glass with a rag. He must be. And also, elsewhere in the book you will find that although it is impossible in life, it is inevitable in the movies that when somebody is placed on the bar during a fight, they are hit so hard that they slide down the entire length of a bar. Try that at your neighborhood saloon and see if it works. Another thing you will find is that it is much more difficult in real life than it is in the movies to put a tankard of beer on the bar and slide it down eight or ten feet until it winds up in front of the person who ordered. It usually winds up falling into the lap of somebody who was two or three feet down the bar.

Siegel: And might lead to a lawsuit nowadays.

Ebert: Yes, and of course all saloons exist in movies in order for there to be a fight there. This is a hundred percent predictor. If the characters go into a bar, there will be a fight. Now, if they go into a cocktail lounge or a hotel lobby or a little café for a drink, then something else could happen. But if it's a saloon, there will be a fight.

W hen Scott Simon interviewed the film critic PAU-
LINE KAEL, he began by reading from one of Kael's
most eloquent and provocative essays, "Trash, Art, and the
Movies." In 1969, she was writing about film in an assort-
ment of San Francisco Bay Area magazines, having not yet
become the film critic at William Shawn's *New Yorker*. She
wrote about the place that movies had come to occupy in
American culture. Simon began the reading; she completed
it. March 18, 1995

Simon: [*reading from Kael's essay*] "In whatever city we find
ourselves we can duck into a theatre. . . . Where could we better
stoke the fires of our masochism than at rotten movies in gaudy
seedy picture palaces in cities that run together, movies and anonymity a common denominator. Movies — a tawdry corrupt art for
a tawdry corrupt world — fit the way we feel."

Kael: [*continuing*] "A good movie can take you out of your dull
funk and the hopelessness that so often goes with slipping into a
theatre; a good movie can make you feel alive again, in contact, not
just lost in another city. Good movies make you care, make you
believe in possibilities again. If somewhere in the Hollywood–entertainment world, someone has managed to break through with
something that speaks to you, then it isn't *all* corruption."

Simon: Ms. Kael, could I get you talk a little bit about your relationship with William Shawn, the legendary *New Yorker* editor?

Kael: It was a very love-hate relationship right from the start. He
courted me for about two years before I went to work for the magazine. It seemed to me too slick and refined for the kind of writing
I did, and yet he persisted and finally he won me over. But the two
of us fought consistently for, oh, twenty-odd years. He had very
squeamish tastes and he could never sit through a movie. He always found something too bloody or too offensive and yet he loved
the idea of movies. But if I tried to review something like *Deep
Throat*, he went into a panic. I had to talk with him at his bedside
to try to review that and I finally gave up. On the other hand, he
was a great editor. If I turned something in, half an hour later he

would have read it and would phone me to tell me his reactions. That's unheard of for a big-time editor. Most of the time, you turn in copy and you never hear a word and you don't know whether you've made an ass of yourself or not.

Simon: May I ask, I didn't know until reading your foreword to this collection, that you could cause quite a stir when you used to go out in New York City?

Kael: I pretty well abandoned it and moved to a small town in Massachusetts about twenty-five years ago and commuted to New York for the days I needed to turn in copy, because too many people wanted to get me. They weren't used to having themselves described, or having their performances, rather, described in a slick-paper magazine unflatteringly. Anyway, rather large and substantial movie actors threatened to beat me up and the people who were escorting me had a hell of a time removing ourselves from the vicinity.

Simon: John Cassavetes once gave you a hug, which seemed to go over the bounds?

Kael: Yes, I felt he wanted to crush every bone in my body. George C. Scott was less than charming to me. There were a number of people who had private reputations for beating women up anyway. It was about all they could beat up. It began to be a little threatening, and sometimes it was just unpleasant if you were sitting in a restaurant and you looked over and seated at a table were two young actors you'd been unkind to. It gets pretty awkward.

Simon: We'll get to a lot of the other stuff, as they say, "in a moment." I would just like to begin talking to you about some of the pieces in this collection, if I could. Because going through it, I kept turning back the pages of something that struck me, something I wanted to talk about, and interestingly enough, it's mostly about films that you've loved. For example, I might say, I have you to thank for opening my eyes years ago to Robert Altman.

Kael: Oh, I'm — I feel blessed.

Simon: And, you know, I guess if I had to pick a single Altman film that most affects me, it would be *McCabe and Mrs. Miller*, clearly a classic. But your piece about *The Long Goodbye*, which is not one of the Altman's films that gets mentioned a lot — it's of course based on the Raymond Chandler mysteries, a Philip Marlowe mystery.

Kael: Right.

Simon: A lot of people were upset by it, felt it wasn't good Chandler.

Kael: I think it's because Elliott Gould played the hero, and they imagined some Waspy, handsome fellow in the role. It was very funny with Elliott Gould in the role. People have forgotten how good he was in those years. Indeed, how good he still is in, for example, his small part in *Bugsy*.

Simon: One of the scenes that keeps coming back to me in *The Long Goodbye* — well, I think about even a simple a thing as Elliott Gould as Marlowe shopping for cat food.

Kael: That cat food scene is a classic.

Simon: Exactly.

Kael: There are scenes like the one with Mark Rydell as the petty gangster, breaking the bottle against his girlfriend's face. They're incredible scenes in the movie that upset people and yet said something.

Simon: In that scene (you know, I must say I got a video and so I saw the movie again just a few months ago), as I recall, you do not really see the bottle striking the woman, the gangster's moll.

Kael: Thank goodness, no!

Simon: No, but what you do see is the look of horror on the faces of the professional men of violence who are surrounding them.

Kael: Right.

Simon: Let me ask you then about Francis Ford Coppola's *Godfather, Part II*. This, of course, came out, I guess, what, about twenty years ago?

Kael: Right.

Simon: At a time before sequels were reflexive. It confirmed for you that Coppola was working in what amounted to an operatic scale.

Kael: I think *Godfather II* is simply one of the great American movies. Particularly if you take it together with *Godfather I*. But even by itself, those scenes of early New York with DeNiro as the young godfather have never really been matched, I think, for emotional substance. The whole movie has scale and richness. I mean, it has so many operatic characters. It has a whole American complex and, of course, it does speak of what goes wrong in American culture.

Simon: I want to ask you about the classic essay from which we quoted to introduce you here. "Trash, Art, and the Movies" appears in this collection. And let me get you, if I could, to talk a little bit about that. You note that when people get together, they often talk less about good movies than what they love about bad movies.

Kael: Right.

Simon: What is it that we love about bad movies?

Kael: Because, for one thing, we feel that we make discoveries in bad movies. The good movies, everything is generally presented to us because they work at all cylinders. Whereas, the bad movies we have personal, oddball relations to, and if someone else has noticed some obscure little point that was ludicrous or that was wonderful, we feel an attraction to them. I think one of the great things about growing up is learning which friends you can go to movies with and which ones you can't, and which fellows you date you can go to movies with and which ones you can't.

Simon: You write in this collection about a couple you know that broke up over *Dances with Wolves.*

Kael: I shouldn't laugh at it, but it is funny. I don't think I could be around somebody for long who likes *Forrest Gump.* There are certain movies that are sort of touchstones of how you react emotionally. There are certain actors. I mean, if I were around someone who says that Tom Cruise was his favorite actor, I'd have a rough time.

Simon: Now, but wait. I'm not about to say Tom Cruise was my favorite actor, but one of the things your criticism has done over the years is defend kids who would rather go to that old picture *Wild in the Streets*, as opposed to something worthwhile, because you say that connects to their lives.

Kael: *Wild in the Streets* has certain kinds of vitality. Let's give it a modern equivalent. *Dumb and Dumber* I enjoyed thoroughly. It's a very astute, slapstick comedy. Very, very well acted, and it's got some of the funniest scenes I've ever seen in it. There is a tendency for people to think that a movie has to have a worthwhile content. People are often saying that they regret that Americans don't make movies of ideas, and very often what they really mean is they prefer the greater control that they had at the theater. The theater was often about ideas, where people sat in a room and talked. And they really want to go back before movies made them feel that they didn't control things.

Simon: You believe in star power. That's a phrase that comes back in several of your reviews.

Kael: There are certain people who have extraordinary gifts of magnetism. They don't necessarily have it off the screen, but they have it on screen. What's held movies together and what's kept us going are the actors. I think if we hadn't had, oh, Steve Martin and Robin Williams, Bill Murray and Bette Midler and half a dozen other performers who brought us something new into movies, we couldn't have gone to see those pictures because they were basically so much like pictures we had seen before. But it's always the power of the human face and the human body to hold us there, and it's not something we should fight. I mean, Michelle Pfeiffer has a great camera face. It would be stupid to deny it.

Simon: Does a good movie make you feel alive, uplifted still?

Kael: Alive, uplifted, I don't know. It makes me feel great. I think good movies do that for people. The terrible thing is when good movies don't do that for people and you feel they've somehow been so cousined by lousy pictures that when they see a good one, they tend to resent it because they feel things they don't understand.

You simply cannot categorize the movie director SID-NEY LUMET. Nominated for more than fifty Academy Awards, his credits include *Network, Murder on the Orient Express, Serpico,* and *Prince of the City.* Lumet made his moviemaking debut in 1957 with *Twelve Angry Men* and has worked over the years with many of the world's finest actors and screenwriters. Lumet told Bob Edwards that he never knows how a particular performer will respond to direction until he starts rehearsals. April 18, 1995

Lumet: Part of my job is to become whatever the actor needs. I can speak many different acting languages. If you're a method actor, I can talk Stanislavsky. If you're a Royal Academy graduate, I can talk to you in those technique terms. So that is my — part of my — job to become whatever helps that actor fulfill what they're doing.

Edwards: With Ralph Richardson it was music.

Lumet: Yeah. I didn't know it at the time. This glorious actor — for me, he was the finest actor in the English-speaking theater, and I didn't know that when he was appearing in the theater he would warm up in his dressing room by playing the violin, and when we were working on *Long Day's Journey into Night,* he asked me a question, and I tend to talk a lot, and about thirty minutes later I finished, and he looked at me and said, "I know what you mean, dear boy. A little more cello, a little less flute," and it was not only an enchanting putdown of me, but I understood immediately that he works from really an auditory perception. And from there on we talked in musical terms. "Ralph, a little staccato." "A little more legato." "A little more bass, Ralph." "A little more treble." And it was glorious. It was shorthand and it worked quickly and we had a complete common language.

Edwards: With Brando, you wanted to help him through the thirty-sixth take on a line, and the key was to leave him alone.

Lumet: Yeah. You know, actors have a very, very painful time when they're working, and I know people don't believe that. They think, Oh, they're just showing off, or it's a bunch of exhibition-ism. Not so. If they're good, there's a tremendous amount of per-sonal revelation involved, and that's painful, always. And in this instance, Marlon was going up on a line that I knew very closely related to his own personal life, and I didn't feel I had the right to violate the confidence he had given me, even if it would help him get over the block of that line. I'm not his analyst, I'm his director, and I let him struggle through it.

It was extremely painful, and when we talked about it afterward, after the shot was completed and we were going home, and I said, "You know, Marlon, I was debating whether to tell you what I thought might help you through that block, 'cause I think it had to do with what we talked about last week," and so on. And he looked at me and he smiled, and, you know, when Brando smiles you think the sun is coming up, it's glory, that man, and he said, "I'm very glad you didn't," and gave me a hug and we went on home.

Edwards: You like writers, you respect writers, and enjoy work-ing with writers. You had some good experiences there. Probably had some bad ones too.

Lumet: Not many, not many. I guess that that comes from the theater, you know? In the theater — that's my background — the writer is it. So that that automatic respect for what the writer has done, that's just built in to me.

Edwards: I think it would have been great fun to be with you and Paddy Chayefsky on the set of *Network*.

Lumet: It would have been a ball because we had a ball. He was incredibly funny. He coined that phrase, as far as I know, of "rubber ducky school of drama." Rubber ducky meaning, "Somebody took my rubber ducky out of my bathtub when I was two years old and that's why I'm the deranged killer that I am," you know, that kind of dumb attempt to explain people. There was another marvelous thing that he said once. He was a very litigious fellow, as far as studios were concerned. The first question about anything, when the studio called up was, "Can I sue?" And he wanted always to put them down whenever he could. He used to say, "Look, I know what you guys want. You want a pet-the-dog scene and a kick-the-dog scene." And I'd say, "Paddy, what's a pet-the-dog scene?" And he said, "Pet-the-dog scene, that's for the hero. Kick-the-dog scene, that's for the villain." He said, "Unless you got a pet-the-dog scene and a kick-the-dog scene, they're too dumb to know who the hero and the villain is." He was just filled with that kind of funny hostility and — and it was such a joyful time working with him.

Edwards: And you could watch it today and wonder where the satire is. It's all true, isn't it?

Lumet: But, you know, Bob, we maintained that from the beginning. People would say, "Oh, what a brilliant satire," and we'd say, "What satire? It's sheer reportage."

Edwards: If you had a couple of film cans and you were standing at the Pearly Gates and your entry into heaven depended on showing a film, what would you show?

Lumet: Whoever was in charge, I would have to give them the same answer: "You have to pick it." Because by naming a favorite, you sort of make orphans of the others, so it's one of the few questions I duck all the time.

Edwards: Has it changed?

Lumet: I don't know because I really don't look at my past work much. My daughter-in-law gave me for my birthday a set of videos of all my movies, and I think on almost all of them the cellophane is still intact.

With her mod look, blond hair, mini dresses, and white boots, PETULA CLARK was the very image of 1960s British pop. Young and sophisticated, with a beautiful voice, she became an international pop star with such recordings as "I Know a Place" and "Downtown." In fact, she had been a star abroad for more than two decades. When she was only ten, Petula had her own radio program in England, called *Pet's Parlor.* Two years earlier, during World War II, her father, convinced that Petula could be a singing star, got her onto a BBC radio program. During a rehearsal, an air raid began, and, as she told Liane Hansen, to calm people down, Petula sang. January 22, 1995

Clark: It was a special show for kids who had relatives serving abroad. You know, I had an uncle who was serving in Iraq, I think, at the time. I represented all the kids who'd been left behind in England, just as Vera Lynn did, I don't know if you've heard of her —

Hansen: Oh, sure.

Clark: She was the force's sweetheart. I was the force's little girl.

Hansen: Do you remember the song that you sang?

Clark: Yes, of course I do. It was "Mighty Like a Rose." You know, [*sings*] "Sweetest little fellah, everybody knows, don't know what to call him, but he's mighty like a rose."

Hansen: Thanks for doing that so early in the morning.

Clark: It is a bit early, yes.

Hansen: I think people would be surprised to find out that you have been in show business a very long time.

Clark: Oh, yes, a very long time.

Hansen: You signed a movie contract when you were eleven years old, with the Rank Organization, very famous British film distributors, and you worked with people like Alec Guinness.

Clark: And Peter Ustinov. Yes, I've been lucky enough to work with some really great people. Alec Guinness — I was in a movie which I think was called *The Promoter* over here. It was called *The Card* in England. And I gave him his first screen kiss.

Hansen: [*gasps in surprise*]

Clark: Yes. A momentous thing. He was extremely shy, and so was I. It was a good movie. Glynis Johns was in it, Valerie Hobson. It was good.

Hansen: So by this time you were on a show biz track.

Clark: Yeah. You know, after that famous thing on the radio during the war, I went on to do a lot of radio. And then I did television. And then I did movies. And I was a child star. And I went on working all through my adolescence.

Hansen: But then you came back with a bang when you were in your thirties, actually, what, almost thirty years ago, with "Downtown"?

Clark: When "Downtown" hit, I was already extremely busy. I was married and I had two small children. Really, "Downtown" came almost as a kind of intrusion into my life. I was getting these calls from the States, saying, "You've gotta come, you've gotta come," you know. You know, "Ed Sullivan wants you." And I said, "Who's Ed Sullivan?" You know. And I just couldn't do it. You know, I couldn't get over here. And eventually I came. And I remember that first *Ed Sullivan Show.* I arrived totally jet-lagged, of course, you know, straight from the airport because my plane was late. I went straight to the studio, which was a theater. In fact, that's where they do *The Letterman Show.*

Hansen: Right, *The David Letterman Show,* sure.

Clark: And the audience was in, and the orchestra had rehearsed without me. And I walked onto the stage with no makeup, no — you know, with the clothes I'd been traveling in. And they started playing the music, and it was a standing ovation. I mean, before I even started to sing. I thought, Wow, what's this? You know, This is America. And that was my first introduction to the American public. It was extraordinary.

Hansen: Was it a little strange for you to be in your early thirties and be emblematic of a time, you know, the swingin' sixties in London, a time when, you know, we weren't supposed to trust anybody over thirty. All the teenagers listened to you. Oh, it's true, they did. I did.

Clark: Did you not trust anybody over thirty?

Hansen: For a few years I didn't, but now I trust them all. But do you know what I mean? I mean, here you are, married lady, you had two children. And here's this, you know, image we had of you in little white boots, you know.

Clark: Oh, well, that's who I was. I mean, you know, I mean, being married and having two kids doesn't mean that you're, you know, a frump. And I certainly wasn't. You know, I was leading the most extraordinary life all over Europe. And I wasn't putting on an act at all. That's who I was. And in a way, that's who I am, you know. I don't think you can fake that.

Hansen: In 1993, you made your Broadway debut as Mrs. Johnstone in Willy Russell's musical *Blood Brothers*. The story is about the Johnstone twins, separated at birth when their mother is forced by economic necessity to give one of them away. You have said you didn't feel up to playing the mother at first because you weren't quite sure you understood who this woman was.

Clark: It may sound silly, you know, because I am, after all, I'm an actress. So, you know, one should be able to play anything, you know, more or less. But I didn't feel that I had that experience inside me to be able to really play this woman sincerely. As Olivier would say, "Well, act it, my dear, act it," you know. But you have to be able to find that something inside you to make it real. In fact, of course, I do know who this person is. Certainly the Welsh side of my family was very poor. My grandfather was a coal miner in South Wales. And when the bombardments got a bit too much in London, myself and my sister would go to Wales, where things weren't quite so bad, and we would live with our grandparents. And it was a pretty poor existence, although we loved it. Of course, I don't think children are ever aware of the surroundings, you know. I mean, we used to live in air raid shelters when we were in London, and thought it was great fun. So I really had seen this kind of life, but I had forgotten it. You know, you sort of bury all this stuff inside you. You know, I've gone on to be quite wealthy and successful and travel first-class and limos and all this, you know, all that stuff that comes, all the trappings that come with it. And a part of my life is sort of — I've forgotten. And this has brought it all back to me.

Hansen: Is it true that you don't like your name?

Clark: Yes.

Hansen: Really?

....

Trial lawyers are taught to ask only questions to which they already know the answers. STUDS TERKEL, the great radio interviewer, asks only questions to which he doesn't know the answers. "If I had questions to which I knew the answer, why would I ask the question?" he told Scott Simon. "Astonishment is what knowledge is all about. Wonder is what knowledge is all about." After forty years of eliciting wonder and knowledge on radio, some of Studs's interviews were released on audiocassette in a collection called *Four Decades with Studs Terkel.* His subjects have ranged from Chicago's South Side to South Africa, from Mel Brooks to Bertrand Russell. Simon had witnessed Terkel up close at radio station WFMT in Chicago, where the legendary interviewer's talents were known to desert him when it came to handling recording equipment. January 21, 1995

Terkel: Well, I've got to make it clear that I'm probably the most inept guy anywhere.

Simon: Are your shoes — they're OK. All right. I was checking your shoelaces.

Terkel: Oh, my shoelaces. Do they make you nervous?

Simon: No, no. I was wondering if you'd tied them, frankly.

Terkel: Oh, well, they're tied. Oh, I see. I'm a little slow on the uptake. I don't drive a car.

Simon: Neither do I.

Terkel: Oh, you don't?

Simon: No. We're the last two people, I think. You got a license?

Terkel: No.

Simon: I don't either.

Terkel: But could that be? You're of a younger generation. You don't drive a car?

Simon: I never learned.

Terkel: It's astonishing.

Simon: I think I'd be terrible at it, too.

Terkel: You're an anomaly. I'm a little easier now, not better, but easier, with a tape recorder. Often I press the wrong button. I almost lost Bertrand Russell. Here I was, up in a town called Penrhyndeudraeth, a name that is unspellable, a Welsh name in north Wales, in his little cottage during the Cuban Missile Crisis. Suddenly, I realize, I was just about to begin. I didn't have the button on, the on button. I'm just about to start, and I say, "Lord Russell," and he said, "Oh, what is it, young man?" I said, "Just a moment." And then I'm pressing that button. So I almost lost Russell. I lost Michael Redgrave by forgetting to press the button. But it's an asset at times. When interviewing, say, for the books, these are the not celebrated people, not authors or musicians. This is say, someone in a housing project, and I forgot to press the button. She'd say, "You didn't press that." And I say, "Oh, thank you." At that moment, she feels not only my equal, but my superior. See, at that moment, I'm not this guy with a mike from Mount Olympus coming down to earth to do it, but this goofball with this machine. And she helps me. Some people accuse me of deliberately goofing it up so I can make that other person feel better. That's not so. I'm just inept. It's simple as that.

Simon: You still always read the books of any author you interview, listen to the music of any composer, see the plays of any playwright or actor.

Terkel: I only have on people, I'd say, whom I respect as either writers or musicians or whatever they may be. How can you show any respect unless you know his work, or certainly, if you've read his book?

Simon: You know this. There are people, all the time, who've been interviewing people for years, who are pretty popular at it, no names mentioned, who say they never read the book.

Terkel: Oh, Larry King.

Simon: I said no names mentioned.

Terkel: No, he's proud of it.

Simon: I know he's proud of it.

Terkel: But at least in his case, he makes it quite clear. But there are many who pretend. That's even worse, you see. Nelson Algren, after he wrote *The Man with the Golden Arm*, was interviewed by someone in San Francisco, who obviously hadn't the slightest idea who Algren was or read the book. And he said, "The man with a golden — what's it about?" Nelson said, "It's about the Golden Gate Bridge." And he said, "It is?" And for the next half hour, Nelson Algren talked about the Golden Gate Bridge.

Simon: Oh no.

Terkel: The guy didn't know the difference. I know when I watch a TV show or hear radio and the person is interviewing and you know they haven't read the book, quite obviously. "What's it about?" Right. "What's it about?" "Well, how did you come to write it?" or "How long have you been a writer?" You know that they haven't read the book. But, the point, it's even worse, is that the writer has to play the game along with them. They both pretend.

Simon: We hear a lot in our age that the general level of literacy is declining. Have you noticed, as you interview people, that the general level of conversation has declined?

Terkel: What's happened here, oh boy, so many things. It's easy to say it has. I know it has. But why? I think one reason is technology itself. The very nature of technology. As we become more and more enamored, technology, we know, can help mankind. It has, of course, in labor-saving devices, washing machines, other matters. At the same time, the love of it has overwhelmed us. A case in point. I like cases in point. You've been in the Atlanta airport?

Simon: Yes.

Terkel: It's a modern airport.

Simon: Yes.

Terkel: And they have those trains that take you to concourses.

Simon: The subway you have to take to get to your plane?

Terkel: Yeah, subways. And they're nice and smooth and silent, silent. I'm on it and it's crowded and a young couple are late and they rush in and part the pneumatic doors, just about to close. And as they close, the same voice, oh, it's a mechanical voice. It's a man's voice. You know that. It is a human, but it's mechanical. It's imitating the machine. So as the doors shut and the couple just make it, the same voice, without pause, says, "Because of late entry, we're delayed thirty seconds." Everybody's looking at that couple, you know, and they're just quailing and they're embarrassed. And I had a few drinks. And so I'm saying, "George Orwell, your time has come and gone." And there's dead silence. And then I see a baby sitting on the lap and so I look at the baby, about a year old, and I said, "What is your opinion of all this?" And the baby just breaks into one of those big, wide, FDR-type grins. And so I holler, "There's still hope in the world."

SCIENCE

For all the attention paid to the AIDS epidemic, it is by no means the only, nor even the most frightening of contagious diseases menacing the world. LAURIE GARRETT, a science reporter for *Newsday*, painted a terrifying picture of infectious and deadly ailments in her book, *The Coming Plague: Newly Emerging Diseases in a World Out of Balance.* As Garrett told Daniel Zwerdling, public health researchers generally agree that serious diseases caused by bacteria and viruses are spreading faster and afflicting more people than at any time in history, including such diseases as gonorrhea, syphilis, and hepatitis. February 11, 1995

Garrett: We're also in the middle of the worst malaria epidemic the planet has ever seen. More people are dying of malaria today than in the 1960s when we set out to get rid of it. We have witnessed drug-resistant tuberculosis. In fact, the Centers for Disease Control and the World Health Organization just last week released a study that shows that we're going to have the largest tuberculosis epidemic by the year 2000 that the human race has ever faced. This is supposed to be our age of having conquered and vanquished the microbes, but the reverse has occurred, and a lot of scientists are now saying that conditions for the emergence of diseases and the spread of disease have never been better for the microbes than they are now.

Zwerdling: What's most surprising about the cases in your book is that you argue that some of those conditions that you say are making microbes spread faster than ever are environmental changes such as the ozone hole, deforestation. We knew that these sorts of problems caused more skin cancer and soil erosion, but you're arguing that the same environmental problems are partly responsible for spreading these killer viruses.

Garrett: Well, not just viruses, also bacteria and parasites. As we go into any kind of ecology, we now have become sophisticated enough to recognize that we disrupted, on a sort of macro level, that which we can see. So if you go swaggering into the Amazon and you burn down a chunk of rain forest, you can clearly see it's different than it was before you showed up. What is less clear, and we're only beginning to adequately research, is what happens on the micro level, that level that we can't see. Every single place where the question is asked and studied and scrutinized, using classic scientific methods, the encroachment of humanity does severely disrupt the microecology and often in ways that permit the emergence of diseases that we had not really recognized before.

Zwerdling: Why don't we talk about a specific example, which you cover in one of the chapters in your book. And that is the epidemic of hantavirus. Now, this was what some media, back in late 1993, were calling "Navajo disease," right?

Garrett: Right, the "Navajo flu," a horrible, horrible term applied to it, very unfair to the Navajo people and one that was much resented in the southwestern United States.

Zwerdling: This is an incredible detective story about how a nineteen-year-old Navajo athlete was on his way to his girlfriend's funeral when he suddenly died. Then it turned out that his girlfriend had died of the same strange disease. I want to skip over the details of the detective story because people should read the book to find them out. But let's leap to near the end of this story because you say that researchers have uncovered what appears to be a chain of events suggesting that some of the people who've gotten this disease have gotten it partly because of the U.S. bombing campaign in Korea, during the Korean War at the beginning of the 1950s.

Garrett: It's very interesting. Hantaviruses turn out to be a whole class of viruses, and the particular hantavirus that's now called Muerto Canyon that occurred in the southwest, turns out to just be one of this giant family that we're only beginning to truly appreciate. The first time they really came to our attention was during the Korean War when the United States was doing an intensive bombing campaign. It was the last time that a lot of U.S. troops were hunkered down in trenches. The bombing prompted a particular kind of wild mouse to move away from its remote field areas and, to escape the bombings, to come closer and closer to villages, to human habitation. They got into turf fights with rats and in the process of these turf fights, they bit the rats. It appears they transmitted this previously very, very rare and remote virus into urban rat populations. Then those U.S. troops in the trenches, where they were exposed to the mice, and people in the cities who were exposed to the rats, came down with this very dangerous disease. A certain percentage of these people proceeded to die. It is a hemorrhagic syndrome.

Zwerdling: How did it get from Korea to the Navajo reservation and now to the East Coast, apparently?

Garrett: Well, it's not the same virus. The one that was in the Navajo reservation is a member of the family, but it's not the same virus. The one that turned up in Baltimore and in Philadelphia and in New Orleans and, for that matter, in every single port city of the United States where anybody has bothered to look, turns out to be the Korean virus. It appears it was carried by rats that were inside of shipments of automobiles from South Korea.

Zwerdling: The case of the hantavirus shows how an unlikely chain of events in one part of the world apparently creates disease on the other side of the world. In this country there has been a lot of publicity over the last decade about Lyme disease, an illness almost unheard of ten years ago, which now makes people afraid to go on a picnic or strolling through the woods in New England because it's carried by ticks and it can, if untreated, disable you for life.

Garrett: This is a classic one as well, where you can see how disrupting our macroecology made us make changes in our microecology that we didn't even know about, didn't pay attention to, didn't anticipate. And bingo, we have a new disease syndrome.

Zwerdling: In what way?

Garrett: Well, when settlers came to the northeast, in particular to Massachusetts, they colonized immediately and started chopping down trees for fuel and to build. Pretty soon, they had done such an incredibly efficient job at denuding the northeast. What eventually grew back to replace the huge forests in the northeast were what Andrew Spielman, a wonderful biologist at Harvard University, likes to call "an ecosphere about as natural as your average parking lot." The improper, aggressor species have taken over; you've got this low scrub and these little scraggly trees. The great timber of the past will never return. In a similar way, the animals that took over are different because we eliminated the predatory species. So now we have deer with no predators. At the micro level, we have various aggressive species with no predators. The overall result was a totally disrupted, artificial ecology, in which a particular tick population that thrives on the deer and on a certain kind of mouse, and the bacteria that's carried by that tick, managed to flourish. Now, in these places that people aspire to live in because they want their suburban, wooded environment, it's dangerous.

Zwerdling: You can look at any situation in life in the glass-is-half-empty or the glass-is-half-full mode and when I get caught up in the details of your book, it's easy to be in the glass-is-half-empty mode. I get a dread feeling that we're all on the verge of being wiped out by exotic diseases. There seem to be more and more illnesses which can't be treated by the usual antibiotics. On the other hand, it seems to me that you could look at all of your stories in a glass-is-half-full way by saying, "Hey, folks, we have great news. There are lots of scary viruses and bacteria out there. But you know what, most people are not, in fact, getting them. Most people around the world don't have HIV. They don't have hantavirus. They don't have cholera."

Garrett: Yes, but if you combine cholera, drug-resistant malaria, drug-resistant tuberculosis, HIV, hepatitis A, B, C, D, E, F, and G, and a host of other things that are spreading around the world, I'm sorry, but most do. The majority of the world's population is today facing infectious disease problems. We may not feel it so much in our comfortable, suburban homes in the United States of America right now, but I'll remind you that last year four hundred thousand people got sick in Milwaukee drinking their tap water. This goes back to your first question, Why do some scientists think things have never been more favorable to the microbes than they are today? We are seeing a rise in the antibiotic-resistant microbes, in chlorine- and disinfectant-resistant microbes. We even see bacteria now that can live on a bar of soap. We couple that with the fact that we are really in a global village now and that there is no such thing as a place too remote for human beings to go to. What this all means, coupled with population growth, is that we are witnessing an ever increasing and rapidly accelerating set of circumstances that are ideal for the microbes and that make our job, as humanity, to control the situation, more and more difficult every year.

Zwerdling: So suppose President Clinton reads this book, and says, "Oh my gosh, we've got to do something. Laurie Garrett, you're right, and so are the infectious disease researchers you write about all around the world." What can President Clinton do now with this information?

Garrett: You have to recognize that disease emergence is a national security concern. If you define security as the right of the average citizen to feel safe, to feel that no outside threat will come their way, this is a national security concern.

Zwerdling: So you're arguing that when the federal government decreases funding on malaria research overseas, as it has been doing the last few years, you're saying that's a big, big mistake.

Garrett: It's imperiling us. I think people have this tendency to view, at least health aspects of foreign aid, as fitting in with all these sort of liberal, do-gooder projects, and we just, as a nation, can't afford to be liberal do-gooders anymore. I think that would be a fair summary of how a lot of people in the United States and, I might add also, in other wealthy countries, view the situation. At the same time, we are witnessing a situation where the notion that diseases have anything to do with national boundaries is becoming increasingly artificial. What was yesterday in Zaire could be today in Los Angeles. And if we continue to see the issue of public health as a political partisan issue, we will be defeated. We will lose.

JODY HEYMANN was transformed one day from doctor and health policy analyst to patient. A week after receiving two degrees from Harvard, an M.D. and a Ph.D. in public policy, she was hospitalized for a seizure caused by bleeding into the brain. After brain surgery that she was told would take less than two hours but took ten, she found she would have to learn to live with seizures. Her doctors said they could not find any lesions on the surface of her brain, but they had removed something. Heymann's experience of medicine from the patient's perspective led her to write *Equal Partners: A Physician's Call for a New Spirit of Medicine*. In an interview with Linda Wertheimer, she talked about rethinking the relationship between the providers and recipients of medical care. The book begins with the story of her own diagnosis and surgery. March 28, 1995

Heymann: It was almost two years before my father could talk with me about that day. He reopened the journal he filled the week of the surgery. This is his writing: [*reading*] "Mom and I got up around four-thirty in the morning and drove down to the hospital. I remember we saw you for about a half hour before they started to give you the series of sedatives. I remember them wheeling you down the hall to the operating area, and again your spirits were very good. There was something — an excruciating sweet, proud, frightening feeling — about seeing you so brave and so upbeat going into something that was so frightening."

I remember trying to cheer my parents up. But I also remember not being afraid, having the courage of a pilot who had studied war at the Air Force Academy but never fought — at least never fought on the side that gets injured. It's frightening what a lack of perspective one can have even after medical training and working in hospital wards.

Wertheimer: What happened next was really gruesome and horrible. The surgery went on for much longer than it was supposed to. The lesions in your brain that they were attempting to remove they couldn't find. And then you described the process of waking up and the pain, which you didn't expect either.

Heymann: I woke up. I was in terrible pain. My fingers were gripping the side rails until my knuckles were white. And the pain medication, as too often happens, was being given too infrequently to work. My husband tried to get it to be given more frequently but wasn't even able to see a physician who would speak to him about it. At the same time, I was having terrible hallucinations. I asked numerous people about them and what might cause them and their answer was "We don't know. We've never heard of any patients having them." Later, I realized, talking to patients, that these were fairly common. Had people simply listened to patients' experiences, known about them so that they could tell me how common these were, then I would have known that they would be only temporary, I would have known I wasn't going out of my mind.

Wertheimer: When you finally did go back to work, apart from your own continuing struggles with seizures and so on, you knew more at that point about what patients go through than you had learned to that point in medical school. You tell a lot of stories in the book about other patients. People whose situation you understand because of your own experience. But where does that lead you? What should health policy do to compensate, to help integrate the kinds of things that you learned into normal practice?

Heymann: I think changes need to occur in two different spheres. One is in medical education. And we need to have medical students learn more from patients about what it's like to live with a health problem and to live with the health treatments we prescribe. A second thing that needs to happen in education is giving new physicians the understanding that when they can't figure out what's wrong it doesn't mean the patient is making it up. That's on the education side. The other side is clearly in changing the health care financing system so that there's enough time for patients and doctors to talk to each other. Right now the average outpatient visit is twelve minutes in the country. Twelve minutes is nowhere near enough time to listen to patients, to share in decision making, to do a physical exam and discuss diagnoses, treatment plans. And yet, many managed care systems, on average, have even less than that twelve minutes.

Wertheimer: The book is called *Equal Partners* because you think that patients should be taken seriously in terms of their own accounts of the state of their health?

Heymann: Yes. I think patients should be taken seriously and I think that patients bring something equal but different to the table. Physicians know more than patients about physiology or microbiology or anatomy. But patients know and will always know far more than physicians about what it's like to live with an illness. What it's like to work with an illness, raise their family, how the treatments as well as the illness itself or health condition affects their lives. They bring that knowledge to the table. And the name of the book is for the need to work as equal partners in decision making and in the discussion of what one's options are.

Wertheimer: You, I would think, would be a special patient. You would be somebody doctors would be anxious to take good care of, the friend of colleagues? Why do you suppose what happened to you happened?

Heymann: I think it's just so common. After the surgery, I had brain swelling. It was being treated successfully with a drug that went straight into my veins. But then when I was changed to a medication by mouth, it didn't work. I began to throw up as the brain swelling got worse until I was throwing up every couple minutes. And I tried, as a physician, as you describe, as that special physician, to say, "I know what's wrong. Clearly I'm not keeping the medicine down that I'm throwing up constantly. Give me the medicine intravenously so that it will stay in." Even as a physician, I couldn't get any help in that setting. When you're in the patient's shoes, you often feel like you're talking to someone who has headphones on and is tuned to another station. The physicians are listening to other physicians, but they're not hearing what patients are saying, whether you're a physician yourself or not.

Manic depression reminds KAY REDFIELD JAMISON of the Chinese belief that before one can conquer a beast, one first must find it beautiful. It is a beautiful distillation of both what is finest and what is most dangerous in human nature. Dr. Jamison is an acknowledged expert on manic-depressive illness and someone who lives with the condition. A professor of psychiatry at the Johns Hopkins University School of Medicine in Baltimore, Maryland, and the author of *An Unquiet Mind: A Memoir of Moods and Madness*, Dr. Jamison spoke with Scott Simon about the illness that has exhausted and frightened her, but also contributed to her very identity. December 2, 1995

Simon: First off, "finest and most dangerous" — those are the words you use. Help us to understand that, if you can.

Jamison: Well, finest, in the sense that I think that moods are so intrinsic to who we are and what we are, as people. Manic-depressive illness is extremes in moods, but it's also all gradations of moods. So in some ways, you have different kinds of experiences and emotional experiences you would not otherwise have. It's basically a dreadful, terrible, lethal disease. It's basically awful, but there are certainly parts of particularly mild manias where things are just extraordinarily wonderful. You feel alert and alive and you take chances you wouldn't take and you have experiences you simply would not otherwise have.

Simon: When did you first begin to feel this way, looking back on it?

Jamison: Looking back on it, certainly in any sort of extreme way, my senior year in high school. As a child, I was intense. I took things to heart, but I don't know so much more than other people. I mean, a lot of children are intense. I mean, childhood is intense, but when I was in high school I just started flying. I was high as a kite for weeks, sort of on natural juices, and everything was marvelous and wonderful and comprehensible and cosmic and I didn't need any sleep, and then I totally crashed, and I couldn't think. I couldn't reason. I couldn't understand or remember anything. I couldn't read something and have it make any sense at all.

Simon: Did anyone think it was a problem at those times, or was it just part of being a gifted teenager?

Jamison: A couple of my friends certainly noticed that there was something wrong with me, and one of my teachers very much noticed and called me aside, but not my family. I think you mask these things. You know, you're an adolescent anyway, so your tendency is to keep to yourself or just share things with your friends. One of the reasons I'm so interested in manic-depressive illness and mood disorders in adolescents is that everyone tends to think that anything goes in adolescence. In fact, what we know is that adolescence is not nearly as abnormal a state as people give it credit for being. It's very abnormal to feel the things that I felt, to be deeply suicidal and unable to function.

Simon: I'm sorry for this. I mean, one of the conditions of this business is that you just meet somebody in a hallway, you drag 'em into the studio, and within minutes, you're getting them to talk about the most painful —

Jamison: No, I absolutely understand. I think you can't write a terribly personal book and then not expect that you're going to be asked personal questions. It's uncomfortable, but that's part of why I'm doing what I'm doing, I think. It's just making it slightly less uncomfortable for other people.

Simon: All of that is preface to saying I would really like to know what those moments felt like, those worst moments of your life.

Jamison: It's hard to describe how dark it is. It's very hard. For one thing, what tends to get not so much emphasized with depression is how lethargic one is. You know, if you're ordinarily sort of bright-eyed and bushy-tailed and energetic, and all of the sudden have no energy and all you want to do is sleep twelve, fourteen, fifteen, sixteen hours a day. For the first time in my life, I could scarcely get out of bed in the mornings, a very strange feeling. And hope went. I'm, by temperament, a very hopeful person and an optimistic person, and I saw no point in anything. It was painful. It was painfully dreary. You know, they did a study once and asked terminal cancer patients, those who had a history of depression as well as those who did not have a history of depression, what the pain of terminal cancer was like compared with the pain of severe, unremitting clinical depression, and they said that terminal cancer pain was much easier.

Simon: You said at one point that the body becomes uninhabitable?

Jamison: Yes. The body becomes uninhabitable. The mind becomes uninhabitable. You become someone that you just, simply, don't recognize and don't like. I mean, I was not used to not liking myself. You, you know, you have a coexistence with yourself, as it were. You have a relationship with yourself and you talk with yourself and you walk with yourself. I mean, you don't think about those things, until you lose it.

Simon: I'm sure this is the least of it, but I remember the anecdote you tell about buying a bunch of paperback books once.

Jamison: You mean the Penguins?

Simon: Yes.

Jamison: Yes. It's a sort of the other side of it. This is the side of manic-depressive illness that is, unfortunately, quite seductive and addictive. I was buying everything that wasn't nailed down.

Simon: Looking for pleasure?

Jamison: No, just buying. I mean, you see something and you think, My God, I have to have that, and there's no limit. You know that you have all the money in the world, and there's no problem. I saw a Penguin book, and I thought, My God, you know, really, this Penguin book really ought to have company. I had to form a Penguin colony, you know? And so I went and bought a whole bunch of other Penguin books so that they would all feel close together and have a colony. So when you're manic, one of the first things, very often, you do is just spend tons and tons of money on stuff.

Simon: How did you ever get done what you got done during those years?

Jamison: Well, you know, one of the nice things about academics is that pretty much, with the exception of teaching, where you've got to show up, and clinical supervision, in terms of publications and advancement within the academic world, nobody much cares whether you get most of your work done within a few months of the year and don't do much in terms of writing the rest of the year. Teaching was difficult. You can show up and look fine, but there's always this terrible abyss between the private experience of despair and the public expression of it.

Simon: Yet, when you sought help and got it from people who were understanding and perceptive, you weren't all that wild about lithium.

Jamison: I wasn't all that wild about lithium. I wasn't all that wild about the idea that I had an illness. I kept thinking, Well, you know, there ought to be ways. This is just temporary. My first psychosis, I thought, I was flamingly crazy. I mean, I was hallucinating and delusional. But you can justify almost anything. You can rationalize it as just being under stress or whatever I rationalized it as. I didn't like the side effects from the lithium. I was on very high doses because, at the time I was put on it, everyone was on high doses of lithium.

Simon: I think we need to say what some of those side effects are, too. Because, to me, they were not widely known.

Jamison: Well, again, this is at high doses, because I'm still on lithium and I owe my life to lithium and I don't have, really, any side effects now that I could even begin to complain about. But at the time when I was on high doses, it definitely affected my ability to think quickly, to respond with a full range of emotions. I think those aren't uncommon side effects of lithium. What I also had was a very uncommon one; it affected my vision. It can do that, and I had spent all my life deeply immersed in literature and had read four or five books a week since the time I could remember first reading, and I didn't read a book for ten years.

Simon: Do you ever, in the back of your mind, play around with the whole sensation of being normal? I know that's what the treatment is supposed to do. But, just, normal — you get up, you throw out the pills. You know, "I need nothing."

Jamison: No, I don't. I used to think that way all the time, and I used to stop my lithium. But no. I'm absolutely convinced. I know exactly what will happen if I stop my lithium. I will get very manic, very psychotic, and then I will want to die, and I'm just not interested in that anymore.

Simon: If psychiatrists, and I'm not speaking just of you alone, but of your colleagues, are as vulnerable as the rest of us, as one of the people sitting on your couch, that must be an awful feeling of mortality, and then some.

Jamison: Yes, I think that's true. Studies have shown that doctors in general are more susceptible to mood disorders — depression and manic depression — than the general population, and it's probably not particularly surprising. The question is, How do you handle it? How do you make sure the patients are protected from judgment calls that may not be good when people are manic, for example, or when they're depressed?

Simon: There was a time when you came to Hopkins that you decided you had to tell the chairman of your department, and I wonder if you could share what his reaction was?

Jamison: Yes. Actually it was quite wonderful because I was dreading it. I was going through the business of filling out forms for my hospital privileges, and I realized that I was going to have to talk to my chairman and tell him that I had manic-depressive illness. So I told him this, and I just waited. There was this long pause, and I thought, Oh, my God, you know. I was just dreading it, thinking, Why do I do this? Why am I in this situation? My chairman reached over and he put his hand on mine, and he said, "Kay," he said, "I know you have manic-depressive illness." Then he started smiling and laughing. He said, "If we got rid of all the professors on our faculty in the medical school here at Hopkins who have manic-depressive illness, not only would we have a much smaller faculty, it would also be a far more boring one." It was really quite wonderful. It was the perfect thing to say, and he has been great from square one.

Simon: There are people who suffer hearing loss who will talk about how irritated they get when they realize people are speaking past them. There are diabetics who are accustomed to getting discounted because everyone says, "Oh, mood swings, insulin and all that stuff." What is it like for you being lithium-dependent?

Jamison: Actually, in sorting through what my major concerns have been about coming out very publicly, at first I just thought of professional repercussions, but on a really personal level, you're given a lot of latitude to be a human being. My concern was, OK, now that people know I have manic-depressive illness, that if I look a little off in the distance or if I look a little tired or a little sad, if I get irritated with somebody or aggravated or impatient, or too enthusiastic, that all of the sudden I'm going to be seen as "a manic-depressive" instead of somebody who's just feeling a little tired or a bit moody. I'm a moody person. I'm glad I'm moody. I've opted to be moody rather than take a superhigh dose of lithium. I don't mind having manic-depressive illness or saying that I am manic-depressive. I do mind being seen through that gauze of people's stereotypes about manic-depressive illness.

In 1995, the American Psychiatric Association revised its standard reference, *Diagnostic and Statistical Manual of Mental Disorders.* One aim of the revision was to accommodate cultural variations in the definitions of mental illness, to let American doctors and therapists know that patients from other cultures who seem mentally ill may be perfectly healthy when seen in proper cultural context; a well-known psychiatric condition in one culture may not exist in another. One of the contributors, an anthropologist named CHARLES HUGHES, told Daniel Zwerdling, "Imagine two patients walking into a clinic. They're both suffering from extreme anxiety. One is American, one is not." January 8, 1995

Hughes: I might say, "I've just been overworked lately, and this is the reason for my stress." But somebody else coming in and feeling stress might well say, "I didn't go through the right cleansing ritual after the birth of a baby."

Zwerdling: This is somebody from another culture speaking?

Hughes: That's right. From East Asia, where there's the influence of the belief in harmony and balance, and if one's body gets too cold, for example, from the wind, this is the Chinese and South Asian kind of wind illness.

Zwerdling: So if I'm a conventional therapist in the United States who doesn't know much about other cultures, I'm not educated about them, and this person from Asia comes in talking about spirits and cleansing rituals and wind, I mean, I might think that person is, well, schizophrenic.

Hughes: Right, really crazy. Would you be right, or would you say, "Sounds crazy to me, but it may be their own normal explanation as to what is the reason for this"? The whole gist is that there are various ways of defining what is illness, what is conceived as illness, and what causes it and what resolves the problem.

Zwerdling: A therapist I know who treats Africans, for instance, says sometimes a patient will come to her, and say, "I've been bewitched."

Hughes: That's right.

Zwerdling: Yes, but it doesn't mean that they are nuts?

Hughes: It doesn't mean that they are crazy because a normal belief is that there are witches out there and they can do things to you. It's a way of packaging and giving concrete form to these anxieties.

Zwerdling: In this discussion, you suggested a couple different things. One is that people in different cultures may be experiencing pretty much the same problem, which is low-level depression or anxiety, but they describe it differently. You have also raised another point, and that is that if we go from one culture to another, we may see people suffering different groups of symptoms. For example, if you go to parts of Asia, say Malaysia, or Thailand, or China, you might see people who suffer from what they call *koro*.

Hughes: Oh, yes. This is something that occurs when, say, a man is sitting around the campfire in the evening, suddenly grabs his penis, and starts yelling for help because he is gripped by the fear that his penis will recede into his body and possibly cause death. So friends and family come and help hold on to his penis so this won't happen. Now, that does sound like decidedly bizarre, strange behavior, a strange conceptualization of body. But the cases that have been analyzed have really raised the question if, again, this is a somatic displacement of some pretty profound kinds of anxieties.

Zwerdling: In other words, the people are feeling emotionally anxious and put it onto a part of their body.

Hughes: That's right, a somatization.

Zwerdling: Let me ask you a very pragmatic question. I'm a therapist in the United States. Somebody from, say, an Arctic Eskimo community or from Southeast Asia comes to me with what I know are a very culture-bound set of symptoms, which I don't see here in the United States. They might think they're bewitched. They blame their illness on ghosts, on the wind being wrong. What do I do about it now? How do I treat them?

Hughes: The first thing you would do, and one hopes this is being built into psychiatric training, is to ask the patient, and one hopes a patient's family is there, "Well, how do you explain this?"

Zwerdling: But then do I prescribe Prozac anyway, or do I tell them to do some ritual that they're used to doing in their own culture?

Hughes: Certainly some medications may well be appropriate, but one should at least work with the idea of accustomed rituals or culturally familiar rituals. Family therapy and things of that kind.

When a series of small earthquakes struck in Wyoming, they had an effect on one of the most famous attractions of Yellowstone National Park: the geyser Old Faithful did not erupt as frequently as it had before. Noah Adams called RICK HUTCHINSON, a geologist at Yellowstone, and they talked while waiting for Old Faithful to go off. July 27, 1995

Hutchinson: An earthquake can cause a shift in the groundwater movement, the hot water that feeds the geysers and the hot springs here. If the rate of flow is altered so that, let's say, the water goes to Geyser Hill, across the river from Old Faithful, instead of directly to Old Faithful, then the reservoirs take longer to refill and reheat between each eruption.

Adams: So an earthquake kind of shakes things up down there?

Hutchinson: Yes, it can change the plumbing system. It can make some geysers more active, and do just the opposite on others.

Adams: And this kind of continues on a year-round basis anyway?

Hutchinson: Yes, Yellowstone's very, very active, earthquake-wise.

Adams: What do you see right now?

Hutchinson: There's a big crowd waiting, and the visitors can see on Old Faithful this occasional splashing, which we call freefall. It's just steaming at the moment, and we're at eighty-four minutes and counting.

Adams: When people drive across the country to see Old Faithful, do they feel like they've gotten their effort's worth, or is it disappointing to some people? How do people react to it?

Hutchinson: You have the whole spectrum of reaction. A lot of people, especially older adults who may have been here in the forties or fifties, remember it being a lot taller. So now, just because of the crowds and concerns of protecting the geyser cone, the trail's a little bit farther away. Of course, first impressions are always more spectacular. It's erupting now.

Adams: What does it look like?

Hutchinson: A very tall, graceful column of water and steam and. . . . One second. Looking at the height — we've got some marks on a tree that we measure it against — it looks like this particular eruption may be somewhere around thirty-three, thirty-five meters.

Adams: So that's pretty good.

Hutchinson: Yes, considering the high winds that we've got today.

Adams: Can you see the people? Are they happy?

Hutchinson: Yes. The interesting thing, though, is it seems like a lot of visitors have short attention spans from watching too much television. A lot of them start leaving about seventy seconds into the eruption, just when it starts dropping in height.

The day Jeanne Calment, reputed to be the oldest person in the world, turned 120, Bob Edwards spoke with a neuropsychologist at the French National Institute of Medical Research, who is one of a team of doctors studying the longevity of the Frenchwoman from Arles. Calment is older than the telephone and the light bulb. She recalls meeting the artist Vincent van Gogh in her father's store when she was fourteen and eating at the restaurant in the Eiffel Tower while it was still under construction. She has outlived seventeen French presidents and her only grandson, who died in 1963. KAREN RITCHIE says that Calment's appearance can be quite deceiving. February 21, 1995

Ritchie: She'll sit quite curled up in a chair, and she'll look very frail. The most surprising thing is that when you actually touch her to let her know that you're there, because she has cataracts and doesn't see, suddenly she sits quite upright and comes alive, and she's immediately interested in who you are and what you want, and she's very eager to talk to you.

Edwards: How did you get involved in studying her?

Ritchie: There was a study of centenarians in France around three years ago, in which they identified this woman as being the oldest person in the study. First, we set about to verify her age, and in doing so became quite interested in her. I became interested in her for two reasons. Firstly, because I work in the area of brain aging, I was interested to see what were the effects on the brain at being able to reach such a high age. Secondly, as an epidemiologist, I was interested to know, given that we expect senile dementia to be more and more prevalent with age, to see in fact if she had senile dementia, as many geriatricians conclude that if we all live long enough, we will all be demented. In fact she doesn't have senile dementia, so she refutes that proposition.

Edwards: What else did you find about the state of her mind?

Ritchie: I think, firstly, there is no history of psychiatric illness. I think also, quite exceptionally, for a very old person who has lost all of her family, there are no symptoms of depression at all. She sleeps well, she eats well, she communicates in a very lively manner. She still has a quite wide vocabulary, but her memory for more recent events, of course, is not very good.

Edwards: So she would be better able to recall her meeting with van Gogh than what happened last week?

Ritchie: Probably, though she sometimes surprises us. For example, when I was trying to see how fluent she was in her ability to use words and find words, I asked her to give me as many animals as she could think of, and she said that was silly. So her physician intervened, and said, "Well, I'm going to buy Christmas presents for my children. Can you tell me some ideas of presents that we could buy for children for Christmas?" She looked at him, and said, "Doctor, you told me last year that you had no children," which is quite true. So every now and then she astonishes us.

Edwards: Is there any way to explain this?

Ritchie: I think the longevity certainly has a strong genetic component. She's really the third generation of people who were destined to live a long time. She herself says that she has been rather fortunate, in that she has been brought up in very bourgeois living conditions and that she has never really been subjected to great stress or to great deprivation, but there's obviously more to it. Many people have lived in much the same living conditions. She has, as we've seen, extraordinary immunity to disease. She has lived through a number of quite severe epidemics and hasn't caught anything. She survived childbirth at the turn of the century, and she's really quite a strong woman.

Edwards: She's a unique case?

Ritchie: She is quite a unique case. We compared her to a few hundred elderly people in their eighties and nineties. We found that on most tasks she performed as we would expect an eighty-year-old person to perform. I think that's probably an underestimate of her true ability, because you have to remember for the last four or five years she has been completely blind due to cataracts. Were she able to see and hear, and receive more stimulation, I think she would perform far better.

Edwards: This is a very interesting news story, but what is the scientific importance here?

Ritchie: The average life expectancy in Western countries is leaping forward very quickly, and one of our concerns is what will the profile be of people who are in their hundreds and above that if that is going to be life expectancy after the year 2000, say? We're interested in the causes for her living such an exceptional amount of time. What is the mechanism behind it? Is it something to do with the environment? Is it largely genetic? I think she's answered very many questions in that regard. We know, for example, that there is a protein that predisposes people to senile dementia, and that she doesn't have it. We know, for example, that the majority of centenarians in France have dark hair and blue eyes. We're not quite sure what the connection is, but she has dark hair and blue eyes. We know that there's not really a dietary factor. She seems to be someone who has very low stress levels, but certainly the genetic component seems to us to be enormous.

Edwards: Anything we can learn from her that might help us extend our life span?

Ritchie: I think probably one of her best quotes is "I'm not afraid of anybody." And I think that's important. I think she is someone of tremendous courage who really takes life in a very positive way, and she doesn't become easily stressed. She's very assertive. She doesn't let people push her around. She does what she wants to do.

Deoxyribonucleic acid, or DNA, was actually the subject of much popular discussion, even on tabloid television shows, around the time that Dr. DOROTHY NELKIN published *The DNA Mystique: The Gene as Cultural Icon*. In the trial of O. J. Simpson, the prosecution introduced extensive DNA blood evidence connecting Simpson to the double murder of which he was acquitted. Liane Hansen asked Dr. Nelkin, a professor of law and sociology at New York University, about society's fascination with DNA and the DNA fingerprint. March 5, 1995

Nelkin: Well, a lot of the fascination deals with the role of DNA as evidence, as a means of identification of the individual. However, my interest is in the fact that DNA can tell you much more than simply who a person is. It has the capacity to tell a great deal about a person's predisposition, for example, to many diseases.

Hansen: And predisposition to criminal activity?

Nelkin: Well, I think that that claim has been exaggerated, and the purpose of writing this book was to explore not the biological meaning of this entity but its social meaning, and its social meaning is rather extraordinary. If you look at popular media, genes are responsible for obesity, for criminal behavior, for alcoholism. There are genes for sinning, there are couch potato genes, there are genes for nearly every behavior that one can imagine.

Hansen: Getting back to the Simpson case, do you expect that perhaps the interpretation of the results of just this identification, this evidence, this fingerprinting, might make this a landmark case?

Nelkin: I think DNA evidence for purposes of identification has been very widely accepted in American courts. The problem that people worry about for the most part is whether laboratory practices are adequate to do this sufficiently. This, again, is a very particular use, and I think more interesting is the social interest, the social appeal, of genetic information as a way to avoid future risks. For example, for insurers, for employers, even in educational systems it's a means of diverting responsibility from the institution to the individual.

Hansen: Do you expect that defendants in future criminal cases could actually stand there, and say, "My genes made me do it."

Nelkin: Well, it's not just the future. There's a number of cases in which DNA defenses are used to mitigate punishment. In the state of California, for example, two former alcoholics were on trial during the same year, and one pleaded a genetic defense and his punishment was less than the other's, and they were very parallel cases. Similarly, in Georgia there is a genetic defense that is currently under way in order avoid the death sentence.

Hansen: What do you see as the dangers if society has begun to medicalize social problems?

Nelkin: I think the risks are a continuation of the current political tendency to divert responsibility. One of the chapters of our book is called "Absolution," and the idea is that there is no need to worry about remedial education. There is no need to worry about improving the circumstances of individuals. It's all in the genes. By diverting the responsibility, this absolves the society, it absolves parents, and even in a sense absolves the individual from responsibility, and I think that is a major danger. It's the place we look for the solution to social problems, and I think that's misplaced.

Hansen: And it could be very misplaced if social policy is based on this genetic information.

Nelkin: Yes, and there seems to be tendency in this direction. If you look at the influence of this recent book *The Bell Curve*, that's the direction in which it is going, and it has, obviously, a great deal of appeal.

Hansen: Is science on a runaway train, do you think?

Nelkin: I don't think so. There's beginning to be a great deal of distress among geneticists that people are running away with these images. It's kind of interesting that the Genome Project puts three percent to five percent of its resources into looking at the social and legal implications of genetics research. To my knowledge, this is the first time any major scientific project has systematically, from the very beginning, tried to address these problems precisely so it would not become a runaway science.

Hansen: There were some researchers in the Genome Project who asked people what they thought would happen in the future.

There was a list of ten predictions, and number one was mapping the human genes for personal identification and an eye toward treating diseases before they actually occur. Now, this sounds very good, but are there some underlying things that must be considered here?

Nelkin: Well, I think there's a lot more promise than reality to gene therapy. First of all, in terms of cost it would be available for very few people. Genetic diagnostics, genetic testing, is far, far ahead of any capacity that we have to be able to cure, so I think that one has to not be overly optimistic about the meaning of those promises because I think they may be very far in the future. Meanwhile, the problems of diagnosis, the problem of testing, when you can do nothing about it and when that information may be available to insurers or employers, is in itself very problematic.

When the television screen shows a thorny and sinister protagonist, advancing to the accompaniment of dramatic music and the explanatory prose of a deep, English-accented voice, it can only be a nature film by Sir DAVID ATTENBOROUGH. Sir David's photographs and films of the natural world for the BBC have become a staple of American public and cable television. Like his brother, the film actor and director Sir Richard Attenborough, he was knighted for his achievements. Upon the release of a film and companion book on *The Private Life of Plants*, Attenborough had this conversation with Scott Simon. October 7, 1995

Simon: Sir David, this program, this book, is dedicated to the plant's point of view, as you say. From their point of view, do they run this place?

Attenborough: Well, I guess if you were to invoke, what shall we say, an independent witness and an independent judge — say some superintelligence from outer space looking at this planet — it would conclude that the most successful kind of organism on the planet, from many points of view, are those green things. After all, some of them live longer than those things that dash about all the time, those animals. They live in places where the animals can't live. They are able to live on the simplest things. They can travel through time in a way that the animals can't in the sense that between one generation and the next may be a century or so. And, of course, without those green things, the other things, the animals, can't exist at all. So I reckon that the extraterrestrial's judgment would be that the successful things on planet Earth are those green ones.

Simon: And they use us, to put it kindly?

Attenborough: Certainly they do. If you pick a blackberry, if you think about it at all, you may say, "How bountiful of nature to provide me with this nice sweet mouthful." But, of course, what is happening is that that sweet mouthful is a comparatively cheap wage provided by the blackberry plant to persuade you, or any other animal that might eat it, to transport multiple numbers of its seeds, maybe a mile, two miles, three miles, four miles, and then excrete it elsewhere. So that you have done a transport job for the plant. We are undoubtedly, in those cases, the servant of the bramble.

Simon: Now, one of the things that you point out in the book and the series is that one of the ways in which plants have been able to not only survive, but prosper, is that unlike, say, us, they have a multitude of ways of scattering their seeds.

Attenborough: Certainly do.

Simon: I was particularly intrigued by the story of the sea bean.

Attenborough: The sea bean uses sea transport.

Simon: I had never known that was possible. In fact, I would have assumed that that would have been bad for a seed.

Attenborough: Well, many plants do that. I mean, the most famous, of course, is the coconut. The coconut goes to sea very well equipped for the trip. I mean, it has water on board, it has food on board, which is inside the coconut, and, of course, it has a good vessel in a fibrous coating, which is, as it were, a raft. And the coconut can travel for hundreds of miles through tropical seas, and if it eventually ends up on a seashore, that's where it grows and that's why the coconut, in the wild, grows only along seashores and lines the beaches of that paradise island which you've got in your mind.

Simon: There's a particularly arresting scene in the first program where you depict a bramble growing. The camera follows it at close range. You see it nosing and coursing through the woods. It reminded me of some of those elaborate videos we see from the Pentagon showing the cruise missiles, the so-called smart missiles. This seems to be a smart bramble, if you please.

Attenborough: It's a smart bramble, OK. The thing that it reminds me of — when you film this in time lapse and move onto the time scale of a plant, as it creeps along the ground moving from side to side — is a blind man finding his way with a white stick. When it detects the right kind of place for it to clamber up, it sticks in one of those thorns which snag our flesh, and it creeps upward over a wall, over a rock, over another plant, if necessary. It is an extremely

aggressive creature. When this series first came out in Britain, and I
said that the blackberry is an aggressive plant, people said, "You
can't call plants things like aggressive." Well, by any definition,
that blackberry is an aggressive empire builder.

Simon: A technical question about how you used elapsed-time
photography. To take a look at something like this bramble with
the naked eye — it's just lying there. You say it grows at much as
three inches a day.

Attenborough: That's right.

Simon: How do you shoot this stuff? Is there a cameraman behind there for two weeks in succession?

Attenborough: No. If you want to travel alongside the tip of a
blackberry shoot, you have to move the camera at the same speed.
And you can't possibly do that manually. So what you do is to build
rails, and you put a little carriage on the rail in which you mount
the camera. The carriage has a motor, and the motor is controlled
by a computer, so every time you take a frame, after the frame has
been taken, the camera advances a micromillimeter, or whatever it
is you program it to do, to keep up with the blackberry. That, of
course, can go wrong because sometimes the blackberry decides to
put on a turn of speed, and you aren't there to notice it, and sometimes it goes in a different direction than you thought it was going
to go. So there are things that go wrong, but if you can get it right,
and when you get it right, the effect is quite riveting, really.

Simon: Sir David, how many blackberry plants did you have to
go through to get that one shot?

Attenborough: The blackberry was OK, actually. It's so tough
that we didn't have a lot of problems. We had other problems. I
remember particularly we were producing some shots, nice shots,
of some buds opening out into leaves, and they were just moving in
a normal sort of time lapse. Moving beautifully, growing upward,
and opening, and gently spreading their green expanse toward the
light, when suddenly, in time lapse, a posse of slugs tore in from
the left-hand side and consumed the lot in front of the camera's
eye. So we didn't actually see this until we took the film to the lab.
Disaster.

Simon: Slugs'll do that, though, won't they?

Attenborough: Yeah, they do.

Simon: I wanted to ask you about a single line that you have in this book, which since reading it yesterday, I have been quoting to people. Might I read you some of your own prose?

Attenborough: OK. Yes. I can hardly say no, can I?

Simon: So you can marvel at it, as I did.

Attenborough: And I'll say, "My, my goodness, what wonderful choice of words," yes.

Simon: You say, in a section called "Flowering," "Orchids have made something of a specialty of sexually bamboozling their pollinators." I like to think the key to life is somewhere in there, but explain this if you could, Sir David.

Attenborough: We all think of orchids as those big, glamorous things from the tropics, but there are also small orchids which grow, quite a lot of them, in Britain and certainly in Europe, which grow about a foot high. They have little, comparatively modest, flowers, but if you look at them closely, they closely resemble female wasps or bees. There are a number of them, and each has its own particular mimicry. You can see the brown body of the bee. It has yellow marks on the side which look like wings. It has a little shiny knob at the top which is its head, and to make the mimicry even more perfect this orchid produces a perfume which chemically is exactly the same as the perfume produced by a female bee when she is sexually receptive. So male bees, swarming around, suddenly catch hold of these molecules, trace them to their source, see what they think is a female bee sitting there on a stalk, and they land on its back —

Simon: Don't do it, guys, don't do it.

Attenborough: Well, well —

Simon: All right, I'm sorry. It's necessary for things to grow.

Attenborough: Yes it is. And they then copulate. And the vigor with which they copulate releases a little click within the mechanism of the flower, which releases a hammer, which comes down loaded with a great lump of yellow pollen, which bongs the bee on the back of its neck. You can actually see the bee saying, "Whew, not at all what I expected. But see if I can do that again." So it flies off to find another orchid, and when it lands this time, that great gob of yellow pollen on its head clicks onto another receptive thing on the next orchid plant and, hey-ho, the orchid has reproduced itself, which is more than you can say for the bee.

Simon: Goodness gracious. One other point you make in this project is that what sometimes might interrupt us from understanding the true nature, or, as you might put it, the private lives of plants, is that they function in a different time frame than we do. We inhabit the same earth and the same space, and yet we don't really recognize the ways in which they live according to a different clock.

Attenborough: Yes, and that's why I had the nerve, or the cheek or something, to call it private. I think that it is impossible for us, under normal circumstances, to comprehend the intimate life and processes of a plant precisely because they live on a different time scale. In between species of animals, there are, quite definitely, different time scales. A hummingbird lives on a quite different time scale from an elephant, and you can calibrate it, really, by heartbeat. A hummingbird's heart beats extremely fast. I've forgotten what the figure is, say two, three, four times as fast as a human being's. If you film a hummingbird and slow it down by that factor, to match, as it were, our heartbeat, not only can you see all kinds of behavior when the two hummingbirds display to one another, but their song, which at the moment to our normal ears sounds just like a very, very high-pitched squeak, and a short one at that. If you slow that down and make it much longer, you can see that actually it's quite a complex song. The other time scale is an elephant, of course. An elephant's heart beats much slower than a human being's, and in correspondence it lives much longer and the sounds it makes are very low-pitched sounds, very deep rumbles, which we can hardly hear. Now, if you speeded them up, then you hear those in a different way, as is the case with whale songs. Plants, as it were, are beyond whales and elephants in the time scale. They are way down there, and it's very difficult for us to appreciate the life of plants. Except, we can speed them up on film. When you do that, you see that these are active organisms, seeking, questing, gaining territory, mating with one another, strangling one another, poisoning one another.

Simon: I hope you don't mind a family question.

Attenborough: Depends what it is. Do you want advice?

Simon: That's very kind. Perhaps I do. Of course, we need to explain that you're the brother of Sir Richard Attenborough. There cannot be many families in which two brothers have been knighted for their own distinct achievements.

Attenborough: Well, I guess that's true. I mean, I can't think of another. It's not a big deal, you know. It's not a very big deal.

Simon: Well, not to you.

Attenborough: No, I don't think to anybody, really.

Simon: I think the queen would like to think it's a big deal to her, though.

Attenborough: Well, she smacks the shoulders with a sword of quite a number every year, you know. There are people who go reeling out from Buckingham Palace.

Simon: Do you call each other Sir Dickey and Sir David, or anything like that?

Attenborough: I certainly do. Absolutely yes. Of course I do. I won't tell you what he calls me.

SCOTT SANDFORD put a cliché to the test of science. There is no more familiar dismissal of an inapt analogy than the charge of comparing apples with oranges. Judging, however, from Sandford's research, very few people have made that comparison with scientific exactitude. A scientist at NASA's Ames Research Center in California, he tested a Granny Smith apple and a navel orange, using a spectrometer and, as he told Noah Adams, he found apples and oranges to be amazingly alike. April 4, 1995

Sandford: I needed to remove a lot of the water from them because the water is a very strong infrared absorber, and I wanted to just see the materials themselves. So I took a little slice of apple and a slice of orange, and I stuck them in my oven at home at a low heat for a while to desiccate them, just to dehydrate them, get the water out. Then I took each of those slices and I ground them up in the presence of potassium bromide, which is just a salt, basically. Ground them up so that the particles of apple and orange were dispersed and then crushed that mix into two different pellets, one for the apple and one for the orange, so that I have a little disc, basically, of apples and oranges suspended in salt. Then I put those in my spectrometer in my laboratory and took their spectra. And then I could compare those spectra in the computer or on a piece of paper.

Adams: Were you surprised?

Sandford: Yes I was, actually, a little bit. I guess I hadn't given a whole lot of thought to how they would look, and I guess sort of naively assumed they would look a lot different because, hey, they look different in the visible. But once I thought about it, I realized I shouldn't have been surprised that they do in fact look very, very similar in the infrared. And that's because they basically contain the same chemicals, which is what the infrared is sensitive to. So apples and oranges, in fact, look like very much alike.

Adams: I'm looking at the graph, and you're right, the apple graph looks exactly like the orange graph. Let's say you take away the orange and put in there a walnut, grind it up, and treat it the same way. What would it look like?

Sandford: Well, I would hesitate to guess on a walnut, but there would be a lot of similarities because virtually anything that's food, for instance, contains a lot of organic compounds, a lot of carbon and hydrogen, so many of the absorption features you get in the infrared will be very similar. A lot of things will look alike, and then if you want to tell the difference between one and the other, you have to look for subtle details, little features and wiggles in the graph which are distinctively different from one to the other. In fact, that's what I spend a lot of my time doing at NASA, looking for the little wiggles because they're the ones that give away the more detailed information.

Adams: So a graph like this would give you a good starting point?

Sandford: Yes. For instance, if I were to take a spectrum through a telescope of dust around a star, and it were to look like the graph you have in front of you, I would know from that graph to say, "Hey, I may have discovered fruit in the interstellar medium," but I would know well enough not to say, "I've discovered apples" or "I've discovered oranges" because they look so much alike. Instead, I would have to look at the apple and orange spectrum and look for some subtle difference between the two and then go back to the telescope and see whether the dust around the star had the detailed characteristics of one or the other.

Adams: Let's say for rhetorical reasons you're looking then for a more apt comparative analogy of what substance would give you a completely different spectral graph reading compared to the other.

Sandford: From an apple or an orange?

Adams: From an apple, let's say.

Sandford: Any mineral. For instance, dirt would look very different. You know, diamonds would look different, chalk would look different. If you stuck DNA in there, it would have a few similarities, but it would have a very characteristic spectrum which would be different from an apple and an orange and so on. On the other hand, DNA from different things would look almost identical.

Adams: So if you really wanted to draw an apt comparison, you could say, "Well, that's as different as apples and diamonds."

Sandford: Right, if you want the analogy to follow not only an invisible range of the spectrum, where you and I see with our eyes, but also to extend in the infrared, we need to change it from apples and oranges to apples and diamonds. That's not a bad idea. We'll see if that phrase catches on. I suspect it won't.

ANIMALS

The appearance of manatees off the Atlantic Coast anywhere north of the Carolinas is a rare event. These walruslike mammals swim north from their coastal Florida home for the summer, but not usually so far north as Chessie the manatee has traveled. In the summer of 1994, Chessie earned his name by swimming all the way to the Chesapeake Bay in Maryland. Scientists airlifted the ten-foot-long, twelve-hundred-pound manatee home. The following summer, wanderlust struck Chessie once again. He swam all the way to New York Harbor, the northernmost point at which any manatee has ever been sighted. JIM REID, a biologist with the Interior Department's National Biological Service, monitored Chessie's progress and talked about it with Bob Edwards. August 15, 1995

Reid: He continues to travel north. He's been making as much as twenty or thirty miles per day, sometimes spending less amount of time traveling, but his general pattern has been to continue north.

Edwards: Is that good speed?

Reid: Well, at twenty to thirty miles per day, that's what we see for other manatees that are making long-distance movements, a pattern that we see in Florida of manatees traveling south for the winter.

Edwards: The itinerary so far has sounded like a boat cruise of the East Coast: Savannah, Charleston, Myrtle Beach, Norfolk, Atlantic City, New York City, now Connecticut.

Reid: He's hitting all the hot spots, it seems. While we think that's pretty remarkable for an individual manatee to make that long of a movement, and we have no documented sightings of manatees this far north, the activities along the route are pretty normal for a manatee spending time traveling, feeding on salt marshes, and occasionally resting. So in that regard it's normal; it's just on a much bigger scale than we've ever seen.

Edwards: Any idea why he keeps going north?

Reid: The water temperatures are pretty warm. This has been an exceptionally warm summer. The backwaters especially are in the mid-seventies. So there's really been no reason why he can't travel this far north, but it's really difficult to put a reason on why he's made such a long move.

Edwards: So he's not in danger now?

Reid: No, he's a shy individual, and we're concerned about human activities, but that's the same concern that we have for manatees in Georgia and in Florida. It's really the water temperatures that we're looking at as a concern. Right now there's no problem with that.

Edwards: Do you think you'll have to intervene as you did last year and fly him home to Florida?

Reid: Well, we'd really like to let him make the trip back on his own. The effort and the risk to the animal that would be taken in order to capture him, if we could capture him, are significant, and biologically we're learning a lot about what manatees are capable of. If this one's capable of moving this far north, perhaps he can do the same and travel back south.

Edwards: Maybe he set the pattern last year and he'll head north every summer now.

Reid: This could get old if we were having to intervene every summer in order to return him back to Florida, so that's another reason why to let this go, not to risk the animal but also to let him make the opportunity to move back south.

Edwards: Some reports have suggested Chessie may have begun his travels in search of a mate.

Reid: That's really not the case. We've been tracking manatees for the National Biological Service for over fifteen years and we've learned a lot about manatee behavior and reproduction. "In search of mates" — it would be reaching it to say he was doing that. We do know these are curious animals and they like to explore their environment, and perhaps he's just doing that on a grander scale.

D r. JANE GOODALL says that as a child she read the Tarzan novels and envied the fictional Jane for her life among the wild apes. Goodall grew up to become the world's leading authority on chimpanzees and a passionate advocate on their behalf. While she spends most of each year in the field, she regularly lectures throughout the United States. Alex Chadwick interviewed her during one of her tours. May 6, 1995

Chadwick: It's thirty-five years since you've been studying this one group of chimpanzees in the Gombe reserve on Lake Tanganyika in East Africa. And in that time you've been able to look at families and tell their stories. It feels like an epic saga the way you talk about these chimpanzees.

Goodall: In fact, the extraordinary thing is that every single chimpanzee has his or her own unique and vivid personality. So what we've done over these thirty-five years is collect up a whole series of case histories and family histories and we're learning about the tremendous importance to the child of the kind of mothering that he or she gets and what a difference that can make to the behavior of the adult.

Chadwick: You tell a story about a particular chimpanzee, Mike, who was not really doing very well and yet emerged to be the dominant male of a band. And how did that happen?

Goodall: Well, Mike was even past his prime and he didn't weigh much compared to the other males, ten of them, who were all his superiors. But he had this incredible motivation to change his rank, to improve it, and he was unusually intelligent. So this was back in 1963 when the chimps were regularly coming to my tent. Sometimes there were empty kerosene cans lying around for my little, you know, cooking things and lights. And he learned to use three empty kerosene cans, hitting and kicking them ahead of him to enhance this charging display that the adult males do when they career across the ground with bristling hair and bunched lips, ferocious skull, dragging branches, waving the vegetation, making themselves look bigger and more dangerous than they may be and trying to intimidate rivals in this fashion. Adding cans to that display just did it for Mike.

Chadwick: You were interested in observing wildlife from a very early age, a ridiculously early age. There's a story about your first encounter. Would you tell that, please?

Goodall: There were two actually. One was taking earthworms to bed with me to watch how they walked without legs when I was eighteen months. And the second was when I was staying with my father's family in the country. One of my jobs was collecting the hen's eggs each day in a little basket, and I kept looking at the egg and looking at the hen. Apparently I was always saying, "But where does the egg come out? There isn't a hole so big." I decided I would have to find out for myself, I suppose, because I can vividly remember waiting crouched at the back of a little henhouse in the straw until a hen came in. And I can still remember to this day exactly what it looked like to see how a hen laid an egg.

Chadwick: When you took earthworms to bed as a little girl, your mother responded by saying what?

Goodall: She came up, she found the earthworms, and instead of saying, "Ugh, get rid of these disgusting things," she said, "Jane, if you leave them here they'll be dead soon because they need the earth." So I ran back with them.

Again, she was frantic when I was in the henhouse. Nobody knew where was I was. And I was in there for four whole hours, aged to about four and a half. They called the police. They were looking for me, searching for me. And my mother had one last desperate look as the dusk fell and saw this excited little girl with straw all over her. Instead of sort of grabbing me, and saying, "How dare you go off without telling us, don't you know how worried we've all been? Don't do it again!" she saw the excitement and sat down to hear this wonderful story.

Chadwick: You're a lucky girl to have a mother like that.

Goodall: Unbelievably lucky. Of course in those early days, when I began dreaming of Africa, it was fifty years ago and young girls, young boys, didn't go tramping off into the African wilds to write about animals, which is what I wanted to do. But although other people thought this was foolish, my mother always said, "Jane, if you really want something and you really work hard and you take advantage of opportunity and you never give up, you'll find a way." Just like Mike.

Chadwick: You talk about the qualities of these animals in the way that they greet one another with kisses, in the way that they reach for one another just to touch a fellow being, if they're frightened or scared by something that they don't understand. These are human qualities, or certainly we think of them as exclusively human qualities.

Goodall: Yes, the chimpanzees show many behaviors that we used to think unique to ourselves. And as you say, the nonverbal communication patterns: kissing, embracing, holding hands. It's not only that they look like ours, but they appear in the same context, and it's a little humbling because it makes us realize that we humans, after all, are not completely unique.

Chadwick: Where do you see things going in the next ten years, the next fifteen years, as regards chimpanzees?

Goodall: Well, I see that many, many more across Africa will disappear. The tragedy here is it's not only individual chimpanzees who disappear, but whole cultures. Even Gombe only has about 160 chimps within thirty square miles. And that is really not a large enough population for long-term viability. Yet outside the park, all the forests have gone, it's just cultivated fields. Soon this whole area along the lake of once beautiful, lush forest will be a rocky desert. So even though everyone is now trying to find imaginative ways of reversing this trend, it *is* going to continue and a lot more chimpanzees will disappear.

Chadwick: When you go back to Gombe and see the chimpanzees that you know, did they recognize you?

Goodall: Oh, yes. It's a bit hard to tell now because there are so many people there and tourists come. But in the early days when the chimpanzees began to get used to me, and I would be away for a while, I'd go back perhaps with someone else and they would just immediately accept me, but they would run away from the somebody else, which always made me feel good. I was their friend by now. But today they've now got so used to people, they won't run away from anybody.

NATALIE ANGIER is another case of a career inspired by a childhood fascination with animals. Unlike Jane Goodall, whose love of the wild led her to a lifetime of researching chimpanzees, Angier was drawn to the very creatures that terrified her in her youth: cockroaches. Angier is a science writer for the *New York Times*, a Pulitzer Prize winner, and the author of *The Beauty of the Beastly*. She described the origin of her interest in bugs to Daniel Zwerdling. August 19, 1995

Angier: I first started, in fact, writing about cockroaches some time ago, as an attempt to get a grip on my own fear of roaches. Once I started investigating what it is about cockroaches that makes them such great survivors, I began to admire them. I realized there was probably a lot to be learned about the beastly items among us. All the species that we normally try to ignore. So I made that a specialty.

Zwerdling: You're being serious about this. You're not just saying that for dramatic effect? That you started writing about bugs partly to combat your fears?

Angier: Yes, absolutely. I've always been afraid of insects, and I think this is certainly not uncommon. But I just decided that since they do own the planet, it was probably better to understand them than to just ignore them. Plus I just think that they, once you start to look into them, because they're so numerous, they've just developed so many spectacular ways of sort of getting their own little niche in order.

Zwerdling: One of the most amazing bugs you write about is something that just about all of us can find in our own gardens or in the lawn next to our apartment building, the common roundworm.

Angier: Well, you probably wouldn't see them unless you had a microscope. They are about a millimeter long. But if you were to pick up a scoop of dirt or go to your compost heap and spread some out under your microscope, you would find them. They're these beautiful, little transparent worms. You can see through their skin and you can see their muscles and you can see their cells. You can actually see everything pulsating. And the way they move is very beautiful. They sort of slither. The reason why these have become so interesting is because biologists have sort of taken it upon themselves to turn this into a kind of workhorse of understanding the basic processes of life.

Zwerdling: This is what really struck me. You say that scientists are convinced now that if they could just understand and map the genetic structure of this teeny-weeny roundworm, they would finally understand and map the genetic structure of humans. You write that in this international project to map human genes, fifty million dollars is devoted to this roundworm.

Angier: In fact, it turns out that when they start looking at these genes, they find the same genes in our genetic code as are dictating certain features of the roundworm. For example, the nervous system. You would think that it would be completely different. After all, it's just this invertebrate worm and it's only got about nine hundred cells in its nervous system compared to trillions for our own. But it's still giving us a handle on how these things actually start. You have to start really small. You have to start simple and you have to have some way of being able to trace the beginning, middle, and end of the picture of development. And this roundworm is great because it's transparent; they can see these cells move. And they also have fewer genes to work with and then they can start scaling up, and saying, "OK, well, this does this in the worm. What does it do in a human?"

Zwerdling: One of the most historic things in your book is that you shatter some American myths. You basically challenge the English language. Right? You probably know the part I'm talking about? "Busy as a bee." "You're a busy beaver." Researchers have found that, in fact, bees and beavers and other animals and insects that supposedly are tireless workers are not.

Angier: Well, this has been a very interesting development. The problem is that throughout the history of studying animals, we always look at them when they were moving because, after all, you have to have something to study. Then when they started actually following these animals through entire days of their lives, not just looking at when they're moving, but saying, "Let's chart your whole day," they looked at every single thing the animal does throughout the day. It turns out that most animals spend most of their time doing nothing at all.

Zwerdling: And scientists actually dissect the nest, or slip microscopic video cameras up into the hives?

Angier: If you actually tag any of the individual insects, tag an ant or bee, and see what it's doing throughout the day, you will find, most of the time it doesn't do anything. It just kind of sits there. So that this idea of activity comes from looking at the hive. And they take turns doing a lot of these tasks. So it's not that they're busy as a bee; it's busy as bees. So each bee has a lot of time, downtime, to rest. Now, you may think, Well, why should they do that? Well, each bee or ant turns out to be like a battery. It has a fixed amount of energy.

Zwerdling: So it's not like if the bee eats the right nectar that day, it can gain more energy?

Angier: Right, it has a fixed amount of energy to devote to whatever tasks the nest or the hive need. So if it turns out that the nest or the hive needs a lot of work done quickly, all these animals get going and then they all die quickly. But if there isn't that need, the best thing for them to do is nothing at all. To save themselves for when there actually might be demands on their time. So when you look at one of these things that's just resting, you have to feel, Well, it's actually prolonging its life.

Zwerdling: Now, anybody who has had a cat or a dog has at some point said, "Boy, rough life! All it does is lie around all day and sleep." So what is the evolutionary purpose of that?

Angier: Of sleeping?

Zwerdling: Well, yes, of the cats and dogs sitting around all day sleeping, and doing very little.

Angier: Because they don't have to do anything.

Zwerdling: You mean you and I don't have to be here.

Angier: The whole idea from evolution's point of view is to make more animals and to keep things going. Now, keeping things going, you try to do it as cost efficiently as possible. So if you don't have to be doing something, if you're not in the middle of your mating time, if you don't have to fend off any predators, the best thing to do is to lie low and save your calories because then you might actually do better when it comes to something really important, like feeding your offspring. So I think that this idea of working at something that is ingrained, everything has to have a purpose, and in most cases, with most animals, most of the time, there isn't a reason for it to work and so it doesn't.

While the study of animal behavior is a well-established science, the study of animals' feelings is another, more speculative, matter. The psychoanalyst JEFFREY MOUSSAIEFF MASSON and the biologist SUSAN McCARTHY collaborated on the book *When Elephants Weep: The Emotional Lives of Animals.* Once again, the work of adults draws heavily on childhood encounters with animals. Jacki Lyden asked the two authors about their intent in writing about the emotions of other species. July 16, 1995

Lyden: Did you go into this, if you'll allow me to say this, with a prejudice aforethought. Did you think, I know animals have emotions and I'm going to prove it.

Masson: I had dogs and cats and birds and lizards and mice and rats and hamsters and gerbils and tortoises and snakes and everything as a child, and I was absolutely persuaded as a very young child that these animals had strong emotions. It never occurred to me, really, until fairly recently that anybody would object to that statement, although we have encountered that to some degree. Some scientists have not welcomed the idea of studying emotions. One reason is that they feel it can't be measured. It's not easy to study scientifically. Of course, that's true of many things, including human emotions.

Lyden: Susan McCarthy, what stories of animal emotions prove to you that they have emotions quite similar to humans?

McCarthy: What we mostly did was look at observations of wild animals by scientists who were studying all kinds of things from dominance hierarchies to foraging strategies. We asked whether their data also told us something about emotion. One of my favorite examples comes from a biologist who was studying peregrine falcons in the Rockies. She had what's called an ethogram — a chart with different categories of behavior — and every time one of these behaviors occurred, she checked it off in one color depending on whether it was the male or female falcon. They had a nest with five babies in it. And one morning, she suddenly realized that her notebook was filled out in only one color, that the female falcon was missing. The notebook also showed that the male falcon's behavior was changing, that he was spending longer and longer periods at the nest, looking around, looking into the nest, making inquiring calls, but the female didn't show up. After three days, he was sitting on a rock by the nest, and he suddenly let out a terrible cry, a sound she had never heard a peregrine make before. It sounded to her like, just, a wail of agony and despair, and then he sat there motionless until the sun went down. It wasn't until the fifth day after his mate had vanished that he pulled out of this and suddenly went into a frenzy of hunting, from dawn 'til dusk, catching food for his young. Some biologists climbed down to the nest a week later, and they found that three of the young peregrine falcons had died, and two of them were thriving, and, in fact, their father was able to rear them and fledge them successfully in the autumn. She later discovered that the female had probably been shot off of a telephone pole. Now, I think the sadness of this falcon, as evidenced by his behavior when his mate disappeared, is fairly evident, and the fact that three of the nestlings died shows that the sadness, itself, did not particularly have survival value, but was probably intimately connected with the affection between the pair.

Lyden: Jeff Masson, you make a contention that we know that animals have emotions. Anyone who's ever had a pet or been around one knows that, but scientists choose to disdain this, and say, "They may, but they're not the same as human emotions." What is the split? What are scientists so skeptical of?

Masson: Well, I think it depends on the scientist, and I do think there are some scientists who would be perfectly prepared to admit that animals have emotions. I think that the scientists most reluctant to admit that are the ones who, in one way or another, profit from the use of animals in what I particularly think is not a very nice way — namely, doing painful experiments on them, because if animals are capable of suffering, are capable of feeling sorrow and loneliness, and even despair, then, of course, it raises all kinds of ethical questions about whether we should be doing painful experiments on these animals. Now, I understand that reasonable people can differ in their view on this. Even Susan and I differ. But we both agree that it's very important that people not deny that the animal they're working with does have these feelings. I choose, on the

Noah Adams was intrigued by the following item on the Reuter news service: "Scottish police are looking for a hypnotic dog whose disappearance had halted a sellout Edinburgh Festival Fringe show." The runaway dog was named Oscar and billed as the world's only canine hypnotist. According to his owner and costar in this singular act, Oscar ran off while being exercised. HUGH LENNON, the human half of the duo, issued a warning to anyone who might see Oscar: "Do not look him straight in the eye." Noah Adams asked Mr. Lennon about how Oscar performs his hypnotic duties. August 23, 1995

Lennon: The people on stage are asked to go. They're told that Oscar the Hypno-Dog is coming on stage to hypnotize them. When he comes on, we ask for quiet from the audience, and also ask for volunteers to go and kneel one by one in front of the dog and look into his eyes and concentrate on his eyes. The time that it takes for Oscar to hypnotize those people varies, depending on how much the person believes that he will be hypnotized.

Adams: You bet.

Lennon: Some people go almost straightaway. Others may take as long as maybe twenty seconds or thirty seconds.

Adams: And Oscar just stares at them?

Lennon: He sits there and he stares at them. In fact, what gave me the idea in the first place is that I noticed that when he was a pup, he used to sit down and stare at people. He used to stare at everyone. So he's got a very dominant stare.

Adams: Do you figure he knows what's going on here?

Lennon: I doubt it. I think he just likes to stare at people, and he stares. The fact that these people go into that state, he doesn't quite understand, I don't think, what is happening. We think that there's a possibility that the chap that found him could have been hypnotized by him because he actually gave up his sandwich.

Adams: The young boy who found him?

Lennon: Yes, gave the dog his sandwich.

Adams: Well, that's quite likely, I would think.

Lennon: It's a possibility.

Adams: The news report said, as I understand it, "Be careful if you see this dog, Oscar, because he may hypnotize you if he looks you straight in the eye."

Lennon: Yes, I've been asked that question many times by the media when they contacted me to find out what's the story about the dog, their main concern was whether people could be hypnotized by him if they looked into his eyes. Well, I did explain that there is only a very slight chance, that if a person has been hypnotized by Oscar or if they've not seen the show before, and that person believes that Oscar's eyes could hypnotize him, then he would certainly go into that state.

Adams: How are you going to convince Oscar to stick closer to home now?

Lennon: I'm buying him a long chain and padlock.

There are many more breeds of dog than those on display at the Westminster Kennel Club Dog Show. Noah Adams explored the seemingly infinite variety with BRUCE FOGLE, a London veterinarian and the author of *The Encyclopedia of the Dog*. The encyclopedia includes the Peruvian Inca orchid (a hairless hot water bottle of a dog), the lurcher (from Ireland), the dunker (from Norway), and dogs from dozens of countries and every continent. Matchmaking breeders are responsible for many of the varieties, while others, like the Carolina dog, are the offspring of more independent parents. November 2, 1995

Fogle: The Carolina dog is a strange story because Lehr Brisbin, Dr. Brisbin, who's a biology professor at the University of Georgia, discovered these dogs at a Department of Energy site in South Carolina. Dr. Brisbin feels that these dogs have been breeding independent of human intervention for quite some time, and he feels that this is a true primitive dog, that is the descendant of dogs that were brought by Asian people when they crossed the Bering Strait eight thousand to ten thousand years ago. Their looks are, oh, not unlike crossing a Labrador and a German shepherd, although they're smaller than that.

Adams: They are light brown with pointed ears?

Fogle: Yes, beige, brown eyes, rather sleek body. But the color is very similar to the most common color of a dingo in Australia, for example.

Adams: I thought that I knew about a lot of dogs, but I have never heard of the Plott hound — country of origin, the U.S.

Fogle: I had never heard of the Plott hound either. There's the treeing walker coonhound and there's the Catahoula leopard dog. I hadn't heard of any of those. The Plott hound is the only coonhound in the United States that doesn't have a British or English origin. Its origin is in Germany with the Plott family, who brought some of their dogs over with them and then selectively bred their dogs for a high-pitched voice, a very curious, sonorous, bawling type of voice, which is very common to most coonhounds, and selectively bred the dog as their family breed starting in the 1700s in North Carolina.

Adams: Do you think you could go down there and find somebody named Plott who's still breeding these dogs?

Fogle: Apparently there are still members of the Plott family who are still breeding the Plott hound.

Adams: There is yet another family sort of dog, and whenever I turn the page and come across this dog I have to laugh. This is — I'll try to say it — the Alapaha blue blood bulldog?

Fogle: Lana Lou Lane is the principal breeder of this dog. The Alapaha blue blood dog looks like a cross between an English bulldog and a boxer dog. And, in fact, that makes it look a little bit like an American pit bull, although it has a cuter face. The face is pushed in more than the American pit bull, and there are very few of them.

Adams: This dog has kind of a quizzical look on its face because the genetic pool is so small, bred by one family.

Fogle: This is always the problem. If you look at that dog closely, you'll see that its lower eyelid is rolled inward, and that's an inherited defect that's called entropion. When the lower lid, or the upper lid, for that matter, is rolled in, the skin rubs on the eye and causes chronic irritation to the eye. Now, that's a problem that has a high incidence in this breed. And the Lane family should be able to eliminate that with careful breeding.

Adams: They have to get some outside blood in. How do they do that, though? This is the only place the dog is bred?

Fogle: I'm quite certain that the old-fashioned English bulldog, the type you see in Victorian etchings that has a much smaller head, was used in the original breeding of this dog. And the Lane family would simply get one of those dogs, and they could introduce that type of bloodline in.

Adams: It's surprising to me that you can actually make a new breed of dog so quickly. How soon can you do it if you have a couple of dogs you'd like to put together before it becomes a breed?

Fogle: Oh, you can do it in one generation if you want. The Labradoodle is a good example. There's been a breeding program in the state of Victoria in Australia for guide dogs. In Victoria, they cross standard poodles with the Labrador to reduce the incidence of hip dysplasia in the Labrador, to get rid of a genetic fault, and to try and reduce molting, shedding fur. The standard poodle sheds less than the Labrador does. They try to maintain the trainability of the product. If they hit it first time around, there you have a new breed — the Labradoodle — and you don't have to go any farther.

Adams: That's what you can do, but should you do it? Couldn't it be a dangerous thing to do? Why should you be doing that much tampering with good old dogs?

Fogle: Well, because we are tampering with bad old dogs that we've already tampered with. The great big genetic soup of mongrels, or — if you've noticed, I've dubbed my one little bit of political correctness, I've called the breeds of dogs "purebreds"; and something like a Labradoodle, a "cross-bred"; and the mutts and mongrels have become "random-breds." The random-breds are the great genetic resource for dogs, as long as random-bred dogs remain the most common dogs in the world, as they are. Over fifty percent of dogs in the world are not selectively bred, they're randomly bred, and that maintains an exciting genetic pool.

Adams: OK. I'm going to put you on the spot here. Let's say you want to come home from work and you want to have a good laugh as soon as you open the door. Now, I think one of the reasons to have a dog is because they're funny, but what's the funniest dog for you in this book that you've found?

Fogle: The Prazsky Krysavik. It was just completely unexpected.

Adams: Oh, I just found it in the book.

Fogle: Now, you're not supposed to laugh. But you can't help it. I mean, if you come home to your own little personal Prazsky Krysavik, you have to smile because you look at this little thing, which weighs somewhere between two and six pounds, and is a Czechoslovak breed. You say to yourself, the wolf is the parent of the dog. You look at the Prazsky Krysavik, which means in Slovak, "beautiful Prague dog," and you figure there's no way that there's wolf in this. There's no conceivable way that a wolf had anything to do with producing a little thing that looks like a cross between a miniature pinscher and an emaciated Chihuahua.

Adams: It looks kind of like a small deer, even.

Fogle: Long legs, Bambi-type eyes, but they're funny little things, and they're a giggle. They're just fun to have around.

T here are breeds of cat and then there are provisional breeds of cat, types recognized by many fanciers, but not yet granted full status by the authorities. Such is the status of the Munchkins, a breed of cat whose provisional recognition by the International Cat Association provoked no small controversy. Munchkins are low-bellied creatures, the feline equivalents of dachshunds. While they now fetch as much as twenty-five-hundred dollars, their roots are humble and as short as their legs. They all descend from a pregnant stray cat rescued by a Louisiana woman in 1983. PAUL McSORLEY, the secretary of the International Cat Munchkin Society, discussed the breed with Scott Simon. July 29, 1995

Simon: You own a Munchkin?

McSorley: I own several.

Simon: What do you like about them?

McSorley: Well, I like their uniqueness. They're very affectionate. They have a very sweet expression. They have big round eyes, and that's appealing to me.

Simon: Can they do everything a cat usually can and needs to?

McSorley: They can mouse and hunt and run and jump. They corner swiftly, and short, strong legs make climbing easier too.

Simon: There are some people, as I don't have to tell you, who are quite uncomfortable with this and say that this has been a breed that's been developed just for the delectation of human beings, and that's just not a fair thing to do to the animal world.

McSorley: This is a natural, spontaneous mutation. What you see is what you get. We have not created the legs to be short. It's just the way it is. We can't make them any shorter or any longer than they already are. We've heard a lot of squawking going on, and I'm sure it will continue. But the bottom line is that these cats are very natural and healthy and they're here to stay.

Simon: I am told, Mr. McSorley, that in the thirties and forties,

RELIGION

Karol Wojtyla of Kraków, Poland, is the world's most influential religious leader. The former quarry worker, actor, poet, and playwright became a priest, and later the archbishop of Kraków. At age fifty-eight, Karol Cardinal Wojtyla was presented to the crowds in St. Peter's Square as the 264th pope, the first non-Italian pontiff since 1523 and the youngest since 1846. He took the name John Paul II. His biographer, the former *New York Times* correspondent TAD SZULC, enjoyed unprecedented personal access to the pope and many previously confidential documents. Szulc discussed his book *Pope John Paul II: The Biography* with Scott Simon. June 24, 1995

Simon: You are Polish-born.
Szulc: Yes, I was.
Simon: You explain many times in the book that intrinsic to understanding John Paul II is understanding what it is for him, for the pope, to be Polish.
Szulc: Because he brings to the institution, to the church, and to the world at large a culture that is very specific, very little known, and in a sense, quite alien and foreign to the church constituencies from this country to Latin America, to western Europe. So I thought from the very beginning, unless you explain what it is to be a Pole you will have a hard time explaining him or understanding him. It's kind of a basic foundation of his personality.
Simon: What is it to be a Pole and in what ways do we see that in his life and his reign?
Szulc: In his case, it is a whole catalogue of things. It's being patriotic, obviously religious because Catholicism is the predominant religion of Poland. It's being romantic. It's being politically acute. It's being ready for rebellion. It almost sounds like an eastern European version of being Irish, except more so, as some people have pointed out.
Simon: The one most consistent character trait I noticed through

the way you present Karol Wojtyla's life, is his capacity for deep, profound, consistent daily prayer.

Szulc: It is said by his closest friends that he prays on the average of seven hours a day, which does not mean that he is on his knees for the full seven hours. He could be praying in the car, in the plane, the helicopter, during Mass. It's his sort of interior process of being engaged in prayer. He explains prayer is the sustenance which has made it possible for him to work endless hours after getting run over, shot, fallen off things, hurt, damaged. So that is very crucial, again, in the personality.

Simon: Let me read something that he wrote, apparently describing his time as a small-town parish priest in Poland. He wrote, "You go out in your cassock, your overcoat, your alb and biretta over beaten path in the snow. But snow will cling to your cassock, then it will thaw out indoors, and freeze again outside, forming a heavy bell around your legs, which gets heavier and heavier, preventing you from taking long strides. By evening, you could hardly drag your legs. But you have to go on, because you know that people wait for you, that they wait all year for this meeting." That's a wonderfully vivid image.

Szulc: It's a very wonderful, vivid image, and that is something that he has always lived up to, the image. I'll give you a quick example. When we went to Denver in August of ninety-three, almost two years ago, he made a point of standing and shaking the hand of every single American bishop who came down to Denver for the occasion of the World Youth Day, because he said, "They came from all over to see me, it's my obligation to stand here and shake hands and chat with them, even if it takes hours and hours and hours." And I think that kind of goes back to the passage that you just read from his early years as a parish priest.

Simon: As head of the church over the past seventeen years, the pope has left two distinct impressions. I won't refer to them as a contradiction. Some critics have. On the one hand, this man is a stalwart proponent of human rights, who was unafraid of taking on not only military dictatorships but prosperous Western cultures when he feels the values they're promoting are dehumanizing our societies. On the other hand, there is this man who is perceived by other people as being intolerant of dissent and inflexible in his reading of personal idiom and religious ideologies. Do you see any contradiction? And how does he bring that together in the same personality?

Szulc: To him, you see, there is no contradiction. To you, to me, as we observe it, as we listen to him, as we read him, there seem to be glaring contradictions. I think millions of Catholics in this country and elsewhere perceive it as a contradiction. He does not because in his own mind all this forms part of the basic belief which he holds, which is the sanctity of life. He opposes the death penalty. He opposes all kinds of violence in human beings. His explanation for his absolute obsessive opposition to abortion is that it is the sanctity of life that is at stake. Artificial contraception, to his way of seeing things, it's also consistent, because life is not allowed to begin where it might otherwise begin. Your question takes us into the area of, is he or is the church losing constituents? Are they losing Catholics? And the answer is they are losing. But he will tell you over and over again that he will not change his views, his approach to all this, to please anyone. If the church is to become smaller but more rigorous, more disciplined, so be it.

Simon: Let me not proceed on the premise that there's something contradictory between being against abortion and being in favor of human rights. There are some people, you yourself, who would notice contradictions in the Holy Father's own human rights policy. For example, he was of no encouragement, or very little, to Archbishop Romero in El Salvador. He was of no encouragement to Father Aristide in Haiti. As much as he reviles military dictatorships, he seems to accept them more easily than he does advocates of liberation theology.

Szulc: I think the record certainly shows that. Archbishop Romero of El Salvador left a diary recounting his encounters with the pope, which were very sad, during which he was treated badly by the pope. I think the answer to this is, as I understand it, that he comes from eastern Europe. The theology of liberation is a Latin American contribution to church philosophy, church doctrine. He knew very little about Latin America, and I think he was convinced much too quickly by people who had different political agendas that the theology of liberation equals Marxism, pure and simple. Now, here's a man who comes out of Marxism, out of Communism, and is being told that those priests in Latin America, in the picture of Che Guevara, are Marxist priests. Therefore, he never intellectually accepted the notion that theology of liberation need not be Marxist, need not be a damaging thing to the church. And to the contrary, if treated intelligently, it could be a very powerful rebirth for the church. I think that this is one of the great misunderstandings of his career. I think it's a very sad thing because it has damaged an awful lot of people in and out of the church that should not have been damaged and should have been encouraged.

Simon: Some people in the West have been surprised that this man who identified himself as an opponent of the dehumanizing aspects of Marxism would now take on capitalism. He refers to it as savage capitalism.

Szulc: He's been doing this from the very outset. And he has made a point of having said, even in the Encyclical See 1990, that there was a reason why Karl Marx appeared on the world scene when he did in the nineteenth century, because of the exploitation of the workers and the peasants during the Industrial Revolution, and that's why he annoys a lot of, let's say, right-wing ideologues in our country here. He feels that capitalism, if carried too far, can be as dehumanizing as Marxism at its worst. I think, curiously, his sense of values, when he preaches family values, come closer and closer together to the values that we are rediscovering in our politics, be it President Clinton's speech to black ministers in Memphis in November 1993, or the Contract with America. I think that he is very much a part of this whole evolution of moral values. I cannot tell you whether he and Senator Dole would join in criticizing Time-Warner. But, quite seriously, this is exactly the view that he would take because he believes that those are values which are terribly damaging to modern society in the context of what he calls "savage capitalism," which he would perceive such a corporation to be.

Simon: Is John Paul II's health good enough to be pope for another five years? A grisly question.

Szulc: Listen, literally, "God knows" is the answer. He's seventy-five years old. Let me put it this way. There's nothing in his health, as we understand it today, with all the limitations of having no access to his medical records, that it is not at all impossible he will be here four and a half years from now at age eighty, which is less than previous popes when they died. He is the pope who, this year, has instructed all the cardinals to prepare for year 2000, for the millennium, essentially rewriting the entire history of the church to point out where the church, the Roman Catholic Church, has been unjust, unfair, insulting, damaging to people, over the past centuries, with its religious wars, inquisitions. He thinks for the church to be seriously acceptable to the new generations, the church has to come clean. It has to admit its errors. He grows with the world. He grows with his church and, above all, I think he wants the church to grow with him. And very, very much, I think this is very important, he has brought the church into the world in a way in which the church had never really been present.

Simon: The overwhelming impression a reader gets at the end of your book is whatever his contradictions, whatever his inflexibility, this is a great guy. I was reminded of what Antony said of Brutus, "The noblest Roman of them all . . . the elements so mixed in him that Nature might stand up and say to all the world, 'This was a man.'" His capacity for belief, conviction, passion, prayer, his enormous energy — what a life.

Szulc: It will be a huge, enormous impact on the history of the twentieth century, no matter how it's analyzed, no matter where the pluses and minuses are assigned. He will have been one of the great personalities of our time, of the century, secular or otherwise. And I think he will be remembered perhaps the way Gregory the Great of the sixth century is remembered, as one of the great fathers of the church, for better or for worse.

When Pope John Paul II visited the United States in 1995, huge crowds greeted him. In New York City's Central Park, on ground soggy from rain, a crowd estimated at a quarter of a million gathered to celebrate Mass. The enthusiasm for the pontiff contrasted with the evident lack of enthusiasm among American Catholics for many of his ideas. According to public opinion polls, more than eighty percent of Catholics held a generally favorable opinion about him but most strongly disagreed with his positions on premarital sex, abortion, birth control, and the role of women in the church. Daniel Zwerdling went to the Catholic University in Washington, D.C., and asked theology students DAN KOONTZ and MARY BEAUDOIN, "Who is the pope to you?" October 7, 1995

Koontz: For me he is a voice, I think, among so many voices in our culture. He has something to say that I think is important. He represents a voice, not God's voice per se, but a voice that people resonate with.

Zwerdling: When you say "a voice," though, you are speaking of him almost as you might speak of a great political figure, of the American president or the president of France.

Koontz: He is that. He is a political figure and he has a political voice, but I think that he has something in addition to that, too, and that is he is a calming presence. Just his presence in America seems to say that there is some hope, there is some inspiration in our humanity for the future. We're not going to just fall apart in a world that seems to get less stable as time goes by.

Zwerdling: So far we've heard the pope is a political player. He is a soothing presence.

Beaudoin: He is also the person who symbolizes in a way the unity of the Catholic Church throughout the world, that this is the leader of the Catholic Church. Maybe that has to do with the stabilizing presence. We know that as a church we are going to hang together because there is this leader.

Zwerdling: Let's talk for a couple of minutes about this notion of unity and about this message you are talking about. If you look in the newspapers this week, and I am sure you all have, you've seen that there is a huge gap now between what the pope believes and what American Catholics say they believe. I'm going to run down very quickly through a *Washington Post*–ABC News poll that just came out. This poll says ninety-three percent of Catholics surveyed say that you can use birth control methods other than the rhythm method and still be a good Catholic. Eighty-five percent said you can get divorced and marry somebody else without church approval and still be a good Catholic. Sixty-nine percent said a woman can have an abortion and still be a good Catholic. Just over half said you can be a homosexual and still be a good Catholic. Another poll that just came out in *Time* magazine said that most Catholics favor allowing priests to get married, allowing women to become priests. And most Catholics favor, at least some of the time, sex before marriage or say that it doesn't mean that you are not a good Catholic. What's going on here?

Beaudoin: A friend of mine said that the church is kind of like a big dysfunctional family and that we all may disagree on things and some people may be ostracized, but in the end we all hang together because we are family and we do care about each other. I don't know that that analogy is really good, but sometimes that helps me to understand what is happening because I know even when I have disagreements with my own family, I will work on it and try to bring things back together and try to heal the people within the family.

Zwerdling: Does it worry you at all that there is such a disparity between the pope's beliefs and most American Catholics' beliefs, at least according to these polls?

Koontz: It's worrisome, yes, because it can be divisive. The unity that we try to encourage and nurture in the church can be divided by these differences. So I guess it worries me. But it's not an altogether unhealthy situation because it is a kind of relationship of disagreement that maybe we can come to a better understanding of what the revelation is and what the teaching is or ought to be.

Zwerdling: What has brought Catholics, at least in this country, to the point where so many do disagree on so many points with the pope and still consider themselves to be good, devout Catholics? In the old days, people didn't speak out and say they disagreed with the pope.

Beaudoin: I would say that all of those issues by and large need to be open for discussion. I think that that would be my one major disagreement, that the issues cannot be closed because — I'm not sure that the revelation is complete. I just really believe that God's spirit is still active and that the case isn't closed on all of these issues. I think that there is much more discussion that needs to happen.

Zwerdling: So therefore you are implying, I think, that if Catholics have this sort of public debate about what can a Catholic do and still be a good Catholic, what behavior is acceptable, what is not acceptable, that you may actually help discover the word of God, the true word of God, better among yourselves than the pope can deliver.

Koontz: I was just thinking that with all of these issues, nobody has a complete understanding of what they all are and what they all mean or what places to look for in these issues in the revelation of God, not even the pope. The pope would, I'm sure, admit, of course, that he doesn't have a complete understanding of all of this. So as Americans, when we don't understand, we want to talk about it, we want to discuss them. I think that the things the pope has to say on these particular issues bears some thinking about as well as the other sides of all these issues as well. They bear some thinking about. In that thinking and discussing and trying to understand the word of God in these issues, we come to a better, more complete understanding of what God's intention is for humanity.

Beaudoin: I would just say that there have been good Catholics throughout history who have been in trouble with the pope, who have disagreed with the pope, and who have even been excommunicated. I think for me to be a good Catholic means to, as Dan said, take what the pope says and really value that and really work with that, but also to be true to your own conscience and to question those things.

Zwerdling: Can you tell me what is the ultimate purpose, what is the ultimate goal, of your beliefs?

Koontz: I guess for me the core of it would be just to center around Christ and in a community of faith that seeks a kind of solidarity in terms of human fulfillment and relationships and that would be the center. Christ would be the center as the human person who we ought to take as our example. From that would flow all the rest of what it means to be a good Catholic.

Zwerdling: A friend of mine who grew up in a Catholic family, said, "In a way when I think of the pope, I think of him being sort of like a wonderful grandfather or grandmother, somebody we revere, somebody we respect, somebody who we need in our lives, but it's OK we don't agree with him about everything."

Beaudoin: It's very good to have a grandfather figure around in your life because it's a tradition to turn to, it's a tradition that gives you a home, it's a place to go to ask questions, to find guidance. I think that's very important and very comforting. I think that's why many people want to consider themselves to be good Catholics even if they disagree with grandfather.

Volume I of the Schocken Bible took EVERETT FOX twenty-seven years to produce. Fox was a graduate student when he decided to undertake the project: a translation of the Hebrew Bible into English. He was inspired by reading a translation from Hebrew to German, by Martin Buber and Franz Rosenzweig, a translation that captured the spirit and texture of ancient Hebrew in a modern language. So he set out to do the same in English, and produced *The Five Books of Moses*, a massive achievement. More so than other recent efforts, Fox's translation strives for poetry — not the poetry of the King James Bible, but the poetry of the original Hebrew. Fox spoke to Robert Siegel upon publication. December 18, 1995

Fox: Biblical language is absolutely alive. It's compelling. It's not the stilted or pious language that we're accustomed to. So my goal was really to stimulate and challenge readers to come into the world of the Hebrew text. The difference between this translation and most others, at this point, is that it tries to present the texture of the text, the feel of the text, as I read it and hear it. It tries to reproduce the style, the syntax, the ambiguities, the difficulties, the word plays, the meaningful repetitions — all these wonderful things that the Bible uses in order to get its point across and that's designed to help the reader become an active participant in the text.

Siegel: Well, I wonder if you could give us an example, and I'm thinking of a passage that you cite in your translator's preface, which comes from Genesis 32:21–22. And perhaps you can tell us what's happening around this time in the story of Genesis.

Fox: This is a story where Jacob, after many years in exile and having grown up to adulthood, is on his way back home to see his family again. He hasn't seen his brother Esau in twenty years and the last time they met, Esau wanted to kill him. Jacob had stolen his birthright and his blessing. So Jacob is not sure how his brother is feeling at this point, and messengers that he sends to find out what's going on come back, and say, "Yes, Esau, your brother, is coming to meet you. And by the way, there are four hundred men with him." That throws Jacob into a panic and he prepares a gift for his brother to appease him. And what the text says, basically, is "I'll appease him with this present and then when I come to face him maybe he'll be nice to me." The way I hear the Hebrew, it echoes the word *face* many more times, and the movement that's set up by these repetitions of a key word prepares you for the meeting between the two brothers, which in the next chapter has the motif of *face* come back. So let me show you what goes on in this passage: [*reading*] "For he said to himself, I will wipe the anger from his face with the gift that goes ahead of my face. Afterward, when I see his face, perhaps he will lift up my face."

Siegel: All of that repetition of *face*. If we were to hear the Hebrew, what would that sound like?

Fox: That sounds like the following: *"Ki amar akhappera phanav ba-mincha ha-holekhet le-phanai. Ve-aharei khen eh'eh phanav ulai Yissa phanai."*

So you hear this *phanav* or *phanai*, which comes back in the next chapter or even in the next section when Jacob wrestles with the angel. He calls the name of the place of the wrestling match *"peniel"* — the face of God. He says, "I have seen God face to face and my life has been saved." Now, the clincher occurs in the following passage when Esau and Jacob meet at last. Jacob says to his brother, "For I have after all seen your face as one sees the face of God and you have been gracious to me." So all these confrontations, divine and human, are drawn together by the use of a word. If you translate the word out more idiomatically as "I will appease him" instead of "I'll cover over" or "I'll wipe the anger from his face," then you lose that wonderful connection in the text.

Siegel: Part of what you're doing here is something that's familiar in a way to people who have gone from writing for the eye to writing for the ear in radio. You're working repetitions back into the text.

Fox: Yes, that's exactly true.

Siegel: That sounds better than we're accustomed to seeing it look on the page.

Fox: I suppose that's true. If you wrote this way as a schoolchild, you get your paper back with all kinds of red marks. The teacher would say, "Too much repetition. Let's vary the language."

Siegel: We find that right away in the first chapter of Genesis, where we've been taught in English to alternate *God* with *He*, but actually you give us all the *God*s in there. How does it read in your translation?

Fox: This is from the first chapter. [*reading*] "God said, 'Let there be light,' and there was light. God saw the light, that it was good. God separated the light from the darkness. God called the light 'day,' and the darkness he called 'night.' There was setting. There was dawning one day."

Siegel: A big change in this translation is that the book of Genesis here is not the story of Abraham, Isaac, and Jacob, but of Avraham, Yitzhak, and Ya'akov. Why the Hebrew names?

Fox: The Hebrew Bible uses names very often in a meaningful way. Names are used almost as puns and so to retain that sense of the way names can be played with in the text, I've kept more conventional Hebrew pronunciation of the names. Also, I hope it gives the reader a chance to realize that this is not the familiar book that we take it to be, but it is a very ancient book and that our assumptions need to be reexamined.

Siegel: The biggest name question, obviously, for any translation, is what to do with the name of God.

Fox: There's a four-letter name of God in the Hebrew Bible, which is usually translated as "The Lord." Some people have translated it as "The Eternal." Others use various other possibilities. But the most common historical one is "The Lord." This is a name which already in antiquity was not pronounced by the general public. It was limited to the high priests, and at some point we've lost the pronunciation altogether. Ancient Jews wound up writing it in the manuscripts and in the Bibles we have originally without vowels at all. So we can't even reconstruct the pronunciation so easily. That makes it a name which is in a sense not a name. What I've done in this translation is to keep it with uppercase YHWH instead of writing it out erroneously as Jehovah or euphemistically as "The Lord."

Siegel: I wonder if you could read to us from some of the passages that you found to be the most challenging or that in translating

them you felt that you had succeeded best in doing what you set
out to do with the text.

Fox: Let me read a very short story, which is Genesis 22. This is
known as the binding of Isaac. It's the difficult story where after
many chapters of God promising Abraham a son, he finally has one,
and in the next chapter he's asked to give him back. So this is
Genesis 22. [*reading*]

> Now, after these events it was
> that God tested Avraham
> and said to him:
> Avraham!
> He said:
> Here I am.
> He said:
> Pray, take your son,
> your only one,
> whom you love,
> Yitzhak,
> and go-you-forth to the land of Moriyya/Seeing,
> and offer him up there as an offering-up
> upon one of the mountains
> that I will tell you of.
> Avraham started-early in the morning.
> He saddled his donkey,
> he took his two serving lads with him and Yitzhak his son,
> he split wood for the offering-up,
> and arose and went to the place that God had told him of.
> On the third day Avraham lifted up his eyes
> and saw the place from afar.
> Avraham said to his lads:
> You stay here with the donkey,
> and I and the lad will go yonder,
> we will bow down and then return to you.
> Avraham took the wood for the offering-up,
> he placed them upon Yitzhak his son,
> in his hand he took the fire and the knife.
> Thus the two of them went together.
> Yitzhak said to Avraham his father, he said:
> Father!
> He said:
> Here I am, my son.

He said:
Here are the fire and the wood,
but where is the lamb for the offering-up?
Avraham said:
God will see-for-himself to the lamb for the offering-up,
my son.
Thus the two of them went together.
They came to the place that God had told him of;
there Avraham built the slaughter-site
and arranged the wood
and bound Yitzhak his son
and placed him on the slaughter-site atop the wood.
Avraham stretched out his hand,
he took the knife to slay his son.
But the Lord's messenger called to him from heaven
and said:
Avraham! Avraham!
He said:
Here I am.
He said:
Do not stretch out your hand against the lad,
do not do anything to him!
For now I know
that you are in awe of God —
you have not withheld your son, your only-one from me.
Avraham lifted up his eyes and saw:
there, a ram caught behind in the thicket by its horns!
Avraham went,
he took the ram
and offered it up as an offering-up in place of his son.

Siegel: You have made many choices of English words that are different from other translations. Why, for example, do you call the place where Avraham would have sacrificed Yitzhak, or Isaac, a *slaughter-site* instead of an *altar*?

Fox: One of the things that happens in this translation is to dig a little bit deeper into the roots of the language and to reflect the fact that this was a place of animal sacrifice and animal ritual slaughter. That's in the root of the word. *Altar* has a much later ring to it and sounds a little bit different than what was done on these altars, so to speak.

Siegel: Were there any times during the translation when you

Scott Simon interviewed one of the editors of a new translation of Scripture, *The New Testament and Psalms: An Inclusive Version*, published by Oxford University Press. In the interest of removing language that might give offense, this version of the Bible sacrificed such familiar phrases as *God the Father*, *son of man*, and the *right hand of God*. Its version of the Lord's Prayer begins, "Our Father-Mother in Heaven." Simon asked the Reverend BURTON THROCKMORTON, JR., what was wrong with a phrase like *God the Father*? September 2, 1995

Throckmorton: Well, there are several things wrong. I think the main thing is that the church has called God "Father" so much in prayers, in hymns, in Scripture, that at least many people in the church no longer understand *Father* to be a metaphor. They understand that they go from calling God "Father" to believing that God is male. All branches of Christendom have denied that God has a sex or that God is of some particular race. God is believed in all Christendom to transcend all that. So if we combine *Father-Mother*, with a hyphen, then the metaphor is broadened, so God can be seen through either lens.

Simon: I understand that, for example, in this new New Testament, you tried to reduce references to *the Lord*. You use *God* more frequently.

Throckmorton: Yes, also partly for the same reason. It's a way of avoiding again, a male-oriented term every time one refers to Jesus or God.

Simon: Reverend Throckmorton, I opened this new New Testament and almost immediately turned to the Twenty-third Psalm, and the way you folks have it just sounds a lot different. May I read?

Throckmorton: Of course.

Simon: I'll just read the first section. [*reading*] "God is my shepherd, I shall not want. God makes me lie down in green pastures."

You have removed the reference to "He maketh me to lie down in green pastures." [reading] "And leads me beside still waters. God restores my soul. God leads me in paths of righteousness for the sake of God's name." This is just an aesthetic judgment, but I don't find the music there so much.

Throckmorton: No, you're quite right. I think there is aesthetic loss. I think there's no doubt about that. But women who are not addressed hardly are concerned about the aesthetics of not being addressed. So I think we have to sometimes give up, lose aesthetically, what we gain on the question of justice.

Simon: But, a question: for example, as I understand it, this new New Testament does not refer to anyone sitting on the right hand of God.

Throckmorton: Right, the church again, does not believe that God has sides and a front and a back. That's, of course, again a metaphor. Now, I know some who are left-handed who don't feel this way at all, but I understand that some left-handed people wonder why all good things have to be put on the right hand of God and evil things and evil people on the left hand of God, as though the left hand were inherently evil and the right hand were inherently good. That, of course, is not literally the case. By right hand, it's not meant literally right hand, but simply near God. So we have said "by the mighty hand" or "by the side of" sometimes.

Simon: Reverend Throckmorton, are you a little sensitive about having this referred to as the P.C. — politically correct — edition of the New Testament?

Throckmorton: Well, of course. P.C. is a put-down term. It's always used pejoratively, and I think it carries with it the connotation of "unimportant." And I think the matter, for example, of addressing women is not a matter of being politically correct. It's a matter of being correct.

Simon: Recognizing your eagerness not to cause offense, who has told you over the years that they are offended?

Throckmorton: People on radio talk shows.

Simon: Oh, you can't believe anything you hear on the radio, Reverend, you know that.

Throckmorton: I've been on a lot of radio talk shows in this country and in Great Britain.

Simon: Have any women called you up, and said, "I don't like

God being represented as the Father because I feel that that locks me off as a woman from understanding"?

Throckmorton: Oh my word, I get that all the time. Oh yes, I should say so. There's much more of that feeling out in the world than I think some people realize. And therefore, I expect this New Testament to sell widely.

JACK MILES undertook a task as daunting as translating Scripture. He wrote *God: A Biography*. Miles, a former Jesuit and scholar of religion, became a book columnist for the *Los Angeles Times*. His approach in the biography is neither that of the theologian nor the historian, but of literary critic. His subject is the Hebrew Bible, which he discussed with Liane Hansen on Easter Sunday. April 16, 1995

Hansen: Briefly tell us the difference between the Hebrew Bible and the Old Testament.

Miles: The Hebrew Bible, called by Jews the Tanakh, has the same contents, but it orders them somewhat differently.

Hansen: This isn't a continuous narrative, is it? You refer to it as a series of testimonies?

Miles: A sequence of testimonies. It is a continuous narrative from the Creation of the world to the fall of Jerusalem. After that point there isn't a single story that links everything together, but people either talk about God or God speaks in his own name, talking to human beings. You can get a sense of what someone is like, both from what he says and from how people speak to him. In the latter chapters of the book of Genesis, we encounter for the first time the God who was not referred to by any name but by the name of his worshiper, as "God of Abraham, God of Isaac, God of Jacob." When I was in graduate school it came as a great revelation to me that scholars were prepared to believe that once upon a time these were three different gods and that the blinding theophany to Moses in the burning bush — when a voice said to him, "I am the God of Abraham and the God of Isaac and the God of Jacob and the God of your father, and my name is I am who am" — this moment of fusion of all the divine personalities in one personality was rightly honored as, in a way, the birthday of God. And Moses is something like the father of monotheism. What gives our God the character he has is that he is both responsible for the loftiest matters of the cosmos, for the most difficult arrangements of politics, and for the smallest details of your personal life.

Hansen: So in answer to the question about God posed by Tony Hendra in his parody "Deteriorata" — "God . . . hairy thunderer or cosmic muffin?" — it sounds like he's not only both, but, and I don't want to sound irreverent here, he sounds like Sybil.

Miles: Sybil, yes, a multiple personality. In literature a character who has more than one personality, and who has, as a result, an unpredictability, has great interest. If the interest lies in his being sometimes wonderful and sometimes horrible, you might even call him compelling. I think that the simplified God, in which the darker side has been left out, is safer and perhaps more comforting but less compelling.

Hansen: You say that God is an amalgam of these several different personalities, and it's this tension among the personalities that makes God difficult but compelling and addictive. You write about God, what he says himself, and you say in the beginning he was talking to himself, essentially. Then he begins to talk to humans. But what happens to God by the time we get to Job?

Miles: Well, the Book of Job is the climactic moment in the entire story. Back at the beginning we saw at the flood that he had a demonic or destructive side but past that point, his demonic side seems to be held in check. At the beginning of the Book of Job, a devil in a personal form makes an appearance, tempts God, and God yields to the temptation, a temptation to his vanity, and permits the devil to torture an innocent man. Because earlier this man had said, "The Lord God gives. The Lord God takes away. Blessed be the name of the Lord," God thought he would be uncomplaining. The innocent man, to God's surprise, isn't uncomplaining. He accepts it, but he says, "I'm sure God wouldn't do a thing like this, and I ask him for an explanation of why he is doing it." Having heard this at great length, God rises in power and thunder and might and tries to change the subject: "Let's not talk about whether I'm right or wrong. Let's not talk about whether I am unjust or just. Let's just talk about whether I am strong or weak." Traditionally this explanation has been read as adequate for Job, adequate to make him say, "I'm sorry. I shouldn't have brought the subject up." My longest footnote, about eight pages, is on my reading of Job's final lines as, in fact, a sticking to his guns. He doesn't back down. He acknowledges that God is powerful. He does not acknowledge that God is just. And then God does not just restore his fortunes but doubles them, and God's last words to him are, "You have not spoken correctly of me, as has my servant, Job." The name Job is the last syllable that crosses God's lips in the Hebrew Bible, the Tanakh. He never speaks again.

Hansen: And then we get a glimpse of God near the end, where he is. You call him "the ancient of days."

Miles: That's right. In the book of Daniel, which is very near the end of the Hebrew Bible, God is seen. He hasn't been heard from and he hasn't been seen and he hasn't done anything now for seven or eight books. Now we see him with white hair, seated silent on a remote and lofty throne. His angels are communicating with Daniel, and they indicate to Daniel that God knows in detail what will happen down to the end of time. In a way this God, silent and remote, is in contrast with the creator God of Genesis, who was all power, but didn't seem to be so long on total understanding. He was capable of being surprised. He was capable of making mistakes. After all, he made a man, didn't get it quite right the first time. He had to keep trying. What is it that's wrong here? You know, finally he thinks of woman. This God wouldn't do that. He knows everything, and yet he's doing nothing.

Hansen: I know I'm going to get letters because you keep referring to God as "he." But "he" is the literary character that you are picking up from the Hebrew Bible. You also say in your introduction that knowledge of God as a literary character neither precludes nor requires belief in God. Now, ninety-six percent of all Americans believe in God. And they're going to listen to you, and they're going to say you are being blasphemous, first of all, on this holiest of days, Easter. How do you answer them?

Miles: I wonder if you've ever visited any of the great cathedrals of Europe. You can enter the Cathedral of Chartres and fall to your knees in prayer. It was intended to bring you to that state. It was intended to create a prayerful mood in you. You can enter St. Peter's and stand beneath that gigantic dome and feel yourself small, as Michelangelo intended you to feel. But then you can also go back in and talk about the dome as a dome. You are not committing blasphemy if you analyze the architecture. The glass in Chartres Cathedral is much discussed by those who appreciate stained glass as a form of art, and no blasphemy is intended. I intend no blasphemy in talking about the monument of language that we have in our Bible. Here is a work of literature that has been read aloud weekly for thousands of years. But what I find striking is that they were learning lessons from it that they hadn't set out to learn. They intended to admire God for his justice and his patience and his mercy, but at the same time they were also observing, whether they consciously were or not, all of these internal differences that I'm talking about. So that it comes about that we in the West have an ideal of character that actually celebrates internal division. When you meet a new person, you're anxious to know, if you actually become curious about that person, What is it like behind the eyes? What is it like inside the mind? What sort of conversation is going on in there, and what's the struggle? Most of us feel we have some sort of struggle going on. Not all cultures take that as much as a matter of course as ours does.

Hansen: You thought about this for twenty-five years. It took five years for you to write the book. Has all of this scholarly work had any effect on your faith at all?

Miles: First of all, I am a practicing Christian. I attend the Episcopal Church now. When I worship, what I think about is the fact that human beings are limited. Our intelligence is limited. There are sounds we can't hear, but a dog can hear. There are things we can think, and a dog can't think. There is undoubtedly some kind of limit on our intelligence, overall. It seems to me we are a very special species in that we're capable of formulating questions that we cannot answer, thinking always past our own best answer. That's what draws me to wish to worship. It's a kind of public acknowledgment of what we can't do. The Bible as a formulation of God is a failure. It does its best. All of those writers who worked, who were inspired, perhaps by God and perhaps on their own to put these words on paper, succeeded, but only to a point.

JOHN P. MEIER is a Catholic priest, a leading scholar of the New Testament, and a writer attempting to reconcile religious belief with historical fact. Father Meier had just published the second volume of *A Marginal Jew: Rethinking the Historical Jesus* when he spoke with Liane Hansen. Volume II of his study is subtitled *Mentor, Message, and Miracles.* He began their conversation with a definition of his subject. January 8, 1995

Meier: By the historical Jesus, scholars usually mean that Jesus whom we can reconstruct or recapture by using modern historical, scientific scholarship applied to ancient texts. Now, I stress, of course, and immediately you can sense this quotes the historical Jesus and he is going to be a hypothetical reconstruction. By its very nature, it's subject to revision, and it's not terribly surprising that different scholars come up with different historical Jesuses.

Hansen: I have to admit that the scenario that you set up for your book is almost like the beginning of a very bad joke: take a Catholic, a Protestant, a Jew, and an agnostic, lock them in Harvard Divinity School library, and don't let them out until they've arrived at a consensus document. You view your work as that consensus document. Briefly, why was it necessary to take this approach to the work?

Meier: What you refer to, I call sometimes the un-papal conclave. They're also put on a very Spartan diet to get their work along. It was just a very graphic, concrete way of trying to get across the basic rules of the game. Now, obviously, if you had such a group of people getting together to write a consensus document, the basic rules of the game would be that any claims made must be able to be supported by historical, critical work. Any arguments that are made about the data, any conclusions drawn, must be able to be sustained by scholarly argumentation. Or, to put it negatively, no one may make claims that are drawn rather from the insights of faith, as opposed to something that any historical scholar of any persuasion could not accept. Now, that creates a great limitation that will mean that things that each member of that mythical committee might want to say, agnostic as well as Christian, cannot be allowed because it comes from the faith or antifaith perspective of that individual. Therefore the consensus document, indeed therefore this book, will never represent the fullness of what might be said by one individual who is allowed to bring his or her whole worldview, his or her whole faith vision to the topic. It is a severe limitation, but I think it's a limitation that has a purpose. If, indeed, we deal with concrete data according to fixed rules of research, always arguing by strict historical reasoning, then therefore you create some sort of common ground whereby people of very different views — Catholic, Jews, or what have you — may be able to dialogue, and therefore, I think, there is for all the restrictions a very positive payoff, in that it makes dialogue possible among people who, very sadly, for centuries, have not been on speaking terms.

Hansen: There is, aside from the Four Gospels, one nonbiblical source you draw upon, the writings of a first-century Jewish historian named Josephus.

Meier: He is the one who has given us our major sources for the history of Judaism and Palestine, apart from the New Testament. Two of the most prominent people in the whole of the Gospels, certainly Jesus and John the Baptist, both receive brief but passing references in Josephus. Obviously, as you said, we are here on the ground of history at this point, not in fables.

Hansen: John the Baptist is the mentor in the subtitle of your book. Could you elaborate just a little bit on the effect of John the Baptist on Jesus?

Meier: I think it's very important to realize that John the Baptist was, first of all, an independent Jewish prophet in the line of Jewish prophets, in his own right. Christians, naturally, knowing John the Baptist from the Gospels, see John the Baptist only in relation to Jesus, only as the forerunner, the witness, to Jesus. But we have to appreciate that Josephus, a Jew of the first century who had been in Palestine, was quite capable of writing about John the Baptist totally apart from Jesus without any mention of Jesus. For Josephus and for many other Jews, John the Baptist had his own autonomy, his own meaning, his own religious significance. And so there's a whole chapter simply on him, not allowing Jesus even in the door, so that at least for the first chapter, Jesus remains marginal to his own book; and then, secondly, only in the second chapter do we then get Jesus with and without John. What I do is try to bring together all of the material in all Four Gospels, plus Acts, where Jesus and John intersect. My whole point there is Jesus certainly had no other person of his time who had greater influence on him, who indeed launched his whole career, if I may put it that way, than John the Baptist.

Hansen: We have talked about the mentor, John the Baptist. You also deal with the message. Is it possible for you to condense what that message is?

Meier: Well, in one sense, of course, it is impossible, even in the whole book, to condense it, because what I try to say is the heart of Jesus' message is the coming of the kingdom of God. Now the funny thing about kingdom of God, anybody who has read the Gospels, that is of course a key phrase — Jesus is using it all the time — and it's one of those things you grow so used to. You have to stop, and say, "Now, wait a minute, what does that mean?" There is no one neat definition of *kingdom of God*. It is what scholars would call a "tensive symbol," not unlike a Jungian archetype. There is no one neat definition. It is one of these grand mythic symbols that encapsulate a whole story. In fact, for Jesus or for Jews of this time, *kingdom of God* could easily encapsulate that whole story of what Christians would call the Old Testament. It is the story of God choosing Israel, of bringing it to the promised land, the history of the kings who turn out to be false kings and not subject to the one king who is God, the punishment of the Babylonian exile, the return from exile, and then this yearning that once again God would regather the scattered tribes of Israel, ten out of the twelve lost. There was this great promise in the latter books of the Old Testament where God finally would bring all of the scattered tribes back again to the Holy Land, and he would rule over Israel again as the one true king of the empire.

Put into a nutshell, and a terribly small nut, that is what is summarized in that phrase. But notice you can't define it, because it's a whole story and it's a whole bundle of hopes of Israel, that God would finally bring Israel's story to a grand, joyous conclusion.

Hansen: If the message, then, is the kingdom of God, and if that is still the message today, what do you see as the kingdom of God today?

Meier: Of course, in a sense, a good part of the New Testament is a struggling with that message because, of course, the original message is given simply by Jesus to his fellow Jews in Palestine, and then, of course, suddenly, with the death, the Resurrection, the spreading of the gospel message, within a hundred years, a group of Jews for Jesus turned into the emerging Catholic Church at the beginning of the second century, and obviously, along with everything else, the meaning of *kingdom of God* has undergone an incredible revolution, whereby, by the time you get to the Gospels being written, that *kingdom of God* means that all the peoples of the earth are called by the good news of Jesus to gather together as God's one people awaiting the culmination of history when God will indeed rule over the whole earth as king. And while, of course, that is expressed in mythic images of the time and place, I think that basic hope, that in the end God's goodness will triumph and that all the warring peoples of the earth will finally be brought together in one loving community under God, perhaps beyond this world as we now understand it, that hope is, I think, what still drives believing Christians.

Hansen: Critics of the Jesus Seminar, which concluded that only about twenty percent of the statements attributed to Jesus in the Bible were actually said by him, have said that the members of the seminar are often unlikely to consider the miraculous in their discussions. Robert Funk, the founder of the Jesus Seminar, would counter, by saying that those who believe in miracles won't consider the whole idea of invention. What do miracles mean to you? How do you view the miracles that are reported to have been performed, and how are these miracles compatible with this academic approach?

Meier: As you may know, the third part of my book, the part on miracles, actually in bulk takes up half of the 1,118 pages of Volume II, precisely because I feel this is a topic that is often just passed over, or treated very inadequately. Either many scholars will feel they can just dismiss the whole question, or apologists on the other side will write books trying to show that every miracle took place just as it happened. One must be open, honestly, to both possibilities. I don't think we can keep repeating today the famous credo "Modern man cannot believe in miracles," or I think, probably today, "Modern men and women cannot believe in miracles."

De facto, in 1989, I think it was, George Gallup did one of his famous polls of U.S. citizens and he found out that eighty-two percent of Americans, presumably modern men and women, would say yes to the affirmation that, even today, God works miracles. Now, notice the "even today." You would tend to think if he had said, "Only at the time of Jesus," you might have gotten more than eighty-two percent. So first of all, simply, that credo often repeated in religious studies departments, "Modern man cannot believe in miracles," has been sociologically falsified. That simply is not true. Maybe they shouldn't believe. I'm not saying this automatically proves that miracles happen or that people should believe in miracles, but we must be open to that possibility. I don't think we can say eighty-two percent of Americans are just stupid and irrational people. On the other hand, Professor Funk is perfectly right; believers must be open to the possibility that at least some of the miracle stories in the Gospels may be creations of the early church trying to express, in symbolic form, the meaning of Jesus for them. And, therefore, the only way to go about things is not with general statements, but to ploddingly go through every single miracle story of the Four Gospels, applying the usual criteria of historicity that you apply to the sayings and deeds of Jesus otherwise. It can neither get special exemption nor easily thrown out, be treated in the same way, and you must go, story by story, attempting an evaluation. After initial studies of the general question, we go through every single miracle story of all Four Gospels. Sometimes I decide, yes, this goes back to some event in the life of Jesus. In other cases, I do think some of the miracle stories may be creations of the early church to express in symbolic form the meaning of Jesus, but there's also that third element that nobody likes to advance — conservative, liberal, believer, or nonbeliever, namely what I call non liquet — "it is not clear." And I think if you're doing historical studies of Jesus, you have to be willing to admit that galling, in-between category that the evidence in some cases simply doesn't prove the case one way or the other, and some of the miracle stories I have to leave that shadowy *non liquet*.

After reporting on the civil war in El Salvador, the journalist DENNIS COVINGTON wrote about a trial in Scottsboro, Alabama, for the *New York Times*. A preacher was accused of trying to kill his wife by snakebite. The trial made Covington curious about snake handling, about the verse of Scripture "they shall take up serpents," and about the people who follow that verse literally, descendants of the Appalachian settlers on Sand Mountain. The reporter himself was descended from just such settlers. His curiosity led him to snake handling meetings in Kentucky and West Virginia. When friends asked if he would handle snakes himself, he would reply, "I will only take up a rattlesnake in that way if I am anointed to do it by the Holy Spirit." Covington discussed his book, *Salvation on Sand Mountain*, with Noah Adams. March 20, 1995

Covington: [*reading*] "This was the moment. I didn't stop to think about it. I just gave in. I stepped forward and took the snake with both hands. Carl released it to me. I turned to face the congregation and lifted the rattlesnake up toward the light. It was moving like it wanted to get up even higher to climb out of that church and into the air. And it was exactly as the handlers had told me. I felt no fear. The snake seemed to be an extension of myself. And suddenly there seemed to be nothing in the room but me and the snake. Everything else had disappeared — Carl, the congregation, Jim, all gone, all faded to white, and I could not hear the ear-splitting music. The air was silent and still and filled with that strong even light, and I realized that I too was fading into the white. I was losing myself by degrees, like the incredible shrinking man. The snake would be the last to go, and all I could see was the way its scales shimmered one last time in the light and the way its head moved from side to side, searching for a way out. I knew then why the handlers took up serpents."

Adams: Now, that would have been, when? Two years ago, three years ago?

Covington: Yes, the summer of ninety-three.

Adams: It stays very vivid in your mind obviously, that moment. Have you done this since?

Covington: I took up serpents a total of three times, four different rattlesnakes, and late in the book I write that I will not take them up again. I didn't know that was going to be the case until I actually wrote that sentence in the book, and once I had written it I knew then that I had an obligation to stand by that, primarily for the sake of my family. But also I determined that I didn't want to watch a suicide in church, particularly my own.

Adams: You would think of it as suicide?

Covington: Yes, I would. I have a double mind about all this. I mean, I do believe that the handlers are the believers that Jesus was talking about in Mark 16. On the other hand, I am extremely uncomfortable with the idea of somebody dying of snakebite during a worship service.

Adams: The handlers seem to be in a way fatalistic about it. One said to you, "Just because the spirit's upon you don't mean that you'll live," and others said that they indeed were bitten. In fact you write about people who have been bitten and refused medical care.

Covington: Yes, the idea is that if someone dies from a rattlesnake bite during a worship service, at least they died with the Lord.

Adams: But are you staying away from the churches?

Covington: I've only been back once to a serpent handling church since I finished the book. I may go again, but to be frank with you, my life is moving on. I have other writing projects I'm interested in and also, of course, I have my home church here in Birmingham, Alabama, that I'm very much involved in. It's not that I'm shying away from the churches, necessarily; it's just that this is a time of my life that is over now in a way. My beliefs are the same. I do believe that these are the handlers that Jesus was talking about. I do believe they are confirming the Word, and I think they are a sign to us of the passion and the mystery that lies at the heart of Christianity and without which maybe our belief system is not really Christianity if there's not passion and mystery in it.

Adams: In the book when you write about this particular thought, you add the word *danger* as being possibly a necessary part of Christianity.

Covington: I should have included that word too, and missionaries and the families of missionaries will certainly know what's meant by that. A lot of us nominal Christians who just go and sit in church on Sunday, maybe the idea of danger strikes us as being a little absurd or out of the realm of possibility. But danger has always been a part of Christianity and continues to be.

Adams: On the other hand, could it not be argued that people who are attracted to this sort of thing are looking for an adrenaline thrill. And you, in a way, almost admit this. You say, "I'd always been drawn to danger — alcohol, psychedelics, war." You were four times covering the war in El Salvador. "If it made me feel good, I would do it." Could that not be part of the attraction, at least in your case?

Covington: It certainly could and, of course, that's why I acknowledge that. I'm well aware of that, and I want the readers to be well aware of that too. I did not intend for this book to be about me. When I started out I knew it was going to be a piece of extended creative nonfiction, but I wanted to be simply a camera or a recorder and the handlers would be the main characters who would play out this story in front of me. That's not the way it worked out. I got involved. I became a character in the story, and finally, in ways, the book is as much about me as it is about the handlers. That works, I think, in a good way in that it may make me a more believable narrator than I would have been otherwise because I'm opening myself too in the same way that I'm opening the lives of the handlers. And it's crucial in a book like this, about this kind of subject matter, for the narrator to be a believable witness.

In Uganda, on the outskirts of the city of Mbale, a community of worshippers sing the watchword of the Jewish faith, *Shema Yisrael*, "Hear, O Israel," in the rhythms and harmonies of East Africa. These few hundred people called the Abayudayah claimed no ancient descent from the Hebrews, but for several decades they have worshipped as Jews, in Hebrew and in their native tongue, Luganda. They have had little contact with Jews elsewhere, so it was a historic occasion when a delegation of fifteen American Jews from Kulanu, an organization that keeps in touch with peoples on the fringe of Jewish life, came to visit. Among the visitors was Rabbi JACQUES CUKIERKORN, who told Robert Siegel what he had learned about the Abayudayah and how they took up Judaism. August 3, 1995

Cukierkorn: The story goes that they had a leader who, around 1919, had a vision, a dream, in which he had the Bible that Christian missionaries had brought to him. He looked at the Bible, and said, "Gee, I like this, but I just like the first part. I don't like the second part, namely the New Testament. So I just want to follow that part." The missionaries told him, "You can't do that because the people who do that are the Jews." He said, "Oh yeah. In that case I am a Jew." And that phrase, "I am a Jew," in his language, I understand, is "*Abayudayah.*" So without ever having seen a Jew in his life or met a Jew, he chose to become Jewish.

Siegel: So that is the origin of the name of these people?

Cukierkorn: Right.

Siegel: And after that, what did he do and how many people followed him in becoming Jews?

Cukierkorn: He was the local leader and he had a small group of followers that started proselytizing in the area. He compiled a prayer book. He also compiled a book of guidelines — what his followers should do in order to be Jewish. He only met a Jew, I believe, five or six years later, who in their histories is recalled only as Joseph. He came and started teaching them a little Judaism. And throughout those seventy-five years, they have had very, very few visitors, maybe half a dozen.

Siegel: How many people would now be considered members of this group?

Cukierkorn: There are between five and six hundred. The overwhelming majority of them are children, probably two thirds of them.

Siegel: And what kind of a Jewish life have they developed on their own over all these decades?

Cukierkorn: First of all, somebody sent them prayer books, so they know Hebrew. They taught themselves Hebrew and they have currently four synagogues. They worship every *Shabbat*, every Friday night and Saturday morning. They wear yarmulkes.

Siegel: Skullcaps.

Cukierkorn: The skullcaps are interesting. They look very much like the Muslims' skullcaps, and we asked why. It's because there's a Muslim guy down in the village who makes them, so I have one now. They keep absolutely kosher. It was interesting to be there and to realize that they follow some Biblical prescriptions literally. For instance, they do not cook on the Sabbath, which in rabbinic Judaism there are ways to get around because you can keep a fire on and warm things up. They eat just cold food. They have the Bible and they assume this is the truth and follow what the book says.

Siegel: What is a service like in one of their synagogues?

Cukierkorn: Just like the one in our synagogues.

Siegel: Same liturgy?

Cukierkorn: They have the prayer book, they can read the Torah, they chant it, it's beautiful. The only difference is that somebody sent them the prayer books, but didn't send them the music. So instead of singing the traditional Eastern European tunes that we are used to, they put their African melodies to the Hebrew prayers.

Siegel: For example, you recorded their rendition of the traditional Jewish song "Lecha Dodi" — "Come, My Beloved."

Cukierkorn: It's a cabalistic song that was written in Safed, in Israel, in the sixteenth century. It's a mystical prayer that welcomes the Sabbath, and it's very interesting, the welcoming of the Sabbath in Mbale as the sun sets. There is no light. It gets really dark. You get to hear all the nature songs. The roosters singing, the dogs barking. This is very unlike our synagogues.

Siegel: You sat down and you talked with some of these people and asked them about their Jewishness.

Cukierkorn: They are very committed to this religion that they have adopted. One of the reasons they want to be Jewish is because God loves oppressed people. They want to have a special relationship with God. For me, it was very moving, a very spiritual experience, because everything that we have and we take for granted they cherish so much.

Siegel: Well, rabbis both in this country and in Israel often discuss and try to agree on what is a Jew and whether various people are Jews. You're a rabbi. Are they Jews?

Cukierkorn: No.

Siegel: No?

Cukierkorn: I don't think — no, and they would not say they are Jewish. They have the potential. They have been living Jewish lives for seventy-five years. But if they want to be Jewish, they must be converted.

Siegel: Why is that, if people live for a few generations, attending the synagogue, observing Hebrew dietary laws, following the Torah, learning Hebrew, what is it about them that is not Jewish?

Cukierkorn: I'm not sure if it's a good analogy, but being Jewish is like being a member of the Rotary. You can like the Rotary Club, you can live by Rotary values, and, you know, you can even try to sneak into the meetings. But unless you are a real member and the other members accept you as such, you are not a real Rotarian.

Siegel: What would these people have to do to become Jewish, by your standard?

Cukierkorn: Now, that's what Kulanu is trying to do. We want to send them a teacher to teach them about Judaism and Jewish practice, and then we are trying to arrange to get three rabbis to go there, to make a rabbinical jury, which is required for conversion, to convert them all.

THE STORY OF THE YEAR: TERRORISM

I n a year that witnessed several horrifying acts of terrorism, the March gas attack on the Tokyo subway during
morning rush hour was a shocking advance in the nature
of terror. For the first time, a weapon of mass destruction,
nerve gas, was used against an unsuspecting civilian population in peacetime. The gas was planted in several downtown subway stations; eight people were killed, thousands
hospitalized. Japan faced no domestic insurgencies, was at
war with no foreign enemies. Shortly after the poison gas
attack, Japanese police raided the offices of an obscure religious group, the Aum Shinrikyo, and later charged its leader
and several members. An expert on international terrorism,
Professor PAUL WILKINSON of St. Andrews University in
Scotland, told Noah Adams that the Tokyo disaster had implications for the U.S. and other countries, and represented a
new breed of terrorism. March 21, 1995

Wilkinson: I think that what we are seeing in Japan is an escala-
tion to what has been called superterrorism — terrorist organizations resorting to the technologies of mass destruction, which have
the potential for killing not simply hundreds, but thousands of
people, and there has been a continuing trend, through the seventies and eighties, of increasing brutality. One only has to think of
the change in the threat to aviation from a relatively low lethality
hijacking to the terrible mass murder in the skies that we saw in
Lockerbie or in the Air India sabotage bombing.
    Adams: Would you put the World Trade Center bombing into
this category?
    Wilkinson: I would put that in the category of an example of
highly destructive terrorism comparable to the truck bombings in
Beirut, the aviation sabotage bombings. But even those terrible
bombings, including the World Trade Center attack, would pale in

significance compared to the potential destruction of life that you
would get from the use of biological or chemical weapons in a
downtown area of a large city.

Adams: If you can find a trend in the tactic, can you also find a
trend in the motive or the logic that these groups would bring to
such an act? If they act alike worldwide, what is it that they usually
want?

Wilkinson: Well, I think that this is another important trend over
the last fifteen years. We've seen the rise of fanatical, religiously
motivated terrorist groups. In 1980, there were only a couple of
groups which one could describe as truly religiously motivated.
Today there are dozens of them in many countries.

Adams: What do you think really changed the tactics of the
groups that would try to put pressure on a government? Why did
this change come about?

Wilkinson: One factor is the numbing effect of massive coverage
of terrorist incidents. Small bombs no longer have such a media
impact, so the people who spill the greatest amount of blood capture the biggest headlines. There's the factor that some leaders of
the more moderate disposition, who are genuinely interested in
political and diplomatic progress for their cause, have pulled out of
terrorism and they have given way to hard-line, younger, more
impatient leaders who believe what is needed is not less violence
but more violence. And then, of course, you have the effect of target
hardening. It's a sad fact, but when you harden a target like an
embassy or an airport, you make it more likely that a ruthless
terrorist group, wanting to make an impact, will actually go for a
soft target, and that means a shopping arcade or a truck bomb in a
city street — an attack in a railway station, which is so easily ac-
cessible.

Adams: If you're in Washington, and the news comes about this
sort of action, nerve gas in the subway in Tokyo, what's going to be
your response? How do you protect a civilian target against terrorism of this sort?

Wilkinson: I don't think that there is any real physical protection that could guarantee against this particular type of threat.
The real answer, the only possible approach to preventing this kind
of thing, to effectively combating it, is superior intelligence. If
you have an intelligence system that is ahead of the game, that

Nowhere was religiously motivated terrorism more a problem this year than in the Middle East. After the Palestine Liberation Organization opted for peace with Israel, in exchange for authority over Gaza and most of the West Bank, the militant Muslim groups, Hamas and Islamic Jihad, persisted in terrorism, planting bombs in Israeli cities, undermining support for the peace process. One such bomb went off in the Israeli coastal city of Netanya. Subsequent blasts would terrorize Tel Aviv and Jerusalem. A spokesman for Hamas, Dr. MOHAMMED RANTISI, talked to Robert Siegel about the *jihad*, the holy war or struggle, which he said would continue. January 23, 1995

Rantisi: They [the bombers] are fighting the Israelis as the Israelis occupied their land. They are destroying their lives, disturbing everything in this area. So they are feeling *jihad* is the way to save everything.

Siegel: And in this case, when you say *jihad* is the way to save everything, do you mean that therefore the bombing that killed these Israelis near Netanya was a justified act of war, in your view?

Rantisi: This is a liberation war.

Siegel: A liberation war?

Rantisi: Yes.

Siegel: If these killings continue, killings of Israelis or Palestinians, it's likely that the current peace process between Israel and the Palestine Liberation Organization will not work, that it will end.

Rantisi: We are feeling here, and it is quite clear for everybody, that by the peace process we are losing everything.

Siegel: You're losing everything by the peace process?

Rantisi: Yes.

Siegel: So you would welcome its failure at this point?

Rantisi: Though we believe also by the *jihad* the Israeli forces are to leave Gaza partially, and today, the prime minister, Rabin, asking for full separation between the Jews and the Palestinian Muslims in Gaza. So by fighting and *jihad,* we are going to get our independence.

Siegel: You hear, in Prime Minister Rabin's statement, that there should be a full separation between Israelis and Palestinians. You hear a point of success there for your position is what you're saying?

Rantisi: Yes, yes.

Siegel: Can you imagine any peace between Hamas and a Jewish state of Israel?

Rantisi: We know the mentality of the Jews. They don't want peace at all. So the mentality of the Israelis and of the Jews is to destroy the other people, especially the Muslim people.

Siegel: Well, many Israelis say that the Palestinians, no matter what agreement the PLO enters into, still want to attack the state of Israel, don't accept the legitimacy of the state of Israel. Are they right about that?

Rantisi: The Koran and the God do not accept this state.

Siegel: The Koran and God don't accept the state of Israel?

Rantisi: Yes.

Siegel: What do you have to say now to Mr. Arafat and what do you advise he do right now at this point in his dealings with Israel?

Rantisi: In fact, in a friendly way, I can tell him, "Please go and understand the mentality of the Israelis and the Jews. Don't be bluffed by them. Your way of peace, it is the way of losing everything for the Palestinian rights."

L ater in the year, Prime Minister Yitzhak Rabin was shot and killed by a Jewish assassin who had been connected to a tiny anti-Arab organization called Eyal. The group had attracted little attention in Israel before the assassination and was believed to consist of fewer than twenty active members, most of them under the age of thirty. EHUD SPRINZAK, a professor of political science at Hebrew University in Jerusalem and an expert on the Israeli extreme right, joined Bob Edwards to discuss Eyal and similar extremist groups. November 9, 1995

Sprinzak: Well, it is, indeed, a very small organization. It has been in existence since 1991. It started, surprisingly enough, as a student organization in Tel Aviv University by people who felt they had to challenge the "moderation" of the Kahane people, and that meant that they felt they had to be a little tougher on the Arabs than the Kahane people were. However, they didn't stay for a long time in Tel Aviv because the surrounding area was very hostile, and they all moved to Qiryat Arba in Hebron, which is the natural milieu of all the Kahane groups, and in many respects they became like the other movements. After the massacre in Hebron over a year ago, Eyal was outlawed, just as all other extremist Kahane movements, and they became pretty much the same. That is to say, they were unable to operate openly. They do not have offices, and they cannot work in the name of the organization, and yet they are around and they are very much involved in radical action, but it has mostly been rhetoric.

Edwards: How do they function if they're outlawed?

Sprinzak: Well, they're not outlawed as individuals. They're not sought after as individuals, but they cannot act as an organization. That means that they cannot have an office, they cannot print out leaflets, and they cannot conduct collective meetings. But still, there are many things you can do. You can come to demonstrations, you can, for example, produce a Rabin effigy with a Nazi uniform, you can produce posters, hate literature, from the underground, and stuff like that.

Edwards: The government has proposed new legislation focusing on people who incite violence. Is that overdue, in your opinion, and do most Israelis agree with that?

Sprinzak: Well, it could certainly help, though many people believe that we have all the laws we need to really chase these people and prosecute them, but many of these laws have not been used properly. But I would say this is not the major issue. The job of eliminating them or of reducing them to just a radical rubble is the job of their own community. These organizations are very small. They cannot really function on their own. They're not living in separate communities, and they need the people that surround them. If those people would consider them outcasts, would apply strong pressure to reduce the level of violence, the level of rhetorical violence, I think this could be very effective.

Edwards: The opposition Likud bloc has been accused of tacitly encouraging violence. Is that just politics, or is there some link between the extreme right and Likud?

Sprinzak: I wouldn't go that far. I would say they're guilty by default because some of them, and especially the leader of Likud, Benjamin Netanyahu, have indeed spoken against this extremism and violence in the last few months, but this is about all that they have done. They did not act against these people. They did not kick them out of their demonstrations. They did not tear apart their posters, their hate posters. So this is the problem. It's not by encouraging them, but by not doing enough against them.

On April 19, the United States suffered its most devastating domestic terrorist attack: an explosion at the
Alfred Murrah federal office building in Oklahoma City that
killed 169 people. One survivor of the blast was JAMI
RADACY, who at the time of the explosion was on the job
for the U.S. Department of Health and Human Services. She
was at her desk in one of six cubicles located in the south-
eastern corner on the third floor. Bruised and sore, but not
seriously injured, she talked with Noah Adams from her
home and described her ordeal. April 21, 1995

Radacy: The blast was on the north side of the building, and it ate
back into the building. The front half of our office collapsed. The
cubicle that was connected to mine collapsed.

Adams: Do you recall what you were doing right before the explosion?

Radacy: Yes I do, because I lost my wedding ring. I was putting on
lotion. I had sat down and taken off my jewelry to put on some
lotion, and I was sitting there putting lotion on my hands when
it hit.

Adams: What did you notice?

Radacy: I didn't hear anything. Everyone's talked about how loud
it was, but I don't remember hearing it. I felt something fall, like a
dust, like stuff from the ceiling fell in my hair, is the first thing I
remember. I glanced up and that's when everything started falling
and I tried to ball up and get under my desk.

Adams: Were you able to?

Radacy: Well, I thought I was. But when everything quit falling
— and the stuff that was on top of me, I moved it so I could sit up,
and my desk wasn't there.

Adams: How long did that take, when things stopped moving?

Radacy: It really was very sudden. It didn't take long at all. I'd say
less than a minute. You know, maybe like thirty seconds or so. And
when it first stopped, everything stopped moving, and there was
some stuff above me that kind of had me covered. And I got it off of

me. It was all smoke. All you could see was a real black smoke. It was all you could see. I was facing the north and our office had a north wall, and the Department of Defense had an office on the north side of us. And none of that was there. When I looked out north, I saw the parking lot.

Adams: What did you figure had happened?

Radacy: Well, when I first felt the dust, I thought an earthquake. Then I laughed at myself. We don't have earthquakes. Then as soon as it was over and we cleared everything out, my coworkers and I were yelling for each other. We kept saying, "What happened?" Initially, we thought it was a gas explosion, and we were afraid that it would blow again. And so we were thinking that we needed to be out quick.

Adams: And how did you figure out how to get out?

Radacy: We made our way back to the south wall. And first, we tore our curtains down and there was — I don't even know how to describe it. It was like a cement ledge, just in the design of the building. It kind of angled down, and we used our curtains and held on to our curtains and climbed down them, down this ledge. Once we got out to the edge of the ledge, it was probably about a ten-, fifteen-foot drop down to the ground. And there were men out there. Once we got out to that ledge, they were able to, like, get our feet and our legs and help us down that wall.

Adams: And then what happened?

Radacy: Well, one of the women in our office had a child in the day care center. And she was the first one out, and she went looking for her baby. So as soon as we were all out — there was two other women and I — we wanted to try to find her. And we got out there to our coworker that was trying to find out something about her baby. And her husband worked in the area also. And her husband got there. It seemed like hardly any time at all. I really don't know how long it was. And once her husband got there, they let them stay in the area. But they were trying to push us on out, on down the street a little ways and they wouldn't let us stay with her. So we started heading out. We tried to find phones so that we could phone our families.

Adams: Looking back on it, do you think that you were in shock at this time?

Radacy: I don't know. I was shocked. You know, I don't know if I was in shock, medically speaking. We didn't know what was going on. We didn't know what had happened. And I really think, I didn't realize, when we were trying to get out, I guess I thought everybody was kind of like us. They were OK and they were just trying to figure out how to get out. But once we got out and got out to that curb and they were bringing out the bodies and bringing out people and there were so many people that were hurt so badly, I think that's when it hit me and I realized what had just happened and how lucky I was.

Adams: At that point, could you see that entire side of the building that had been torn away?

Radacy: No. We were on the south side of the building.

Adams: When did you see that sight?

Radacy: Really, I didn't see it until the TV reports.

Adams: What happened in the afternoon? When did you go on home?

Radacy: We were able, once we got out and we kind of headed away from the building, we got to a phone and we were able to call our families. And we told them just that we were OK, but there was no way they could get to us there and we just didn't know where we were going, but that we would try to call them back. One of my bosses lived very close and he was able to call. We knew that they wouldn't be able to get into us up there at the site, so we all walked down, probably five or six blocks down to the Convention Center, and his wife came and picked us up there and drove us to the hospital.

Adams: And you were treated there for scrapes and bruises?

Radacy: Yeah, bruises. No one in my office even had a cut. We were all just banged and bruised. Now, that's everyone but the girl with the child. We haven't seen her since then. We've talked to the family because they still have not found her son. But now I don't even know if she has been treated. I don't have any way to know. We can't get in touch with her.

Adams: Did you have difficulty sleeping that night, Wednesday night?

Radacy: I didn't really try to sleep. I didn't really want to go to sleep because I was expecting to hear about the baby any time. You know, I was expecting them to find him, tell me where they were at, you know.

Adams: You mean your colleague's baby?

Radacy: Yes. And I think that's what really was bothering me more than anything, was wanting to know, you know, what was going on with him. Finally, I got a little sleep the first night, but not a whole lot.

Adams: Have you had a moment's thought, in this three days, about who may have done this?

Radacy: Really, I haven't had time. I've kind of thought a little about why, not so much as how they could do it, but do they even realize what they did? Do they realize the extent of, you know, and did they know that when they planned it? You know, were they just trying to get a little attention or did they intend to affect so many people so terribly, and if so, how they could do it? I just — I really — I've tried not to think about it, really.

The Oklahoma City bombing was evidently motivated by a hatred of the government, a sentiment that unnerved many federal workers. KATIE WORSHAM had worked at the Department of Housing and Urban Development office in Oklahoma City until she was promoted to a job in Fort Worth. After the bombing, she returned to Oklahoma City, where, as she told Scott Simon, there were five funerals to attend for people she knew from the office. April 29, 1995

Worsham: Ted Allen was a forty-eight-year-old father of six and a dedicated public servant. He would always rise to the occasion, whatever it was. Ted Allen's hobby was gardening, and last summer one of the things that I remembered that we used to have such big laughs about — he hadn't had a garden for several years and overplanted on some things and underplanted on others. But he brought in a big sack of tomatoes, cucumbers, squash, jalapeño peppers, and would just put them on the desk, and just say, "Anybody just come. They're for whoever."

Simon: There was a woman named Colleen Guiles?

Worsham: Oh, that was quite a woman. And you're talking about a sense of humor. Of all the employees in the office, that woman was never down. She was a big talker. But she was somebody that truly cared. She was very well respected among our clients that she did business with. She was somebody that, with all of her talking, she had the regulations down pat. But she worked hard to make sure those regulations could help our clients instead of hurt.

Simon: Can I share something with you?

Worsham: Sure.

Simon: We got a letter this week from a woman named Kathy Jones, who says, "My father worked for over thirty years as a field representative for the Social Security Administration in rural Tennessee. For many of the people he worked with, when he set up a card table at their county courthouse to take claims and sort out problems, he was the government man. Often the only representative of the federal government they ever met. He visited his clients in the hospital, regularly ate lunch at the senior citizens centers, learned sign language to communicate with those applying for disability benefits, even learned CPR to bring his clients back from the dead. I always thought of his as rather noble work." Then she says, "I knew that not everybody felt this way. But it was only recently that I recognized the depth of their animus toward government. Now I have to face the fact that some of the people whom I've heard attack any zoning change, any water treatment regulation, as another effort of big government to take away their constitutional rights, just don't want to rein in the bureaucracy." Then she says — and I understand her emotionalism on this subject — she says, "They actually want to kill my father."

Worsham: Right. That hurts. And that's kind of how we feel. I mean, we had a visit from one of the congressmen in Oklahoma, and I asked him to simply remember when he got back that he would think about the survivors here, when they talk about on the House floor, how government's too big and we didn't have enough staff to get our jobs done, that all the things that had gone on for years were still out there to be handled. I just asked him to just appreciate federal employees a little bit more because we give a lot.

The explosion in Oklahoma City claimed the lives not only of federal employees, but also of citizens who transacted business in the Murrah building that day. When the bomb went off in the federal office building, Brother Gilbert Martinez of the El Tabernáculo de Fe Assembly of God Church was there in the Social Security office with a parishioner, Emilio Tapia. Both men were killed. Brother Martinez's Hispanic ministry was sponsored by Brother JIM MCNABB, who spoke with Scott Simon about Brother Gilbert's ministry. April 29, 1995

McNabb: With his congregation, he had a tent. He would go hold crusades around in the different Hispanic communities with this tent. How he came up with the tent, I don't know, but nothing surprises me. I'd always put Gilbert in charge of procurement if I was in charge of anything because he came up with things when no one else could. He would get involved in the Hispanic community. That's why there were so many people at this funeral the other day. We had about 1,200 or 1,500 people that were there. And here you've got this little Hispanic guy with a congregation of 150 or 200 people. But 1,200 people came to a funeral.

And he would organize all the Hispanic ministers. He would cross denominational barriers. He wasn't so concerned that he couldn't go over with this brother from this denomination or this independent brother and do a common cause for the Hispanic community. He was very unselfish, very unselfish.

Simon: Was it those kinds of activities that helped members of his congregation that brought him to the federal building on that morning?

McNabb: Yes, it was. And the fact that the gentleman he was with, Mr. Tapia, did not speak English well. He had taken this gentleman down to the Social Security office to be the intermediary with the language barrier and to help him get established.

Simon: He was helping a man get a Social Security card?

The Oklahoma City bombing trained the nation's attention on a previously little publicized movement of extremist paramilitary organizations which regard the federal government as tyrannical. Timothy McVeigh and Terry Nichols, who were charged in the bombing, had been linked to such groups. The U.S. Treasury Department reported there were "citizen militia" groups in about thirty-four states, with combined memberships of anywhere from ten thousand to fifty thousand. Alex Chadwick asked BOB FLETCHER of the Montana Militia why people feel the need to form militias. May 12, 1995

Fletcher: The goal is very simple. It's the preservation of constitutional government in the United States.

Chadwick: And what do these groups do to go about achieving that?

Fletcher: Typically, number one, it's educational in nature, and that is for people to bring themselves up to speed on the reality of what constitutional rights are in America, which have slowly, progressively been deteriorated. Secondarily, it is to organize and exchange investigative research information relative to those unconstitutional acts and illegal acts and events taking place by unscrupled persons in our government.

Chadwick: When you say that constitutional rights are deteriorating or being eroded, what rights do you mean?

Fletcher: All of them.

Chadwick: But I mean, specifically, name a few constitutional rights that are being eroded.

Fletcher: The most obvious one, number one, that would come to surface initially is the right to maintain and bear arms according to the Second Amendment, and unconstitutional acts — for example, the fact that there are two hundred treaties inside the GATT trade agreement, that when they passed that without adjudicating each one of them individually on the floor of the Senate and voting on them to be either passed or turned down, those were all, as far as I'm concerned, unconstitutional acts of treason by everyone that signed the GATT trade agreement.

Chadwick: Could there be a difference of opinion that didn't involve treason?

Fletcher: Maybe the word *treason* is not right. How about just *unconstitutional, unscrupled,* and *immoral*? Everyone in government obviously is not doing this; however, there are certain groups or numbers of people in our government that obviously are pursuing what is a one-world government under a totally destructive means by which to attack our Constitution.

Chadwick: So you think there is a group of officials within the United States government who are bent on turning our government over to a one-world authority, or creating a one-world government? Is that correct?

Fletcher: Absolutely. And it's not a matter of thinking, it's a matter of documentation that goes back as far as forty years, since the creation of the United Nations, and as recent as just a couple weeks ago with a brand-new documentation, twenty-some pages, from the United Nations themselves, actually published just a few weeks back, where, in fact, the United Nations clearly defines in black and white in their own print that by the year 2000 they expect to have one-world governance completed. There's not a question as to whether this exists, it is a reality, and the sooner people realize it and understand what it means, the better off everyone will be in America.

Chadwick: Mr. Fletcher, there are fears on the part of a number of people that militia groups are encouraging violence in response to these perceived threats that the government is controlled by conspiracies to do this or that.

Fletcher: We advocate no offensive violence. We advocate no violence whatsoever, other than the fact of maintaining vigilance and a defensive posture, period. That is constitutionally mandated in the Second Amendment, and the Second Amendment was created not to protect the duck hunters and not to protect your family from some fellow coming through a window. The Second Amendment was simply put in on the basis that as long as the people themselves had the rights to have their own people's militia and the right to maintain arms that we would not have to be once again, as we were two hundred years ago, put under a tyrannical monarchy, which at this point in time we would refer to as a dictatorship.

Chadwick: The Constitution speaks about a well-regulated militia.

Fletcher: That's right. We're as well regulated as we can be with those groups that we set up.

Chadwick: Do you have some official relationship to the government?

Fletcher: You're either totally ignorant or intentionally misguiding people. The bottom line is you have to understand what I just said relative to why they put this together. It was to protect against domestic potential tyranny, tyrannical government, that we had created this nation moving away from that structure, and you cannot, for God's sakes, have a citizens' militia run by a government, in an official capacity, and protect against a corrupted government, period. It was not set up for that, it's not the concept of the Second Amendment.

Chadwick: You know, there's a sense that the militias may be a threat to the government.

Fletcher: Certainly.

Chadwick: Do you think that it's true?

Fletcher: Excuse me, to the government?

Chadwick: Yeah.

Fletcher: Or to corrupted persons in government? It's a big difference there. We have no problem with the government, sir. If you would read your history, you would know that we the people are the government, period. We the people. Read my lips. We create government, they do not create us. They are our employees, and when they are doing corrupted, illegal, immoral garbage up there, they need to be fired.

Chadwick: You know, ever since the election last fall, people have been talking about angry white men.

Fletcher: Angry white men. What does that mean?

Chadwick: Well, I don't know. I was going to ask you if you are one.

Fletcher: Am I a white man? Absolutely.

Chadwick: Are you an angry white man?

Fletcher: You bet your tail I am, because of the corruption going on. Does that seem inaccurate? Are you telling me that you're happy with things like executive orders that transfer twenty-one billion of your tax dollars without congressional approval to the Mexican banking elite? That makes me angry, sir. And drug operations by our own government officials with my tax dollars? That makes me angry, sir. The murder of people in Panama to the tune of three thousand under an executive order of the president? That makes me angry, yes, sir.

Chadwick: For the record, Mr. Fletcher faxed two pages from the United Nations document that he referred to earlier. It's a report called "Our Global Neighborhood," issued by the Commission on Global Governance. It talks about how the UN can promote "a global civil society," where governments and aid organizations and educational institutions and the mass media work together to help the people. But to quote from the report summary, "Global governance does not imply world government or world federalism. Effective global governance calls for a new vision, challenging people as well as governments, to realize that there is no alternative to working together to create the kind of world they want for themselves and their children."

A more sinister view of the militia movement was offered by CHIP BERLET, an analyst at Political Research Associates in Cambridge, Massachusetts. Berlet has followed a number of groups that voice similar grievances — about government, blacks, Jews, gays — and similar extreme beliefs that they must arm themselves. Berlet told Scott Simon that many of these people believe that society has pushed them to the fringes of American life. April 29, 1995

Berlet: These are the people who think that America has begun to unravel with gay rights, the feminist movement, the fact that abortions are available, environmentalists, all of these things, and couple with that the fact that in the heartland there is not a full economic recovery. It's built kind of a middle-class populist stew, and the pot's boiling over. You're seeing the really activist people electorally move toward the Christian Coalition. But the people who have had it with the system entirely move into the patriot movement, and the armed militia movement is just the armed wing of the patriot movement.

Simon: The way you describe it, though, Mr. Berlet, people who, in some ways we have dismissed as being paranoid have some grounds for their suspicions.

Berlet: Their theories are paranoid. But they're grabbing them out of desperation, not because they're clinically insane. People who are put under tremendous stress grab on to scapegoats. These scapegoats often involve paranoid conspiracy theories, many of which are anti-Semitic in origin.

Simon: And when it results in a resort to violence?

Berlet: Well, in fact, on the fiftieth anniversary of the liberation of the death camps, it is an indictment of the American educational system that anyone has to debate whether or not hate speech and scapegoating leads to violence. In fact, in an environment where scapegoating and hate speech is allowed to flourish, eventually someone, the most zealous, the most stressed, the most fragile, as President Clinton chooses to put it, will decide that to resolve the problem, the most efficient solution is to kill the scapegoat.

Simon: There are some people who feel that some of this is now a rhetorical overreaction. You know, we used to have more than a million members of the Ku Klux Klan in this country. Now just a handful. We used to have people in brown shirts holding rallies in Madison Square Garden and Chicago Stadium, in behalf of the American Bund, and now American Nazis are a relative handful. Are we overreacting to a tragic event, but nothing that really cuts very close to the fabric of American society now?

Berlet: No. We're in total denial still, and that's what's making me still so concerned. If you read the books by Pat Robertson, it's about the Freemason conspiracy theory and the secret elites and the secular humanist conspiracy theory. I watched a show over Christmas on *The 700 Club*, where they talked about currency redesign and whether or not currency redesign was the sign of the Mark of the Beast. This is much closer to the mainstream than people care to admit, because if we admit it, then we have to admit that a person who purveys conspiracy theories rooted in anti-Semitism helped elect members of Congress.

Simon: What if it develops after an investigation that there was just one or even just three people involved; but the fact is they weren't necessarily related to any militia movement of even fifty people, but just one, two, or three people acting on their own?

Berlet: Terror cells are always less than a dozen, usually less than six. I have no doubt that that will be the case. I also have no doubt that it will be related to the militia movement. But that's not the issue. It's denial to suggest that if we arrest those people, we've solved the problem. James Davidson Hunter wrote a book a few years ago about the culture war, and he said that America was polarizing into two camps and that this was going to be very divisive and it would really tear the country apart unless we learned how to talk to each other about these differences, about abortion rights and race and gender and sexual preference. After no one paid any attention, he wrote a book called *Before the Shooting Begins*, and he argued that we are in a period right now in the United States that's very similar to that before the Civil War. You know, if you're an environmentalist, the shooting war began several years ago. People have been beating up environmentalists. Pat Costner's home was firebombed. She's a Greenpeace toxics expert. Judy Bari's car was blown up. She's an environmental activist. If you're in the abortion movement, you know the shooting war began long ago.

From Lebanon to London, world reaction to the terror bombing of the Alfred Murrah building in Oklahoma City was swift and severe. World leaders called the attack "hateful," "blind," "barbaric," and "savage." Some countries sent rescue teams, and foreign leaders called for greater international cooperation in the battle against terrorism. The carnage in Oklahoma was familiar to many Europeans, who have weathered attacks from ideological terrorists, ranging from the Italian Red Brigades to Germany's Bader Meinhoff Gang to the Irish Republican Army. CONOR O'CLEARY, the Washington correspondent for the *Irish Times*, talked with Liane Hansen about his experience as a longtime observer of deadly urban warfare. April 23, 1995

Hansen: First, when you heard the news about Oklahoma City, what was your reaction? Did it remind you of attacks past?

O'Cleary: I think the one attack that it reminded me of most was the IRA attack on two pubs in Birmingham in November 1974, which resulted in the deaths of twenty-one people, and you had the same scenes on television, of innocent people horribly maimed, their bodies being pulled from the ruins, and the same questions being asked: Why?

Hansen: What it reminded me of, frankly, a little bit, was seeing the Grand Hotel in Brighton, after the Conservative Party Congress, when a bomb went off there.

O'Cleary: Well, there have been so many explosions like this resulting from what we call the Troubles in Northern Ireland over the last twenty years. You had the Birmingham pub bombings. You had pub bombings in London. You had the explosions in the city of London in the last two or three years, which were devastating and produced scenes straight out of World War II, and of course, in Northern Ireland itself, you had countless explosions — car bombs, bombs in shops — to the extent that people radically changed their lives and adapted to a situation where they knew that a bomb could go off near them at any time.

Hansen: Let me ask you, since this is such a new experience for many Americans, this idea of domestic terror, what do you think British or Irish authorities might advise, for example, should it be asked, about protecting federal buildings?

O'Cleary: Well, if you look at the progress of the Troubles in Northern Ireland, you can see a gradual accumulation of security, to the extent that at the height of the Troubles, in the last year or two, you had whole city centers and town centers sealed off. Cars were not allowed to park near buildings or stores unless somebody was left in the car, a passenger was left in the car. When you went to the cinema or into a store to do shopping, your bag was searched. You had to put up your hands and be frisked. And also you had to subject yourself to random stops on the road at night or during the day by the army or the police. And the interesting thing for me is that you gradually become used to this. You become accustomed to a very abnormal situation and it becomes a culture shock to leave that situation and come to a country like the United States, where you aren't stopped at random, where access to public buildings is relatively free, and where there are no, or very few, visible security measures such as we have in Northern Ireland, and also, in London now, following the latest bombings in the city of London.

Hansen: I think people in Washington, D.C., and New York, for example, might be a little bit more immune to the feelings of going through security checks. But in Oklahoma City, people don't have this on their minds.

O'Cleary: No. And, of course, this is an act of violence which couldn't have been anticipated. I think the interesting thing now is what effect this has on the psyche of the people and of the country. The Birmingham bombings produced such outrage that within a matter of days, antiterrorist legislation was rushed through the House of Commons. It became known as the Prevention of Terrorism Act. And it provided for people to be detained, suspects to be detained, for seven days without any access to a lawyer. It also provided for the police to issue banning orders on people from Ireland and Northern Ireland from entering Great Britain. And this has been the subject of a lot of criticism from human rights organizations. So one of the effects also of the authorities trying to mollify a very frightened public was a rush to judgment, and there were several cases in Britain, the Birmingham Six, the Guilford Four, the

McGuire family, all people who were imprisoned as a result of these bombings and subsequently found not to have been guilty. But in the atmosphere of the times, it was very difficult for an Irish man or woman, once they were charged, to prove their innocence.

Hansen: One has to wonder, though, how tolerant people in this country would be to that kind of umbrella legislation that would allow any actions. I mean, given the civil liberties that our system of government provides.

O'Cleary: I think it's dangerous to draw parallels because there's also a long history of special legislation being undertaken by British and Irish governments to cope with a constitutional problem. And you have also in Northern Ireland a large section of the population which is tolerant toward the acts of the IRA. Whereas here you don't have that. You don't have a basic, fundamental constitutional argument, which would mean that a significant section of the population would withhold information about people who are engaged in terrorist acts.

Hansen: Personally for you, has this been kind of surreal, given that you've seen Belfast and now here you are, a correspondent in Washington, and we have an event such as this, when we're talking about the security of Americans on our own territory?

O'Cleary: Well, two thoughts about that. One, I'm quite relieved that it's not an international incident, or doesn't seem to be, because obviously this would affect international tensions in a very serious and major way. And secondly, I think it does point to the fact that the United States has got a problem within itself, within its own society, which needs addressing. And it's not necessarily the remedy that there should be increased legislation to cope with these acts, like the Prevention of Terrorism Act. There are other aspects of this society to be explored to figure out how to cope with the violence, or the type of violent thought, which produced the bombing in Oklahoma.

Although the terror in Oklahoma City sprang from American soil and was evidently conceived as advancing a bizarre but completely domestic agenda, the bombing triggered a backlash against immigrants, particularly from the Middle East. The following day Congress was abuzz with talk of tougher restrictions on immigration. Republican Congressman Henry Hyde, chairman of the House Judiciary Committee, proposed permitting State Department consular officers to deny entrance to the United States to individuals who belong to a terrorist organization, rather than only those individuals linked to terrorist activity. President Clinton had already proposed an anti-terrorism bill that would deport people connected to terrorist groups. Linda Wertheimer asked DAVID COLE, a professor of constitutional law at Georgetown University, about anti-terror legislation. April 20, 1995

Wertheimer: Professor Cole, the incident in Oklahoma City is obviously going to create an opportunity for the Congress to reconsider anti-terror legislation and presumably will create considerable impetus to pass even stronger legislation than President Clinton has already proposed.

Cole: Well, I think that's right, and it's certainly a tragedy.

Wertheimer: Why do you say it's a tragedy?

Cole: Well, the event itself is a tragedy, and I don't think it's appropriate, however, to exploit that tragedy for political ends. And what I see, and what I hear, and what Mr. Hyde has been calling for, and what the Clinton administration has proposed in this bill is not all that different, is to direct repressive measures not at terrorists, not at people who blow up buildings, but at people who are merely associated with the lawful activities of organizations that are unpopular. Under the law that the Clinton administration has proposed, people can be deported for sending humanitarian aid to a hospital if that hospital is run by an organization which has even engaged in any unlawful act. Under that kind of a law, anyone who supported the political activities of Nelson Mandela would have been deported, deportable, because the ANC had engaged in unlawful military acts.

Wertheimer: But the Islamic Jihad and other militant organizations in the Middle East also maintain refugee camps, they maintain hospitals, they do good works as well as the other things they do.

Cole: That's right, and for that reason, just last year, the Clinton administration testified in Congress against a proposal such as Mr. Hyde is now re-raising, and that was to make membership in Hamas an excludable offense. Anyone who's a mere member in Hamas in excludable, and the State Department and the INS came, and said, "You can't do that," because Hamas engages in a wide range of lawful activities, as well as some unlawful activities, and it is guilt by association to exclude someone simply because they are a member. If they have done something wrong, if they have supported terrorist activity, if they are in any way connected to terrorist activity, then they can be excluded, they can be deported, they can be criminally punished. But if someone is simply a member of an organization or a supporter of the lawful activities of that organization, it's guilt by association to hold them responsible.

Wertheimer: Professor Cole, this Congress is disposed to treat those people who are immigrants in this country, particularly if they're illegal immigrants, differently from American citizens, and that's evident in the welfare debates and in other areas that the Congress is willing to move in that direction. I wonder if perhaps the Congress won't see it completely differently, just see that if these people are visitors to this country or illegal immigrants to this country, the fastest and most efficient thing to do is just simply to remove them from this country.

Cole: Well, two points in response to that. First, the Clinton administration's bill does not stop at immigrants. It makes it a crime for any U.S. citizen to support the lawful activities of any organization that is designated as terrorist by the president in an unreviewable designation, so the restrictions on associational freedoms are extended to citizens as well as to immigrants. Secondly, the First Amendment has long been held by the Supreme Court to protect all people in this country; it's not limited to citizens. And all of our First Amendment rights are at stake if the government is suppressing the rights of any of us within this country, so aliens and citizens ought to be treated the same way from a First Amendment standpoint.

Wertheimer: What about the reaction that I think many citizens of this country will have, that we are vulnerable in ways that are horrifying to us and that we want to do something about it?

Cole: Well, we are vulnerable, and I think it's precisely because we feel vulnerable and we feel helpless that we lash out and try to do something. But I think when we try to do something, we should focus on things that are effective. One of the reasons that we have a First Amendment and we have protection for political activities is precisely because it's understood to be a safety valve. If people are free to engage in political activity, they are less likely to engage in more extreme activity. If we start to repress, to clamp down on perfectly lawful political activity, that's likely to drive more groups underground and likely to encourage extremists, so I think this is a counterproductive effort.

Wertheimer: What about the effort to keep people who have engaged in terrorist activity, or are associated with terrorist organizations, out of the country in the first place?

Cole: I think it's perfectly appropriate to keep people out of the country who have engaged in terrorist activity. It's also appropriate to deport them. What is not appropriate is to extend that to people who have not engaged in any terrorist activity, who have not supported any terrorist activity, but are simply linked by association to a group that engages in both lawful and unlawful activity.

Wertheimer: Professor Cole, I suggested a moment ago that the atmosphere in Congress has changed. It's certainly changed by this event in Oklahoma City, but it's also changed by the last election. It's a Republican-dominated Congress; law and order is high on the list of priorities. Do you think that means that different things will happen than might have happened a few years ago?

Cole: Well, I think that certainly different things may well happen, but I think that no matter what political stripe the Congress is, it ought to pay attention to the constitutional constraints that are imposed on it and essential democratic freedoms. I think terrorism is a terrible thing, but if we respond to terrorism by suppressing and repressing the freedoms of people who live among us, whether they're citizens or aliens, I think that's a worse thing.

Wertheimer: At first, reporting about Oklahoma City concentrated on the possibility that this terrorist attack may have started overseas. Then, at the end of the day, we find that the FBI is looking in an entirely different direction, at Americans, which raises the question of how to combat terror when you're dealing with domestic terror. If deportation is just not something that would solve the problem, what then solves the problem?

Cole: Well, I think what solves the problem is having laws against terrorism, and we already have laws against terrorism. Rigorously enforcing those laws, and I'm sure that we will rigorously enforce those laws. But I think — you know, some government official said yesterday that no law is going to stop the kind of crazy person who will do what happened in Oklahoma City yesterday. It's not a law that's going to stop that; it's sort of a frame of mind, and if people feel like their concerns are being understood and aired in society at large, the hope is that these kinds of extreme actions will not take place. But it's when people feel that they don't have it, that this kind of response occurs.

Wertheimer: Do you have any concerns about the possible over-reaction?

Cole: I certainly do. I mean, this wouldn't be the first time. The Palmer Raids in 1920 were a similar response to a series of bombings in the United States, and the Justice Department went out and rounded up six thousand suspected immigrants in thirty-three cities and beat them and tortured them and it turned out that ninety-five percent of them were not deportable and the other five percent were deported solely for their association, so this isn't the first time that there have been attempts to focus on immigrants and engage in a dragnet to respond to fear.

MUSIC

Orson Welles called EARTHA KITT the most exciting stage presence in the world. She became an international singing star, purring her songs at the choicest watering holes of Paris, London, and Amsterdam at the tail end of a time in which many African American performers received greater recognition in Europe than in the United States. When she returned to her native United States she appeared in films with Sidney Poitier, Nat King Cole, and Sammy Davis, Jr., and even portrayed the Catwoman in the television series *Batman*. In 1968 at a White House luncheon, she publicly criticized the U.S. war policy in Vietnam to her hostess, Lady Bird Johnson. Rendered unemployable by her candor, she repaired to Europe. When she released a new compact disc, *Back in Business*, a collection of classic club music from Fats Waller to Stephen Sondheim, Eartha Kitt talked with Scott Simon about her politics, her upbringing, and the time in the 1950s when she was performing at the Persian Room in midtown Manhattan and was invited to appear at the Apollo Theatre in Harlem. January 14, 1995

Kitt: The agents whom I was with at the time told me that I would have to change my act, that the songs that I was singing were too sophisticated, too much above the heads of the people, and that I would have to, well, bring the act down to where they think the people would understand me. I thought it was an insult. My two musicians would not go with me because they didn't want to be embarrassed by a failure, I suppose. But I went up to the Apollo by myself and rehearsed the band that was there. I think it was a sixteen-piece band or twenty-four pieces, and I rehearsed myself, and I did exactly the same act as I was doing at the Persian Room, the same gowns, the same everything. We were supposed to do, I think, three or four shows a day, and we wound up doing five and six shows a day because that's how much the people loved it, and they were in line from the box office up to Seventh Avenue, from Eighth Avenue, waiting to get in, and I was the happiest person in the world because it was like being accepted by your own, not only the Afro-Americans, but also by Americans in general. It was home. The king of all times was there. Paul Robeson was in the box, and when he stood up and gave me a bow, I really felt as though you're paralyzed. I didn't feel that kind of feeling when I was actually doing the command performance in London before the king and queen of England. This to me was a king.

Simon: A real king.

Kitt: A real king because he earned his position. He earned it!

Simon: Do you mind talking about your family experience for a while?

Kitt: Well, I didn't have a family. I was given away, I used to say, by my mother, but as I've grown older I don't have a feeling that the lady that gave me away was really my mother. I think the lady who was up here in New York had an illegitimate child down south, and she left me with who they say might have been a cousin or a half sister or something like that, or maybe it was her sister. I don't know. This lady was very dark, and she had a very dark child. Me being what they call a "yellow gal," not dark enough and not white enough, they say you're a reject, at least in those days. My mother, I suppose, if you want to call her my mother — I remember the first scene in my life and we were walking down a road. It was about twilight in the evening, and I was holding her hand, and she had what they call my half sister in her arms, and we kept knocking on doors asking to stay there for the night, and everybody would say, "No, I don't want that yellow gal in my house," when they saw my color. So we kept moving on, and we wound up in forests, sleeping in the pine wood. When the dawn came I remember seeing my mother coming back with fruit and whatever she could get from whatever nearby farmland, and then we would move on. But we were constantly being rejected because they would look down at me and see what color I was, and my mother would have to move on. Finally we wound up in a cabin, and I was always hiding, and I think until this day I am still hiding, and that's why sometimes I act like I am being difficult. It's because I'm too shy and I don't want to be seen. I know who Eartha Kitt is, but I don't know who Eartha Mae is. Eartha Mae is that little urchin, ugly duckling that nobody wanted. When we wound up in this cabin it was only a few days later that I realized that I didn't have to hide anymore because the lady was blind, and she couldn't see what color I was. While I was there in this house, I woke up one night, and I remember hearing my mother sobbing, and I looked through the cracks of the wall into the other room. There she was on her knees begging this man, who was a black man — for him to accept her children, and he kept saying, "No, I don't want that yellow gal in my house." Eventually I was brought up north by Aunt Mamie who was — she's gone now, too — very fair, about the color I am, and she never had any children and, therefore, she didn't know how to treat a child. So here again I was left alone all the time, fending for myself.

Simon: What would you do?

Kitt: Well, I filled writing paper, envelope boxes. I was a salesgirl, and I didn't know how to count very well even though I did go to school. And then Mrs. Bishop! I never will forget her. She was a schoolteacher that was my color, and she encouraged me to learn a poem, and I didn't know why because nobody ever told me why, and I learned this poem, and then one day she sent me down to the High School for Performing Arts in New York, which was down in the Bowery at the time. I had to say this poem, and until this day I cannot even remember one word of it. I was so scared I had just wound up in front of this class! And say this poem? I was the only girl out of I don't know how many — three hundred or three thousand — who were trying to get into the drama department at the New York school at that time. I was the only girl that was accepted and that's when I began to realize that I was OK, and it was the schoolteachers. I have tremendous praise for schoolteachers, because if it wasn't for them I don't know what I would have done, what would have become of me.

Simon: You know, I have to ask you, given the state of your social convictions and the way you have been willing to be outspoken and, as we've noted, paid a price for it, there were a lot of people who were puzzled when you went to South Africa in the late 1980s and entertained there. This was, we will explain, before Mr. Mandela came out of prison, before there was the change in government.

Kitt: Yes, but here again you have to, I think, have the risk of losing face, the same as I did in Las Vegas, the same as I've done in my own country when they would not allow me to come when I was a dancer with the Katherine Dunham Ballet Company in 1948, or something like that, in Las Vegas. They would not allow us to come through the front door, but when I became a star and was working in the same hotel I walked through that front door a hundred times a day to show that everything was OK. You break a principle, and then it's very difficult to put it back to where it was. South Africa, to me, was like that. They said that they weren't going to hire me in certain places because I went to South Africa, but you have to take your chances to break a law that doesn't make any sense and which is what we did. There are two schools that are now built because my daughter and I walked through the streets every Tuesday and Thursday in every area of South Africa that we were in, begging for money to build schools. The teachers were waiting in line to teach, but there were no buildings. So these are the things that we were doing behind the scenes, pulling the races together, rather than pushing them apart.

Simon: So you thought of yourself as breaking barriers there?

Kitt: I always have all my life, even though somebody said it was wrong to do.

Simon: I guess I have to ask you, finally, people have pointed out there are three or four different accents in your voice. You have pointed out there are a number of different complexions in your face and speak about it as if this must be responsible for some sort of divided identity in yourself, but is that true? You always seem to be pretty much certain about who you are.

Kitt: That's because when I step out of the house I know I have to be Eartha Kitt, but you should see me when I'm just Eartha Mae around the house, because I'm very confused, but I think the fact that I have, my whole life, so to speak, become the Eartha Kitt on the stage. I feel very strong in that character and it's very difficult for me to divide her from coming back to being Eartha Mae at times, as long as I'm in view of a public. But the moment I am back in my dressing room, I immediately want to take the face off and all of my paraphernalia off. I'm back to being an urchin again, and then it's difficult for me to face people. Sometimes people will come into the dressing room after I have gone back into being just that ugly duckling, and then I get scared and I act very funny and I know that, and I keep checking myself because I know that I'm now back into being Eartha Mae and I don't want to be seen. I don't want to be heard. Let me hide. It's very difficult for people to accept that, I know.

Simon: Boy, unfortunately, we have reached the moment where we have to end the interview. I can't think of a more awkward place to end it.

Kitt: Well, now that I get off with you, I can go back to being the urchin again. I can scream as I leave the studio.

Simon: Don't call yourself an urchin.

Kitt: Well, I think the spirit of the urchin is constantly keeping Eartha Kitt *au point* — in French, "a level head" — because she always knows from whence she came.

Reviews of DENYCE GRAVES as Carmen, in the U.S. and abroad, call her "sultry," "glamorous," "sensuous," "exotic," "smoky," and "alluring." A thirty-year-old mezzo-soprano who is known as an "anti-diva," modest, open, approachable, Graves debuted at New York's Metropolitan Opera in the role only after singing it in Washington at the Kennedy Center, where she was received as a hometown hero. She was born in the nation's capital, sang there in church, and went to the public schools where, she says, she never imagined herself as an opera singer. As she told Robert Siegel, it was a junior high school music teacher who heard her and encouraged her to sing. March 30, 1995

Graves: One day I was walking through the hall, and she said, "Listen, Denyce. There's a performing arts high school called Duke Ellington, and I think you like singing. You've got a beautiful voice. I think you should go and audition." And I thought, Oh, well, that's not really what I want to do, and she said, "Well, anyway, just go and make the audition." So I did, and I was accepted.

Siegel: Do you remember what you sang for your audition?

Graves: I sang "You Light Up My Life." Remember when Debby Boone made that famous?

Siegel: Debby Boone's "You Light Up My Life"?

Graves: Exactly. And apparently, that was the hip tune of the day.

Siegel: The largest-selling single female vocal of the twentieth century at the time.

Graves: Absolutely, and I guess it was a big hit that day as well, because the woman who was playing for me in the audition said, "Ay-ay-ay, are you singing this too?" You know, but "Fortunately, you're doing it in a different key," so I think they were getting a little crazy over it as well. But, anyway, that's what I sang, and I was accepted, and I went in the summer of seventy-nine.

Siegel: You know, nowadays, now that every opera singer and classical performer inevitably has a crossover compact disc, you may find yourself again singing "You Light Up My Life."

Graves: You know, I would like that. We've talked a lot about that with my managers because I do it around the house for my own pleasure, you know.

Siegel: Now, Carmen has become almost a signature role for you. Do you like to hear that? Or is it true?

Graves: It's true. It was not preplanned. That's just the way that fate worked out.

Siegel: You've sung it lots of different places.

Graves: Oh, many places.

Siegel: Have you ever sung Carmen in English?

Graves: No, never. I hope never — no, no, no, no, no, no. Actually, when I was a student at the New England Conservatory, we had an opera-scenes program. I did part of Act Two up until "La fleur" in English, and you know, the words are hysterical. "All through those lonely nights in prison . . ." It's just horrible.

Siegel: The way you're staged at the Kennedy Center, you're actually leaning back and seducing your man there, stroking him with your leg. This not only is a phenomenally seductive scene, the way you sing it, but you are in a virtually gymnastic position while singing. This must be incredibly hard to do.

Graves: But I've certainly done much more difficult things on stage with *Carmen*, and, in fact, the director, Ann-Margret Petterson, was holding us back a lot, because Neil Rosenshein and I have worked together in Houston and we've done a revival of a new production that was terribly sexual, terribly violent. So we had explored that with each other and were comfortable with doing all sorts of acrobatics, and we really wanted to let loose and do more stuff, but, alas.

Siegel: Let me ask you something. I read a review of your [Royal Opera House] Covent Garden performance of *Carmen*, and the review in a British daily said, "Some compare her to Grace Bumbry, but I prefer the comparison with a young Eartha Kitt." Wherever you go, are you inevitably only compared to other black singers?

Graves: I hate that. I hate that. But, you know, that's the business we're in. It's not just for me as a black artist, I think it's for everybody. You know, they say, "Oh, the sound of Mary Mills is like a young, you know, Mirella Freni." I don't know why people feel the need to make that comparison. But often, and certainly with me, it's always with other black artists.

Siegel: You're only compared with other black artists, you find?

Graves: All the time.

Siegel: Now, to what extent is Carmen a feature of this? Is Carmen supposed to be a natural extension of the exotic Gypsy woman now translated into a black girl, or is that coincidence?

Graves: No, it's just coincidence. I mean, for me, I had seen a lot of different portrayals of Carmen, and it was really important to me to just let the character come through in my personality. I feel that it's very important to be as natural as possible. For example, if my head itches, I scratch my head. I don't think that, Oh, Carmen wouldn't do this, or if something happens funny on stage, you know, an accident, for example, Don José comes in and trips, and I laugh. I think I should laugh. I think to try and pretend that those things don't exist only makes them more pointed out, and I think that that's really important in a character, to just be as natural and as flowing with the situation as possible.

Siegel: Well, as Carmen, you're presumably the one up there onstage who's the most confident about how she's acting and the most unfettered, you know, a free individual.

Graves: But I don't think she's contrived. She can be very calculating when it serves her. For example, she tries many different ways to get him to untie her, but only when there's something in it for her. Mostly she's not a contrived personality. If she's sitting down on the stairs and her skirt is above her legs, it just is because that happens to be, not because she finds that seductive. What's seductive about her is her — is the energy of who she is, and that's what I think. I mean, out there, there's something intangible about this woman that people want. It's not her body, you know. That's the quickest way or the easiest way that they feel that they can get to her, and if there's something in it for her, they can have her body, but they'll never have her, and that's when the problems come in, especially with the relationship with Don José.

Siegel: I'd like to ask you about one other temptress you've played in opera, which is Dalila from *Samson et Dalila*. I have now heard a couple of recordings of you singing the aria *"Mon coeur s'ouvre à ta voix"* that I confess I first heard as Jackie Wilson singing "Night, here comes the night."

Graves: That's great.

Siegel: A sub-Debby-Boone-level popular song of about thirty-five years ago.

Graves: Wonderful.

Siegel: Do you like singing that?

Graves: I love it. I have a huge confession to make. I'm much more in love with Dalila than Carmen, absolutely. She is very opposite in the fact that she is very contrived, I think, and extremely calculating, and she's evil. Not really, I mean, it's after three times that she has tried unsuccessfully to find out the secret of the strength of Samson, but she hates him as an enemy to her people. You know, that's the thing that's so ironic about the "*Mon coeur*" aria, that it's one of the most beautiful arias in all the operatic literature, I think, and she absolutely hates him in this moment. She detests him.

Siegel: "My heart opens to your voice — "

Graves: "Like a flower."

Siegel: And this is a seduction of a man whom she detests.

Graves: Absolutely, I absolutely love that about Dalila. With Carmen sometimes I find myself going back to the novel and the opera; they're two different works. We know in the novel that Carmen was a bit of a chameleon because she spoke many languages, she could present herself in any situation, you know, as a Frenchwoman, as a Spanish Gypsy, as an Englishwoman, or whatever. But with Dalila, she's been groomed to have a certain stature, and I think she absolutely is evil, unlike Carmen. Carmen's just a natural girl, being who she is, who gets in a little trouble with the wrong man, you know?

Siegel: What's it like coming back to Washington to perform, starring in a big opera like *Carmen*, in this case? This is home.

Graves: It's wonderful. Just to be able to bring that home to my family, my friends, people who know me and really care about me, people who've watched me, you know, growing up — for example, my music teacher when I was in kindergarten. These people came to the performances. So it means something to me personally, and also, to feel really appreciated. I had done a Donizetti opera before arriving here in Washington of *La Favorite*, and the tenor who sang opposite me was from Catania [Sicily], and we were in Catania. He was Catanese, so the minute he walked on the stage, the people were screaming and hollering, going crazy. I mean, they were Italians as well.

Siegel: These were very reserved Sicilians, no doubt.

Graves: Exactly. So, you know, I just thought, Oh, gee, I would love to get home with my people, you know, who really appreciate me and love me.

Siegel: In a few years, are you going to turn into a totally inaccessible diva who won't let us talk to you?

Graves: Never.

Siegel: Never?

Graves: My mama won't let me.

Siegel: Her word goes here?

Graves: She has the last word.

I t is an understatement to say that everything about the baritone BRYN TERFEL is Welsh. Welsh was his first language, English his second. He and his wife are raising their son to speak only Welsh until he starts school. His love of singing, which extends to opera, Schubert lieder, and now a recording of English art songs by Vaughan Williams and others, is a typically Welsh passion. Bryn Terfel instructed Robert Siegel in the pronunciation of his name, which sounds like "Tairville" with a heavily rolled "r." It is a lot harder to pronounce than his real last name. December 15, 1995

Terfel: My full name is Bryn Terfel Jones, but there was already a baritone that was named Delme Bryn Jones from Wales. So I had to drop my Jones.

Siegel: There must be a lot of Bryn Joneses in Wales?

Terfel: Yes, lots of them. If you go to a Welsh convention, and say "Mr. Jones, stand up," ninety percent of them would stand up.

Siegel: And most of them could probably sing.

Terfel: It's in the tradition of Wales, be it in the amateur or the professional. We have choirs in every village. We have singing in the church, locally in the pubs. It's a weird fact in Wales. When you have a rugby international, say if you have the Irish playing the Welsh — goodness, gracious me — that's a wonderful match to go to. Not only to see the match, but after the match. You know, the celebrations. It doesn't matter who won, who lost, whatever. The sort of joining of the Celts is something to be really enjoyed there.

Siegel: What was your early musical life like in Wales?

Terfel: My early music life was really something that I wasn't really conscious of. Music and singing was there, always, in the background. My parents sang in different choirs, my grandparents sang. Most of all I think singing started in the church. You know, we sang not really hymn things, but we sang pop songs and we sort of gradually got into the tradition of Wales. Then I started competing and then we have to start radio programs and then television and sort of the ball started rolling and then I went to London to study and then everything sort of had a turnabout.

Siegel: Edward Rothstein of the *New York Times* wrote of your voice, "There is a potent heft to it. It possesses a momentum that makes it seem as if it will keep traveling without further effort. But what makes it most unusual is that this firmly supported sound is laden with meaning and sense."

Terfel: Could you repeat that, please? I love to hear things like that.

Siegel: You like that.

Terfel: Fantastic, wow, what a description. I have to put that in my curriculum vitae. Whatever, you know, [*singing*] "How to handle a woman . . ." There we go. Richard Burton was the first one to sing that.

Siegel: He was a Welshman.

Terfel: *Camelot*, yes. Very good Welshman. I would have loved to have met him.

Siegel: Tell me about the song setting you have recorded of the Robert Louis Stevenson *Songs of Travel*?

Terfel: I think they are the first songs that I ever learned in college. I had a singing teacher who was an eighty-seven-year-old, a pure gentleman. He had the job of looking after me for the first three years of my college life, which was really the most important time in the development of my voice. He just took his time, didn't push, didn't do anything bad, and gave me all these English songs to sing, and the *Songs of Travel* by Vaughan Williams were the first ones that I did actually learn. And the first one, of course, "The Vagabond," the most famous one, is fantastic. I affiliate myself wholly to this song, "The Vagabond," about how he travels and how he loves the rivers and the roads and the fields and the trees of his homeland. This is me.

Siegel: The songs on this particular compact disc are all in English.

Terfel: Yes. I've chosen some Finzi songs and then some Butterworth songs, two cycles by him, and then three songs by John Ireland which consist of another favorite of mine, "Sea Fever," the John Masefield poem. They had wonderful poets to write from. These composers lived in the same time, they had the same circle of friends, they studied in the same colleges. They, you know, sometimes wrote music for themselves as a birthday present. I think that Finzi's *Let Us Garlands Bring* was a birthday present to Vaughan Williams. So they had all these wonderful poems to write music to. I'd have loved to be there, at that time, just to be a fly on the wall and see if they all joined together and, sort of, had notes on each other.

Siegel: At your recitals, do you typically sing in Welsh as well?

Terfel: Oh, of course. I just did a recital in Atlanta, and there I sang a first half of Schubert songs, and I finished with a collection of Welsh folk tunes that a friend of mine wrote for me. Then, for encores and stuff, I relax and I sing pieces from Lerner and Loewe's *Camelot.* Because I think the last songs that you sing are actually the ones that people go out whistling. You know, if you sing "Some Enchanted Evening," they go, [*singing*] "Some enchanted evening . . ." So it's a wonderful end to a recital, I think.

Siegel: I'm surprised to hear you sing "Some Enchanted Evening" at that register, as high as that.

Terfel: Or [*singing deeper*] "Some enchanted eve —— " No, no. There we go. I've just recorded a whole disc of Rodgers and Hammerstein. This is going to be my next album that comes out. And I had a whale of a time. It was fantastic.

Siegel: My editor thinks it's funny that a Welshman should sing "Oklahoma!" Well, where do we think they came from out there in Oklahoma? Where were they all from before they reached Richmond, Virginia?

Terfel: Of course they were Welshmen.

Siegel: They must have been Welshmen.

Terfel: Hey, Welsh is the language of heaven. We're everywhere. Even in Atlanta, where I've just done that recital, there was a Welsh society there and about thirty people turned up and when they hear the Welsh language sung, you know, they just burst into tears because of this Welsh blood of theirs. We have a word in Welsh called *hiraeth,* and you can't really translate it. It's sort of longing, but it's deeper than longing. So, you know, as an ambassador of my country I sell my nationality and I sell my language and I sing my songs wherever I go so, be it from *Oklahoma!* or whatever, it's still a Welshman that sings them.

The Curriers are a family of composers. MARILYN CURRIER's works have been performed at Carnegie Hall and the Kennedy Center. Her sons, SEBASTIAN and NATHAN CURRIER, are also successful composers, both recipients of the coveted Rome Prize, the only brothers ever to win that honor. Sebastian spent his residency at Rome's American Academy in 1993. Nathan was planning to leave for his stint in Italy when the three of them spoke with Jacki Lyden. Marilyn Currier said her sons' early musical careers were not in classical composition. July 30, 1995

Marilyn: They were very adorable little rock musicians when they were kids.

Lyden: Rock musicians. Is this a secret past life, Sebastian and Nathan?

Nathan: So adorable that the local police enjoyed coming by the house and telling us to turn it down.

Lyden: Thanks for that, Nathan. What did you play?

Nathan: Well, I played, at first, bass guitar, and then keyboards. I was also taking piano lessons from about the age of seven, and I think that just in general, for composing, having the ability to play a keyboard instrument is a great tool. So I started composing when I was around eight. I remember my mother buying me a little notebook. I don't think I put much of anything into it. But by the time I was eleven or twelve, I was composing little things that were sort of half rock and half classical, if you will.

Lyden: Sebastian, what about you? When did you begin to compose? You're thirty-six; your brother, Nathan, is thirty-four. When did you start?

Sebastian: Oh, some time in my teens. A similar experience to what Nathan was describing. My mother didn't mention they tried to get us to play stringed instruments at a very early age. I think I was probably a failed violinist as of age five or something like that. Later on, I started both playing rock guitar and eventually classical guitar, and I do feel, too, in terms of our experience as rock musicians at a young age, you know, the classical tradition when you're learning to read music and play what's on a page very precisely, it doesn't encourage a lot of freedom and spontaneity that you need to compose. I think there was something good about the fact as rock musicians we made up our own things and we really had that freedom with dealing with notes. I always think of that as something that eventually fed in to me being a composer.

Lyden: So no one ever had to tell you young boys, "It's time for your music lesson"?

Marilyn: Oh, yes.

Sebastian: Yes. Absolutely.

Marilyn: We used to pay them to practice.

Nathan: That's right. We were paid to practice.

Marilyn: Family secret.

Lyden: Let me come to you, Marilyn. You've taken folk art at the Museum of American Art [in Washington, D.C.] for inspiration in one of your works. *Throne of the Third Heaven* is a sculpture made out of aluminum foil, and it's something I enjoy enormously when I take a look at it. I was really struck to see it as the inspiration for a musical piece. Were you thinking about certain elements in the sculpture? When one sees this, it's an enormous surprise. There are silver tabernacles, silver chairs, silver altars. Can you tell me just something about that?

Marilyn: That was pure chance. I had been to an art colony in Virginia, and the artists there told me about it and said I absolutely had to stop to see it. But it didn't come from any ongoing interest in folk art. I was quite swept away by it. It was an immensely up piece. I mean, if you've seen it, you know what I mean. It's exhilarating.

Lyden: Sebastian, what about you? Do you compose for specific artists, or are you going for a specific audience? You've created a violin sonata for Anne-Sophie Mutter, for example. Can you tell me a little about that?

Sebastian: Well, that's something that came about just by chance. I had had a violin and piano work of mine called "Clockwork" played at something called the Kennedy Center Friedheim Awards. One of the judges was the pianist Lambert Orkis, who plays with Anne-Sophie Mutter, and he said to me, "Oh, I really like this piece. I want to show it to Anne-Sophie and see what she thinks." She liked it and decided to play it and also asked me to write a piece for her. So I wrote a piece called "Aftersong." And so I wrote that last year, and she's been performing it quite a bit since then.

Lyden: When you write a piece like this, do you take it to the performer, and say, "Here it is, and you cannot change it"? Or does the performer comment on it, and you change it?

Sebastian: Generally it stays quite the same, except for minor details. One learns from experience, long before working with Anne-Sophie Mutter, that it's a collaboration in a way with a performer and one needs to give them some leeway, too. Of course as you probably know, a musical score is just a series of symbols and doesn't really tell exactly what you want. So there's always fine-tuning. There is always discussion. There's always fine points that one could disagree on. As I say, I've found many different times that one needs to let a performer have the freedom to sort of pursue what they see in the piece. Otherwise, you sort of stifle their creativity.

Lyden: When one thinks about the composition of classical music, we tend to think of people who are household names and also dead.

Nathan: Some day I will be dead. I don't know whether I'll be a household name.

Lyden: How does one become a young classical composer in America? Where does your music fit into the American musical landscape, Nathan?

Nathan: Well, I would say first of all that the landscape is changing fast and furious in this country. There's kind of a vacuum right now in music in America. People are taking from all kinds of influences. There is no dominant aesthetic. I see eclecticism as almost becoming a value in and of itself, which is not really something to be proud of because music would naturally be eclectic if nothing prevents it from being. What I think about is connection, how to connect these different things that are out there. We hear so much music of different kinds. Connecting things is like making things come alive, you know? It's like the Pygmalion myth of taking something inanimate. These are just notes we're writing when we write music, but we want to eventually make them so that they reflect our individual personalities.

Lyden: What do you think about the health of American classical music, Nathan, particularly for young composers? I read a piece in the *Washington Post* last week about possible cuts in the National Endowment for the Arts, and it regarded classical music as an endangered species.

Nathan: I have an interesting way of looking at the endangered species of classical music. I think that it's like relativity theory. It doesn't help you to take an eight-hour drive, but at the same time, it doesn't mean that it's useless. In other words, something can be practically useless and theoretically preeminent. When the avant-garde started to die in this country, it was essentially killed on the grounds that it didn't sell. People didn't like it. People don't want to listen to Anton Webern and things that sound like scratching on a blackboard. Maybe they're right not to, but that same logic can be then turned to anything. If ultimately what replaces a so-called elitist establishment is just commercialism and what sells, then everything is vulnerable. If Beethoven doesn't really sell well, if it doesn't sell like Michael Jackson sells, why should it still be around? Will it just disappear? In Europe, there's no thought of Beethoven disappearing because it doesn't sell well. The government has a vested interest because it feels that this is something of value. It's like there's a morality there, for them.

Lyden: Is creating this kind of music going to remain strong in this country?

Marilyn: I feel I've done my share through my sons as well as my own work, so I'm hopeful. I think they're wonderful composers. I should get that in.

Sebastian: For myself, I have to say I really don't know. I certainly hope it will be. I think a lot of that importance lies in just education in this country in general, not just for classical music, but just for culture in general.

Lyden: And Nathan?

Nathan: Well, I think that when we're talking about competition there's a very little pie in the new music world for what everyone wants to get — big orchestras to play their music and stuff. But ultimately, there's no real pie. When we talk about the future and the long term and what's going to happen, the pie can grow. There's room for, you know, pop music to take over and classical music to survive and there will be more and more a plurality of different things out there.

I n the year that Frank Sinatra marked his eightieth birthday, his daughter NANCY SINATRA celebrated with a book about her father, *Frank Sinatra: An American Legend*. The author, a recording artist in her own right, remembered for the hit single "These Boots Are Made for Walkin'" and a duet with her father, "Somethin' Stupid," assembled episodes from his amazingly durable career, from his teenage years in Hoboken, New Jersey, where he set out to emulate Bing Crosby, to his late seventies, when he appeared with the rock star Bono. The book recounts her father's romantic involvements with Ava Gardner, Lauren Bacall, and Mia Farrow; his friendships with Sammy Davis, Jr., and Dean Martin, as well as with longtime Jerusalem Mayor Teddy Kollek; and his loyalties to such diverse figures as Martin Luther King and Spiro T. Agnew. A few days after his birthday, Nancy Sinatra talked about her father with Scott Simon. December 16, 1995

Simon: When you were putting the book together, did you discover you didn't know everything about your father you thought you did?

Sinatra: No, not really. I had actually been working on this indirectly for about twenty years. What I did discover, however, was that he did an amazing amount of work. I mean, I knew that he had, but to actually see it in front of my face with dates and times and guest stars and songs and all of that trivia that makes up a life such as his was a little bit overwhelming for me. I was really astounded.

Simon: The bandleader Harry James wanted him to call him — wanted your father to call himself — "Frankie Satin"?

Sinatra: Yes. There was a lot of name changing in those days. I think this life reflects about a hundred years of American history, and I think to have your name end in a vowel in those days was a sticky wicket.

Simon: You recount a time of young women that were called the "Sinatra Swooners." These were adolescent women who — and I'm sure a few boys, for that matter — who took leave of their senses at Frank Sinatra's public appearances. This is a difficult thing to ask a daughter, but what is this thing that women have for your father?

Sinatra: Early on, it was the fact that a lot of the men in the country were away at war, and he was a symbol, in a way. And I think part of it was that he was vulnerable. He combined a sexuality with an innocence. Aside from wanting pieces of his body and parts of his hair and stuff like that. I mean, they used to pull hairs from his head, you know. He brought out a lot of weird emotions, but, I think, it was primarily the fact that most of the men were away and he, of course, being 4F, was at home.

Simon: Is that why he began to acquire such an extensive wardrobe, because it would get stripped off of him night after night?

Sinatra: Yes. Pockets were torn off. They would take his ties immediately. They always went for the ties, which used to drive my mother to distraction because she made all those ties, those floppy bow ties, and she would just have to make more ties. There is one now in the Smithsonian. Did you know that?

Simon: No, I didn't. It must have been difficult for you kids to live through all of the publicity over the — I guess we need to explain to this generation — when your father seemed to be in intense pursuit of Ava Gardner.

Sinatra: Not really. I think we were too young to really know what was going on. I think, mostly, if we were saddened by it, it was just looking at my mother because she was so sad, of course.

Simon: I think a lot of people listening today either have forgotten about this period of time or never knew about it, but it was during this time, when your father was receiving some adverse publicity and was not getting certain recording contracts and film roles that he wanted, that his career was considered to be in quite a stall.

Sinatra: He called it "a little stroke." He said that his career had "a little stroke."

Simon: That must have been a rough time for the entire family.

Sinatra: I think much more hurtful is the stuff in the press that we could not dispute. We weren't permitted to get into any kind of public display of temper or disappointment.

Simon: Were these the allegations about some of your father's affiliations?

Sinatra: Uh-huh. Yeah.

Simon: Well, yeah, it's a big theme of the book, and I'd like to get you to talk about that, if I could, because you say that your father has been hurt over the years about allegations that he has been involved with organized crime figures, and that people who say this are chancing a stereotype of Italian Americans, and, for that matter, don't really understand show business.

Sinatra: Right. Right because, again, in the history of our nation, you can trace it, and it's very explainable. It's a very simple story of growing up in Hoboken, meeting these people as children and growing up together in the same neighborhood. Hoboken was a city, and is, that is one square mile, period. That's it. It never got any bigger, or smaller, for that matter. And it was ethnically diverse. And then came Prohibition. And for some reason, which I'm really not entirely clear about, it came to Hoboken first. And the speakeasies in the country were run by people who were, I guess, bootleggers. They then, in turn, and, by the way, were not all Italians.

Simon: Yeah, hardly.

Sinatra: The Italians took the rap all the same. They moved from the speakeasies into the jazz clubs — Fifty-second Street, like Carlos and Charlie's — and they migrated west to Las Vegas. But to get back to the subject at hand, if you track that and then you track Frank's career and you see how the parallels are there, then you know that, of course, he will have — he would have been working for these people who owned these places. It's very simple.

Simon: You work in nightclubs, you don't hang out with kindergarten teachers.

Sinatra: Exactly. But you tell me why such a big deal was made of this over the years.

Simon: You, though, tell an anecdote about your father approaching Sam Giancana to help Jack Kennedy's presidential campaign. I think there are historians who will argue that in 1960 no one could be under any illusion about what Sam Giancana was doing or what his help represented. He was the head of the Chicago Mob.

Sinatra: I'm waiting for a question.

Simon: Well, I thought that was a very honest account.

Sinatra: Right, but think back now. Let's go back and trace our story again. My dad worked for a man named Skinny D'Amato. Skinny owned a couple of nightclubs. He also worked a place called the Villa Venice, which Sam Giancana owned. Sam Giancana apparently backed Skinny D'Amato in the 500 Club in Atlantic City. In the old Italian style of one hand washes the other, Frank would go and help Skinny out, you know, if he was in trouble with the club, and try and raise some money for him by appearing there. Later in the sixties, he brought in Sammy Davis and Dean Martin, and they did stuff together that really brought in the crowds. Sam owed Frank a favor. And then, after that big favor, because Sam really was the one they credit with turning the election to Kennedy, then later Frank owed Sam. But it was never Frank being involved in whatever Sam was involved in. You know, guilt by association is frightening.

Simon: May I ask you a couple of questions about far less weighty matters?

Sinatra: Sure.

Simon: If you had to choose a single recording of Frank Sinatra's, what do you think it might be?

Sinatra: *In the Wee, Small Hours*, the album.

Simon: Oh, so you're picking an entire album.

Sinatra: Is that cheating?

Simon: No, no, no. I asked the question.

Sinatra: One song. You want one song.

Simon: I'm thinking of one song.

Sinatra: That's tough. In the deluxe package of this book, there are five CDs. One is the CD that appears in every book, which has to do with radio shows and accepting of awards and that sort of thing. The other four represent his four record labels. I had the almost insurmountable task of picking the songs from each label for each of the discs, and, I'll tell you something — it was more difficult to do that than it was to write this book. But the songs, some of them just pop out at you. "All or Nothing at All" is one, of course. "Someone to Watch over Me." The most definitive vocal came down to one song, which is "Ol' Man River."

Simon: Really?

Sinatra: I put "Ol' Man River" as the last song on the last disc because once you hear "Ol' Man River," nothing else could follow it.

Simon: You were at the concert he gave at Chicago's United Center?

Sinatra: I was. Oh boy. The whole Chicago night meant so much to me because, first of all, I happened in Chicago, my parents told me. Secondly, Chicago's my favorite city. And thirdly, I think it meant so much to Dad, and I could tell, you know, by the way he was approaching each song, and he didn't have to use the TelePrompTers. He was just on that night. He was feeling good, and my brother was great conducting. It was just a wonderful, magical night, and the audience, they went crazy. My father and my brother had, of course, decided not to close with "New York, New York" in Chicago. Naturally, they decided on "My Kind of Town, Chicago Is." And when he started to sing the verse, they were on their feet, which begins, "Now, this could only happen to a guy like me and only happen in a town like this." Well, they know, of course, what was coming, and they were right there. And when the song ended, he was crying. He was in tears and had trouble getting down the stairs of the stage. The stage was elevated. His soundman and his manager helped him down the stairs, and I was crying. Everybody was crying. It was just an exciting moment.

Simon: Crying because there's a feeling that there's not going to be many more of these performances?

Sinatra: I definitely felt that. I don't know about the audience, but I did. If that was to be the last show, I was so happy to see it be such a great show.

The blues musician WALTER "BROWNIE" McGHEE was born in 1915 and traveled around the South, picking up music as he went. Like many other blues musicians of the 1940s, McGhee migrated to New York City, where white record company executives had become aware of the commercial potential of the blues. In 1960 in California, with his longtime partner, singer and harmonica player Sonny Terry, he was invited to a house party. Among the guests were two other famous bluesmen, Sam "Lightnin'" Hopkins and Big Joe Williams. The four of them jammed all night, and the next day had a recording session. At age eighty-one, McGhee talked with Bob Edwards about the rerelease of the album that came of that session, *Down South Summit Meeting*. September 25, 1995

McGhee: Blues is truth, you must remember that. Blues is not imagination. And if you live around to tell it, you'll find it and follow it down, it's a living thing. People live their stories that they sing about.

Edwards: Tell me about that jam session in 1960.

McGhee: Everybody from different states in the same house, and it's all playing music. That was the "Down South Summit Meeting." You can tell we had a lot of fun.

Edwards: That comes through a lot on "First Meeting," you and Lightnin' Hopkins.

McGhee: Well, the story about that is I wrote Lightnin' a letter way early in the fifties, and some guy egged me up to writing him a letter because he wouldn't come to New York and record, and I was recording for the same company that Lightnin' was. He said, "Well, I don't know, if you write him a letter." I said, "I don't know nothing about Lightnin' Hopkins, and he might be one of those dangerous guys." "Oh, it's nothing like that. Write him a letter." And I said, "What am I going to write about him? I don't know." He said, "Well, he's got a very pretty woman, he's very jealous of her. You say something about her, he'll answer it." That was ten years later that I got this answer from Lightnin'.

Edwards: Another one on this album is Big Joe Williams. Tell me about working with him.

McGhee: Yeah, Joe. Joe was great. A little hard to handle sometime on the stage when he got a little too much booze, but we all do that sometime when we get too much of booze, but he was a excellent guitarist, nine-string player.

Edwards: Played a lot of slide.

McGhee: Oh yeah.

Edwards: You didn't play slide.

McGhee: I don't play slide. My daddy had a curious thing in his mind. He played with a knife in the years when I was small, and which I didn't know, but slide wasn't a big thing back then, and he'd put a knife between his fingers, you know, and go up and down the strings. And I heard him do that and I thought it was great, and then I started to tryin' to do it. He said, "Son, learn to pick it. Once you slide, you'll always be sliding."

Edwards: I read a review of you and your partner Sonny Terry once, and it spoke about how well you shared things, you know, equal number of solos, equal number of each other's material. That helps make a partnership last too.

McGhee: Well, the partnership was — when I played on the streets, Sonny wasn't playing on the streets in New York. We lived with Leadbelly at the same time together, and I left Leadbelly before Sonny and moved to Harlem, right off the East Side. I asked Sonny to come up one night because I was raking it on the streets, and I'd been paying Sonny whatever I thought was due him because he wasn't singing, Sonny wasn't singing at that time. So one night I got to sit down and count the money out and I was going to pay him, I always paid him in advance, thirty on up. I said, "You know, you can get half of this money if you sing half of the songs that I sing. If I do ten, you do ten." And so he did, and from that day on we started to splitting down the middle until the day he died. We still split down the middle. And there was no leader in this group, see, that was the thing about it. It was either Sonny Terry or either Brownie McGhee, and I didn't care because we got the same

The musical career of QUINCY JONES defies all limits. He has been a musician, bandleader, record producer, and impresario. Jones produced enormous hit records with Michael Jackson, played trumpet for Lionel Hampton, and led big bands with Ella Fitzgerald and Sarah Vaughan. He indulged his eclectic spirit in the recording *Q's Jook Joint*, which mixes and matches the likes of Nancy Wilson, Bono, Queen Latifah, and Stevie Wonder. He talked about his career and the tradition of the juke joint in an interview with Liane Hansen. November 12, 1995

Jones: There's a saying that the juke joint was to the blues what the black church was to gospel music.

Hansen: Do you remember any of the juke joints you played in?

Jones: Oh yeah. I don't remember the names, you know, but they had strange names like Rosie Mae's and Annie's or Blue Lights or Red Lights. You know, all kind of funny names, you know. Jackson, Mississippi, is full of them, you know. They would change, in fact, change. There was one guy that owned two or three of them, you know. But I remember the moods. I remember the catfish, you know, and they used to come in, and say, "Give us some strawberry soda water," you know, "and a fish sandwich," you know. "Don't let it get cold." It had so much flavor. They played Georgia skin [a card game] and did all these funny dances, and there was always linoleum on this big concrete floor, and jukes are pretty square. And pool tables, a back room for gambling and dancing and eating and everything else. It was a trip. But I didn't realize what it was when I was kid. It was just like a big funky place to me, you know.

Hansen: People nice and loud on a Saturday night.

Jones: Oh yeah. They had dancing, they had great food, they had hard liquor, corn liquor, rather, that they called "ignorant oil" in those days, you know. But it was a great place and it was a very colorful place and a dangerous place in a way. But every African American went there regardless of the social background or anything else because they had no other place to go. So it was a gathering place.

Hansen: You organized this new recording almost like we are going into a juke joint and hearing a set by a lot of different musicians that are in there.

Jones: Well, to me that's one of the fun aspects of dealing with something on a mythological basis, just taking the common man and putting it on in a situation that's bigger than life.

Hansen: I love the little sort of tape you have at the beginning of the recording when you hear someone going, "This is Miles Davis," you know. Now, that's not Miles, is it?

Jones: Yes, it is.

Hansen: It is?

Jones: Absolutely. Every voice on there. Even Lester Young. Every voice on there. The first thing I wanted to do is establish that it's definitely a rural situation. That's why you hear crickets and a distant train and a dog bark in a field hollow, and you know it's not in a brownstone in Harlem or someplace. And then you hear a Model T Ford coming up a gravel road, and in the back seat is a whole array of people, from Lester Young to Stevie Wonder to Greg Phillinganes and Chaka, and it's just mythological and it's wonderful. And we have Charlie Parker in there and Miles Davis and Dizzy [Gillespie]. As a matter of fact, Miles and Dizzy and Sarah were on my last album, *Back on the Block*. And so I just decided it would be just so much fun to have all of these cultures and different generations come together so they're all going to come to the same place. Marlon Brando's even in there. That's from an answering service message he left on my phone two or three years ago. And I love what this is about because it's about pulling together all the little children that scamper around, that try to run away from what the core of African American music's about and pull them all back together so they can play with each other and exchange attitudes and genres and everything.

Hansen: Let's talk about that. We walk into the club and the first thing we hear is Ray Charles and Stevie Wonder and —

Jones: Bono.

Hansen: Bono doing "Let the Good Times Roll." It's an arrangement that immediately that music starts, and your hips aren't moving, then you're dead.

Jones: Well, that's the original arrangement I wrote for Ray Charles in fifty-eight.

Hansen: No kidding.

Jones: Right, when he first recorded, I think it was his second or third album, *The Genius of Ray Charles,* and it was my first Grammy nomination. Ray and I, we've been friends since fourteen and sixteen, so we've been like brothers for all these years. The great part about it is we started out together and we used to share our dreams, talk about working with a symphony and doing films and doing records and everything else, and since then, 1948, we've done all those things. He did *In the Heat of the Night.* I wrote the theme for that; he sang it. We did three or four albums together — *Genius Plus Soul, The Genius of Ray Charles,* many albums, and he's now just signed with my record company, Qwest Records, so it's as good as it gets.

Hansen: Ooh, let the good times roll.

Jones: Right. I wouldn't trade the time I was born for anything because it was just the right time. I got all the good stuff, you know, to work with Louis Armstrong, produce Louis Armstrong, and Basie, and Duke, and everybody. I worked with Billie Holiday. I wouldn't trade it. And still Ice T and Michael and Stevie and everybody else, I wouldn't trade it.

Hansen: You were born right in the golden age of the juke joint.

Jones: Right in the golden, good stuff. So I was very blessed. I feel very fortunate.

Hansen: Are you a good dancer?

Jones: Hmm?

Hansen: Are you a good dancer?

Jones: When the mood hits me.

Hansen: "Rock with You." I mean the cut you've got on this album.

Jones: Well, with Heavy D and Brandy.

Hansen: What a groove for dancing that is, and also to hear that tune again, but remade, made for the nineties.

Jones: And when we sold two million records with Michael on that. In seventy-eight Brandy wasn't even born.

Hansen: I know.

Jones: It's amazing.

Hansen: There's a rap group that you kind of superimposed on that, too, and I think there's something that you want to say about rap right now. I mean, let's take a look at this music and compare it to the music that was being made in the early days of the juke joints.

Jones: You have to remember that the origin of rap goes back to mbongi, you know, in Africa. I was part of the American delegation to Mandela's inauguration, and this is the first time, I think, in the history of an inauguration of a new president that they used mbongi as a praise shouter, you know, to introduce him. And it never happened before because that's really thousands of years old. The griots too, which were all about that, you know, of putting the history, like oral historians. They used to say every time a griot dies another library is burned to the ground. And it's the same thing, you know. They have a strong tradition, and right now that's exactly what's happening. They're putting in a very poetic way and strong and theatrical and dramatic way, telling you what their life is about every day in the street, and it's tough. It's tough. A lot of people can't handle it, you know?

Hansen: Well, yeah, I mean, there's still all this, you know, debate in "polite society" about, you know.

Jones: Right, but it's real. It's real. I'm a one thousand percent supporter of what the latest baby is in our music.

Hansen: I can think of no more dangerous a thing to do on a Sunday morning than to put Barry White's voice on the radio.

Jones: Reverend Barry White?

Hansen: Reverend Barry White.

Jones: He is a master, he really is a jewel.

Hansen: And you've combined him with Toots Thielemans. Now, until I heard "Grace at the End of the Day" from this recording, I never really thought of the harmonica as an instrument of love.

Jones: I love Barry's timing, though. He's got the sonority and the texture of a voice with all that fiber in it. But on top of that, he has Laurence Olivier timing. He's incredible.

Hansen: There's one part in the recording when he says, "That's the way we do it down here."

Jones: "At the juke joint."

Hansen: And there's such a long pause between "down here" and "At the juke joint."

Jones: That's beautiful. Well, let me play this just for you. He's a master.

Hansen: How long has this project been percolating? I mean, from the time you were inspired to do it, getting all the artists to do it?

Jones: We started the day after Thanksgiving and at that time I told all of my crew, "We're gonna do this in three days." Ha! I did *Walking in Space* in three days. I did *Gula Matari* in three days. And *Smackwater Jack* wasn't too much longer, maybe two weeks. We did *Thriller* in two months.

Hansen: Whoa.

Jones: But it changed its face real quickly, and I've always had a kind of saying, you know, it's that we always have to leave a little space for God to walk through the room. I really believe very powerfully in the divinity of what we all do because it's out there in the universe and there's a serious higher power involved, and if you ever don't believe it, you know, try to take over God's job and you'll see. He'll take it back from you.

Hansen: So this one ended up — you started Thanksgiving, you wanted to do it in three —

Jones: Three days to nine months. It was like the same as the birth of a baby. And I'm really proud of this baby.

Hansen: You're getting in multimedia now. You're going to probably be doing a lot of history stuff now, CD-ROM? I mean, what you've done with this recording in terms of the history you provide on the notes and the music that you provide is a bit of a history lesson.

Jones: Oh, it's a serious history. But that's the whole point, you know. I don't want to see any more of the different genres of music, plus the African American music, splitting into little camps. I mean, it doesn't make sense, you know. They all go together. What's interesting is when you put them together like when you hear "Do Nothing 'Til You Hear from Me" with a big band with a song that was written in 1940. It's an instrumental for Cootie [Williams]. Then Bob Russell writes lyrics for it, and it becomes a vocal for Al Hibbler with Duke Ellington, with all those great musicians, Harry Carney and, Jesus, Johnny Hodges, I mean, the best musicians that ever lived. And you hear a contemporary rhythm section playing and you get Phil Collins singing on top and people don't even know that it's Phil Collins.

After leaving the band 10,000 Maniacs, NATALIE MER-CHANT set out on her own, got a new band, a new manager, and recorded *Tigerlily,* an album of songs more contemplative and somber than her earlier music. Merchant added women to her tour, including the lead guitarist Jennifer Turner. When she was in Washington for two concerts, she came to NPR to talk with Linda Wertheimer, who asked whether she had left 10,000 Maniacs to change her life or to change her music. October 6, 1995

Merchant: I started to have a bit of a panic about the fact that I had worked with the same group of people under the same dynamic since I was seventeen years old, and I thought that there was too much complacency on my part, that I was capable of doing more and I should do more. And I put together a new band rather than work with a group of studio musicians. So I think there's a distinctive interplay between these new musicians that I'm working with. But I think, also, in the songwriting, it's more subtle and there's a sensuality to this music, an intimacy, that I don't think showed up much in 10,000 Maniacs. And also, in a pop band I think the interplay between lead guitar and lead vocal is probably the most important and intricate, and I think that Jennifer and I work really well together, we speak very well together. She's a skillful player, but she plays with a lot of feeling and there's not a lot of the ego that I've encountered in some guitar players. They tend to overpower the vocalist.

Wertheimer: It's interesting to hear you talk that way because it's so clear when you listen to 10,000 Maniacs or watch a tape of a concert, you were right in the middle of it. The dominant impression that anyone has of 10,000 Maniacs is Natalie Merchant.

Merchant: But when I look at the studio recordings, I see that there was a competition for a certain frequency range, and it was the frequency range that my voice inhabited. It's also the same frequency range as the electric guitar and also the way that Dennis played organ — he sustained a lot of chords. It's just through making my record, and not having a producer, and having to analyze the sound — this is one of the conclusions I came to.

Wertheimer: You do the keyboard this time?

Merchant: Yes. I played, I think, all except one song.

Wertheimer: There's a beautiful beginning keyboard section to "Beloved Wife." This is one of the songs that is mentioned on the part of the album which is more personal.

Merchant: Well, I think a lot of people call this a very intimate and personal album, but I feel that the things that are intimate on this album are universally intimate and more universally personal. Everyone knows what it feels like to lose somebody, and in "Beloved Wife" I take on the character of an older gentleman who's lost his wife of over fifty years. I saw my grandfather in that state. I was with him when he viewed my grandmother's body and then he proceeded to have a heart attack and died two days later. So I felt it was one of the most powerful emotional journeys I'd ever taken.

Wertheimer: You say that these things are universally intimate, not necessarily autobiographical, but I was very interested to know about "Jealousy."

Merchant: Oh, "Jealousy," I think that's a really funny song. It's, I guess a lot of people think, out of character for me to write that song, but I think it's good to laugh at yourself sometimes, and I think jealousy's one of the most frustrating and laughable emotions I've ever had.

Wertheimer: Did it feel as good as you thought it would feel to be completely in charge of everything? You not only performed on it yourself as a musician as well as the singer, and wrote it, and produced it, you even paid for it.

Merchant: That was the scary part. I'd never had that kind of responsibility before, and some days I just wanted to just be the singer because I was also still writing the lyrics while I was also hiring people and booking studio time and talking to the accountant about the massive budget that was growing every day. And then other days I just felt like my confidence built. All the decisions that I had to make were decisions that would have been made by somebody, and it was a really great education to be involved in and I really feel like it's my record, now that it's done.

W hen *Billboard* magazine's Century Award went to the singer-songwriter JONI MITCHELL, few could quibble. From her debut album, *Song to a Seagull*, to her 1995 album, *Turbulent Indigo*, her poetic and penetrating lyrics have been part of the fabric of American life, whether about love and loss or social issues. A gifted painter as well a musician, Mitchell talked about her art and her life with Liane Hansen. May 28, 1995

Hansen: I know there's a danger in reading too much into a song, but when I first heard "Sunny Sunday" from the new album, *Turbulent Indigo*, as I was driving in my car, I wondered whether this woman that dodges the light like Blanche DuBois might be that same woman who woke up on a Chelsea morning and let the sun stream in like butterscotch and sticked to all her senses.

Mitchell: Well, you know, I think the danger is confusing art with the artist. The songs are really designed, and some are autobiographical and some are portraits. Even if they're sung in the first person, frequently they're portraits. So a lot is written from identification, much of this historically. The truth is, it's a portrait of a roommate of a friend of mine, a fellow that I paint with. But everything I write, I identify with. And then again too, in this particular art form, even with a portrait you can put someone else's eyes in it. You know, it's — like Gertrude Stein, Picasso's portrait of Gertrude Stein. He put his own eyes in it. She said, "It doesn't look like me," and he said, "You will." But I think the point of the songs — I object to a certain degree that the public is more fascinated by the artist than the art form itself, and I think that the people who get the most out of my music see themselves in it.

Hansen: I don't think I necessarily saw the woman as you, though. I just saw it as a character.

Mitchell: Yeah, it's a woman in a frustrated position, and so this is a portrait of a stuck woman who has set herself up this game, a target. You know, every once in a while she shoots at this streetlight. She always misses. You know, the day that she hits it is the day that change will occur in her life. That one little victory, that's all she needs, so it's kind of symbolic of *Waiting for Godot*. For change, you know.

Hansen: I also was thinking about it as I listened to it, and then I somehow got in the mind, I guess, the imagery of the sunlight and, you know, a young woman who embraces it and an older woman who sort of hides from it, and, I mean, do you think romantics grow up to be cynics?

Mitchell: Well, what was the song that dealt with that? "The Last Time I Saw Richard." One of the characters in that song says to the character that I play, you know, like, all romantics, you know, get that way, cynical and drunk and boring, someone in some dark café. You laugh. Look at your eyes, they're full of moons, right? So that character assumes that it's true, and frequently I'm called a cynic and usually by people who can't look at the truth. And there may be a tone when I'm delivering something that resembles cynicism, but a lot of times the things I'm saying when I'm called a cynic are factual. I'm reading a book on van Gogh right now, and much of his discourse is taking place also at the brink of a change of a millennium, and I wouldn't call anything he's saying cynicism, but it's more truth than most people can bite off. Basically, I relate to his frustration.

Hansen: Tell me how. I wondered if there was a comparison to be made.

Mitchell: In the world of painters, innovation and originality have always been criteria, whereas in the world of pop music copycatism is rewarded. They usually shoot the innovator. And it takes about two or three generations of copycats, and by the time they like it you've got a real watered-down kind of insipid thing going on. I kind of cut my ear off many a night over that.

Hansen: You are, I think, as well known for your visual art and the fact that you paint as you are for being a musician, and I wanted to know, do you approach a song like a painting?

Mitchell: I was always an artist. I was always the school artist, and I had a kind of precocious ability to render. And I was putting up drawings for a parent-teacher day in the sixth grade when one of the two great seventh-grade teachers came up to me, and said, "You like to paint?" And I said, "Yes." He said to me, "If you can paint with a brush, you can paint with words." Now, that is a tremen-

dous gift to give a young child. When I met Georgia O'Keeffe, she
was in her nineties, and she said to me, "Well, I would have liked to
have been a musician too, but you can't do both." And I said, "Oh
yes you can." And she leaned in on her elbows, and said, "Really?
You know, I would have liked to have played the violin." I said, you
know, "Well, take it up, Georgia," you know? I mean, you know,
start today, you know.

Hansen: Never too late from a yet-to-be-released album, "Cherokee Louise."

Mitchell: Yeah, it's a collaboration and kind of a fun song. I've
written a lot of songs over a period of years about the bridges in
Saskatoon, which is a city where I lived from the age of ten until
eighteen, when I left home. They call themselves the Paris of the
North. They even have kiosks like for posters on the streets, and it
is a cultured little city in northern Saskatchewan or the middle of
Saskatchewan. "Cherokee Louise" was written about the Broadway Bridge, and "Facelift," which is another song to be released,
was written about a view from the Bessborough Hotel looking at
several of the bridges. Two of them are concrete spans, and then
there's an old railroad bridge, an old metal bridge. And then there's
the grand trunk bridge, where I spent my youth. Well, I spent my
youth on all of these bridges. This is about the railroad bridge on a
stormy night.

Hansen: I love the image in that song, the train going by and
making so much noise that no one can hear these lovers' cries.

Mitchell: This is a song for people who live in an apartment
building. And the lyrics here are not mine. They are from a singer-
songwriter also from my hometown. I don't know all of the scene
there, but Donald Freed wrote the lyrics for the most part, and I set
it to music. I added a little bit just to fit into this structure.

Hansen: The sound of the train going through the night that
you're able to accomplish with only five strings on a guitar.

Mitchell: Yeah, five, because one of them was out of tune. Bad
guitar.

Hansen: I'm sure everyone's calling in because they noticed.

Mitchell: Van Gogh, you know, like, believed in the flawed art.

Hansen: There you go. Real-time, real-life sort of performing. Do
you find when you're writing that now — I mean, as you grow
older, do you find yourself sort of traveling back to, you know, the
home of your youth and things you remember about then?

Mitchell: More than ever, I think, you know, because my folks are getting old and also because of Donald, which gives me a friend in the community. You know, Donald and I, we shared so many peculiar things in common. It's an East Side–West Side town. He's a West Side boy. The history is different on the two towns. And I'm an East Side girl.

Hansen: Were you a rebellious one? I mean, out there sneaking cigarettes and such?

Mitchell: Oh yeah. Well, I started smoking at the age of nine. I had polio when I was nine, and when I got out of the hospital I kind of made a pact with my Christmas tree that if I could get my legs back, you know, that it was kind of — maybe it was God. I don't remember. At that time I'd broken away from the church because I loved stories and they had a lot of loopholes. If you asked the teacher about those loopholes like, OK, Adam and Eve were the first man and woman and they had two sons, Cain and Abel, and Cain killed Abel, then Cain got married. Who did he marry? You know, it did not go over well, and so I refused to go to church in the town for a while, but I had this debt to pay back because I did stand up, unfurl, and walk, you know? So I joined the church choir. And one night after choir practice in the middle of the winter a girl who had snitched a pack of Black Cat corks from her mother and we all sat in the wintry fish pond in the snow and passed them around, and some girls choked and some threw up, and I took one puff and felt really smart. I mean, I just thought, Whoa. You know, my head cleared up. I seemed to see better and think better. So I was a smoker from that day on, secretly, you know, covertly, and still smoking.

Hansen: Don't you worry about your voice?

Mitchell: No. I mean, it's gotten a little huskier, but I sounded like I was on helium when I was a girl. You know, it does thicken the cords. I think I like it better a little rough. My favorite singers' voices were a little rough. Billie Holiday at the end, I love her singing at the end. It's really all in knowing what you're singing about and the heart and spirit behind it, so if it gets a little frayed I think you can still get some beauty out of it.

Hansen: What wisdom do you think you've gotten with age?

Mitchell: Oh, I think that's a myth. I think that's a thing old people say. I think people are most intelligent at nineteen. Like Freud, for instance. I'm not a fan of Freud. The most intelligent thing I ever read that he said, he said when he was nineteen, and he said, "Dissection of personality is no way to self-knowledge." He just went on to get stupider. I mean, he's admired by intellectuals as if intellect was all there were, you know, to intelligence.

Hansen: It is funny when you tell that story about Georgia O'Keeffe, that you're the one telling her that she should go out and do what she wants to do.

Mitchell: Well, you never know who the messenger is going to be. Like, somebody's got to give you permission, especially in this culture, and it's true. If you can paint with a brush you can paint with words. If you're an observer and you're going to describe it. Look at van Gogh. His descriptions of what he wants to paint, what he did paint, are fantastic. They're every bit as artistic as the creations in a way. They move you in the same way. His writing gives me a lump in my throat and his painting gives me a lump in my throat. They're charged with his personal excitement.

Hansen: Well, I think a lot of people would say that they listen to your albums the same way. I mean, and I think your albums essentially have been created to be heard more than once.

Mitchell: Absolutely.

Hansen: There's a depth there, there's a breadth there, and one listening actually doesn't do it justice, you know. But you didn't have that in mind when you were creating it, you were creating what was best for you at the time.

Mitchell: Yeah. You know, at first the music was very sparse, and so I was called a folksinger. I haven't been a folksinger since 1964, and none of the songs on my records are folk songs, you know. They're more like German lieder or something in the beginning. They're more classical than folk. Primary colors is what folk art is made of. These are very sophisticated, broken colors. You know, you can't call it folk music. But it looks like folk music. So appearance in the pop world, it's appearance above content anyway.

Hansen: I think a lot of people still appreciate the fact that you will take on social issues in your music. In the newest album, for example, in "The Magdelene Laundries," you are commenting on domestic violence. You're still willing to get out there with a point of view.

Mitchell: Well, it's not so much willing. To create, you need a tailwind. I always have to work from a strong emotion, whatever that emotion might be, you know?

Hansen: Anger?

Mitchell: Yeah.

Hansen: Frustration?

Mitchell: It's only that that will drive you into this seclusion. Otherwise you'd just rather go out and party. For a long time I was, you know, too eclectic to belong. People usually don't like change. They don't like change, and in an artist it requires that they change too and, you know, either you like change or you don't. Most people don't.

Hansen: Well, welcome to public radio. Change and eclecticism are welcome here.

Mitchell: Oh, thank you. That's why we came.

THE WORLD

At a time when nationalist sentiment was rising in many formerly communist nations of Europe and Central Asia, NEAL ASCHERSON, a British journalist who wrote for many years with scholarly expertise about Poland and Eastern Europe, turned his attention farther east. In *Black Sea*, he explored the lands that border that body of water and the peoples who have lived there: Scythians and Sarmatians, Tatars, Karaites, Greeks and Goths, Russians, Ukrainians, some exiled Poles, and micronations, with such new, independent microstates as Abkhazia. As Ascherson told Robert Siegel, his inspiration for the book came from the role history played, both ancient and current, in his own family legend. October 26, 1995

Ascherson: My impression of the Black Sea, originally, was that my father used to tell me stories about it, because he was a midshipman. He was a very junior British naval officer at the time of the intervention in the Russian civil war between 1918 and 1920, and he served in the Black Sea, and he saw the final defeat of the White Armies. And he used to tell me about these legendary characters, whom he encountered and witnessed, like the great Denikin. He was always frankly in love with the place. Another reason was that because I spent most of my life writing about Central Europe, Eastern Europe, I slowly began to realize that the Black Sea is the kind of unspoken background to all that. It is the Mediterranean for East and Central and Northeast-Central Europe, as the Mediterranean is for the Latin countries, but nobody ever talked about it. So I was curious.

Siegel: It is a cradle of civilization. Does that sound right?

Ascherson: Yes, it's one of them. But it's the cradle of barbarism, as a matter of fact. It's the place where the term *barbarism* began, and where people invented this idea that there was, on the one hand, beautiful civilization, which is us, and on the other hand, frightful, degenerate, luxurious, overspending, cowardly, cruel barbarism, which is them. And this polarization about the other began on the Black Sea.

Siegel: The people who made that distinction, by and large, were Greeks, and this was part of the Greek world at the time.

Ascherson: Exactly. The Greek colonists got to the shores of the Black Sea, particularly the northern shores, in — nobody quite knows — it could have been the eighth or seventh century B.C. They lived quite happily with these totally different people. They were settled, agricultural kind of people. The characters they met there were nomadic, unsettled people, who were pastoralists, who wandered the great plains with their flocks and their herds and, indeed, lived in wagons. They didn't even have permanent homes. But then in the sixth century B.C., this idea was invented by the Athenian dramatists around the time of the Persian Wars that this difference wasn't just that some people are like this and some people are like that, but that it was the night and the day. It was a total moral distinction between one kind of people, who are like us, and others who are like the Persians who are invading Greece, or like the Scythians, who live on the Black Sea, and they are barbarians and they're darkness and evil and everything which we are not.

Siegel: Now, one of the fascinating stories about the people who live around the Black Sea is that of the Greeks, whose ancient history you have just described. They remained there all these centuries, and the Pontic Greeks lived on the shore of the Black Sea in modern-day Russia for centuries.

Ascherson: They are one of the most extraordinary examples of continuity, well, better said, imaginative continuity. The ancestors of the people who call themselves the Pontic Greeks left the Aegean Sea, the neighborhood of Greece, in let's say the seventh century B.C. They went to what's Anatolia. From there they went largely to the Caucasus and then into Russia. Then Stalin deported them into central Asia, and now very nearly three thousand years on these people out there in Kazakhstan say, "We want to go home." And what do they mean by home? They mean Athens, Greece.

Siegel: The point that your book makes over and over again is that the land remains the same, peoples come and go and civilizations change; some of them stay for a long time, but others join them. Yet you write about a theory that had dominated Soviet archaeology that said that there really is no such thing as migration.

Ascherson: You see, Stalin, when he allied himself particularly to old Russian nationalism, said "We don't want to think of ourselves, we Russians" — although he actually was a Georgian, of course — "we don't want to think of ourselves as having been created by inrushes of alien peoples from far off to the east, barbarians coming from the steppes, even by the Mongols; we are the Russians. All cultures started here." And so this extraordinary theory was born and migration was banned.

Siegel: You're saying not just that migration was banned, but that historical theorizing about migration and writing about migration were banned.

Ascherson: Absolutely. If you went on playing with migration theory and saying that incoming Scandinavians formed the first Russian state or that the Tatars arrived from central Asia and made this advanced civilization in southern Russia and Crimea, you went to a labor camp or worse in the old days.

Siegel: Toward the end of the your book *Black Sea,* you write a little sermon about nationalism, about the stories that peoples invent for themselves and the truths that the historian and the archaeologist discover about those peoples. What is the lesson that you would like most to impart about that?

Ascherson: Well, the lesson could sound cynical, but it is not meant to be. A great deal of what nations say about their origins in particular is nonsense. It's fraudulent. It's made up. It's a kind of patchwork of half-truths and half-invented things, things selected and rearranged to make a noble past, which makes national independence in our own time inevitable. There is a great deal of myth in it. The fact that you can ascertain, as deconstructing historians nowadays love to point out, that some nation's version of its own history is errant nonsense does not mean that the nation is not authentic. If people believe in themselves in that way and believe in their common past in this way, that's real. It is real even though in a literal sense it's based on full foundations of falsity. What is absolutely wrong, I think, is for historians to truckle under, and say, "Oh, well, if they all believe it, then of course we had better be quiet and not point out that it's nonsense." There is a middle position, which is the ideal one, and that is to say, "Yes, I believe in our country. Yes, I believe we should be independent and proud of ourselves. But all the same, we don't have to be proud of ourselves by lying about our own history. Let's tell the truth about it, even if it isn't always creditable."

B y the time that the Dayton Peace Accords were signed, it was estimated that as many as 250,000 people died in the war in Bosnia and two million people became refugees as a result of it. The Dayton agreement was an occasion for hope that the war was finally over. MISHA GLENNY, author of *The Fall of Yugoslavia,* had covered the Balkan conflict from the beginning, both as a journalist and as a scholar. Glenny told Noah Adams that he had never expected the war among the Serbs, Croats, and Muslims to last so long. November 21, 1995

Glenny: We all knew that it was going to be bloody beyond belief. What the actual consequences would be in terms of the number of people dead and things like that, we couldn't foresee. At the time, what was interesting was that, talking to diplomats outside of the former Yugoslavia, talking to policy analysts, talking to editors, newspapers, from BBC, the radio where I worked, at the time they all thought that those of us who were warning against this type of carnage were stark, raving bonkers.

Adams: Let me ask you just briefly for a comment about all three parties to the Dayton agreement. Is Franjo Tudjman's Croatia a winner in this situation now?

Glenny: No doubt about it. I have to take my hat off to Tudjman. He understood that when the Serbs and Croats went to war inside Yugoslavia, that if he was going to gain his war aims he couldn't do it by relying on the number of Croats, almost twice as few as there are Serbs, and he couldn't do it on the amount of weapons at his disposal. Either brutal calculation of force inside Yugoslavia left him obviously a loser. He understood that. So instead of that, he anticipated that if this became a bloody war, it would be internationalized. So from the very beginning of this period, he started courting the Germans as a powerful, solid, and reliable international ally. That was enormously important, particularly when President Slobodan Milosevic of Serbia, who had all those advantages to begin with — more Serbs, more weapons — went the other way and chose the worst ally he possibly could, which was the Communist party of the Soviet Union. This was when the war started in June 1991. He lined up with the hard-liners in Moscow, who then collapsed in August 1991 after Milosevic had set up all sorts of deals with them. As soon as the coup against Gorbachev happened in Moscow, Milosevic and the Serbian government came out and welcomed the coup, which meant that Milosevic had earned the undying hatred of Boris Yeltsin at the very beginning of this war. So even though the Russians have supported the Serbs in a limited fashion, there is no love lost between Moscow and Belgrade, not to mention Moscow and Pale. Milosevic got it wrong, and as a consequence Franjo Tudjman is able to clean up. Bosnian President Alija Izetbegovic's greatest tragedy is that he decided to go for the option of war without any means to prosecute a war. As a consequence, his people were trashed. He should not take primary responsibility, but Izetbegovic carries a very important secondary responsibility for the fate of this people.

Adams: And the Bosnian Serbs? Did they overreach, do you think?

Glenny: Well, they were encouraged, first of all, by Milosevic. I mean, let's make it perfectly clear that in both the case of the Croatian Serbs and the Bosnian Serbs, Milosevic initially sacrificed the interests of the Serbian people in those areas for a mendacious desire for more territory. He sacrificed people for territory. He realized he had made that mistake and so he had to pay the consequences, which is allowing the destruction of the Serbian community in Croatia and insisting that the Bosnian Serbs roll back. Radovan Karadzic, leader of the Bosnian Serbs, saw this as a weakness, and for a long time was trying to use his relative strength inside Bosnia-Hercegovina in order to topple Milosevic. He simply was not strong enough to do that and that's why Karadzic is now utterly out of the game. Not only is there the provision in the agreement that he won't be allowed to hold political office because he is charged with war crimes, but he's lost the political game within Serbdom and he's now history.

Adams: When you look at the peace map and look ahead, past the wintertime, after the implementation forces get there, do you see a peaceful Bosnia a year from now, two years from now?

Glenny: Well, this will depend crucially on the mandate that is

I n order to send American peacekeepers to Bosnia, President Clinton needed to sell the American people on a mission that ran counter to popular sentiment. At the core of the plan to end the conflict was a line on a map, a political line drawn to keep warring peoples apart. On one side of the line were the Bosnian Serbs, on the other a federation of Bosnian Croats and Muslims. As former undersecretary general of the United Nations for special political affairs, BRIAN URQUHART saw many lines drawn in his time. He discussed the Bosnia agreement with Liane Hansen. November 26, 1995

Urquhart: I think it's the best that could be achieved at the moment, and the question really is whether there's a possibility of integration again in Bosnia or whether they were simply laying down lines on a map to try to keep the different ethnic groups from each other. It seems to me the trouble with this is that everything in our society really goes in the other direction, goes in the direction of integrating different groups, of mixing them up, of people not living in isolated groups of one sort or another. And so what this really does is to put in a frame the historical rivalry between the different groups in the former Yugoslavia.

Hansen: Have you seen this before when these kinds of lines have been drawn on, you know, strictly ethnic differences?

Urquhart: There have been lines drawn all over the place. Sometimes they were drawn as, for example, with the European colonies in Africa in total disregard of ethnic and tribal differences with disastrous consequences. It's the great problem in the United Nations. You have yesterday's politics pursuing tomorrow's problems and you have a mess as a result. It was very frustrating. My own feeling is that somehow or other the human race is going to have to get past this if it's going to have a reasonably stable future because with communications, with travel, with migration, with the circulation of ideas and so on, the sort of reality of absolutely isolated particular groups is becoming less and less valid, it seems to me. I think the interesting thing is that since the cold war ended you had two trends. One is, in places like Europe where you've had a kind of integration trend, and that's by no means complete yet. And then you have the rise of intense nationalistic feelings or ethnic feelings in quite a large number of places where they had been more or less quiet before. And that is really the source of most of the problems which the world is now trying rather ineffectively to deal with. The question really to me is whether you can solve these problems better by trying to put the genie back in the bottle and draw firm lines and then try to enforce them, which is now what they're going to try to do in Bosnia, or whether you have to try to start building bridges between the different groups and seeing if you can't really encourage a process of integration.

Hansen: But who should build these bridges if not the United Nations?

Urquhart: I think the United Nations ought to be organized to do that better. I've been advocating for a long time that the UN take the old Trusteeship Council, which has worked itself out of a job, and convert it into a sort of council of diversity in governments, which deals with all the groups in the world which aren't nation-states, and tries to give them an airing, tries to give them a hearing in the outside world and a way to discuss their problems away from the extremely sweaty, overheated atmosphere of the local conflict. Nobody seems to want to do that, and I think governments are very nervous about it, but it seems to me something like that ought to be done because otherwise these things are going to go on sort of burning underground and then suddenly break out the way they have done now.

Hansen: You pardon me saying so, Mr. Urquhart, but you seem very pessimistic about all of this.

Urquhart: No, I'm not pessimistic. I'm not very optimistic either. I would be much more optimistic if I thought that in our much-vaunted democracies we were getting used to the idea of taking long-term views of things and even adopting programs which ostensibly at the moment are quite unpopular. I think that the quick fix and the short-term solution are very much the name of the game at the moment, to catch up to the next election or whatever it is. And that's true of all countries, and I think this is bad.

Hansen: Give us some examples of what you mean, what governments could be doing to look more toward the future.

Urquhart: More than a quarter of the world's people live well below the poverty line, and with the communications revolution they know exactly what everybody has got and they haven't. That's an extremely unstable situation. And it does seem to me that governments should take a whole look at the economic balance in the world and how you can conceivably make it a little bit more equitable and produce a situation where whole continents don't simply fall behind, as Africa has now done. That would be a tremendous investment in the future. It's very unfashionable because it doesn't produce immediate dividends, it doesn't produce big results for the next election. It might even cost money. But it does seem to me that's the kind of thing that needs to be done.

W hen the fighting stopped in Bosnia, there remained millions of land mines, an estimated three to six million deadly seeds waiting to explode. They posed the greatest danger to both civilians and troops. Eliminating that danger was the task of de-miners, people whose work is as hazardous, as potentially deadly, as it is vital for the restoration of peace. BOB KEELEY had been working as a UN de-miner in the former Yugoslavia when he told Susan Stamberg about his experiences. December 16, 1995

Keeley: One of the obvious questions I'm asked, one of the hardest to answer: it's not like it is on the films. There's none of this cut the red wire or the blue wire, and mines don't go *click* when you stand on them and you're not required to put a pin in afterward. I'm afraid Hollywood and other organizations like it do a great disservice. Mine clearance is a strange thing and is actually incredibly tedious most of the time because it's all those worst garden chores that you always put off being repeated day after day. It actually requires a man on his knees with what amounts to a sharp pointed stick, poking into the ground ahead of him very carefully at an angle of about thirty degrees. He feels for a discontinuity in the soil, and every time he feels an object, he might pass a mine detector over it to — to see if he can detect metal. But ultimately he has to dig that object up with a — with a very small implement like a garden trowel or even his hands. Then he has to deal with it accordingly. But most of the time he's on his belly in the mud, keeping very bored, and it's not at all the glamorous type job that it's made to be in the films.

Stamberg: Just dangerous and boring. But in Bosnia now, the scale of this is so daunting, three to six million land mines. What would it take to clear the entire country?

Keeley: In some ways, Bosnia is comparatively easy because the people that have laid these mines have laid them in a certain manner, and we have, if you like, a zone of contamination along the former confrontation lines. Mines aren't scattered at random through the country in the way that they are in, say, Afghanistan or Cambodia. And so that means that we can at least narrow it down. But we narrow it down to a strip of about five thousand square kilometers, and if only one percent of the area is mined, our estimate is it will take a thousand land-mine clearers thirty-three years to clear Bosnia of land mines. We are not going to do this before the American army turns up. But that doesn't mean that all of your soldiers are going to come home in body bags or wheelchairs because there's a lot of people taking a lot of effort to solve the deployment issue of American and NATO soldiers. Having said that, three million or so land mines is a problem, and people get very impatient when they hear that it takes one mine clearer half an hour to clear a square meter of ground. Mine technology has improved much better than the mine clearance technology that we use to clear them.

Stamberg: I'm very curious to know how they were able to plant so many land mines in the first place.

Keeley: Land mines are very, very simple devices, and anybody with a few minutes training could put a mine in place. And it's a completely different skill, unfortunately, laying mines to clearing them. And one of the misconceptions we have is people imagine that clearing land mines is just the reverse process of putting them there in the first place, and it's not.

Stamberg: Tell us a story from your own experience, Mr. Keeley, on the ground, in the mud, clearing mines.

Keeley: Well, I tell you one situation springs to mind. In Tuzla Air Base, which we were working on. I was actually in charge of the construction project as an engineer at the time, and we had two mine clearance teams working for us. I asked one of the mine clearance teams working for me to clear a piece of ground so that we could build some accommodation units on the ground. The locals, who worked there for us on the air base, thought we were mad because they had been walking over this piece of ground for a long time. But we found one mine by an apple tree. The locals came up to us afterward and what was quite nice actually was they apologized because they thought we were being stupid. One of the departing Yugoslav army people had left one land mine by the bottom of one apple tree. There it could have sat for a hundred years. They're plastic; nothing can go wrong with them. And this mine would have just sat there waiting as a revenge message.

JODI COBB, a *National Geographic* photographer, got a look inside a uniquely Japanese institution. She had the chance to slip behind the rice paper doors, where geishas do their entertaining, and photograph them. The result was the book *Geisha,* which illustrates what happens when Japan's male elite and their geishas get together. Cobb told Daniel Zwerdling how the evening unfolds. November 19, 1995

Cobb: The men will arrive, and the geisha will be there, and they will take their shoes off for them, put the slippers on, or leave them in their bare feet. They'll seat them at these tables. They'll be kneeling on the floor. The geisha will help them from their coats, and it will all be very stiff and formal.

Zwerdling: Where is "there?" Is this a special house?

Cobb: Oh, tea houses or restaurants. There are several geisha districts left in Kyoto, in Tokyo, and that's probably the only place where you'll really find true geisha entertainment.

Zwerdling: OK, so I'm kneeling now on the tatami mat.

Cobb: And you'll probably be on one of those little chairs that are sort of like stadium chairs, so you don't have to spend your time on your knees. The geisha will be on their knees, and interestingly enough, they have sort of calluses on the top of their feet, from where the top of their feet have rubbed against that sort of rough tatami for so many years. But the men will sprawl a little bit more on these little stadium chairs, and the function of a geisha, then, will be to get the party going. It's probably going to be a business obligation that will be fulfilled.

Zwerdling: You mean a business meeting, we're negotiating a deal?

Cobb: It'll be business or government officials or something, and this is where a lot of their actual business gets done. So the sake will be poured and consumed very, very quickly.

Zwerdling: Get them a little looser.

Cobb: Right, and then everybody really loosens up, and then they'll start playing party games, like rock, scissors, and paper, to get people to drink even faster.

Zwerdling: You mean the sort of silly party games we played when we were in junior high school?

Cobb: Well, to me, it was a fraternity party. That's all I could think of at these events. One of them ended up with the men playing a little strip game, a baseball strip game, you know, and sort of clothes flying around the room.

Zwerdling: These are the rich and powerful of Japan. And then?

Cobb: And then the door will slide open and a gorgeous geisha, dressed in full traditional costume of the formal kimono, the black wig, the very white face, will come in and do a beautiful dance, and there will be a geisha strumming a samisen, which is like a banjo, a three-string musical instrument, and she'll be playing that.

Zwerdling: One of the things that really struck me in your book was that these geishas are trained in all sorts of traditional arts and that they need to study these traditional instruments and traditional songs, right?

Cobb: Right. Well, the word *geisha* means "art person" or "person of talent," and their place in Japanese society is sort of the guardian of the highest of Japanese traditional cultural arts now, and they will study the arts of dance, of samisen, tea ceremony, calligraphy, and conversation. But their biggest skill is sort of pampering the male ego.

Zwerdling: I also found this surprising, and I'm not sure I believe it. You say that the men you talked to claim, and that's your word, *claim*, that what they appreciate most about geishas is their art of conversation.

Cobb: In fact, they pride themselves on that, and it's how they emerged in history in a very poor and rural country. Most people were not educated then. Especially women were not educated. Marriages were arranged for them, and they stayed home for the rest of their lives, raising their children. They did not socialize outside the home with their husbands, and even though they are educated now, they still do not socialize outside the home. So it was in their role of society hostess that the geishas originally were the entertainers for the courtesans in the brothels of the pleasure quarters.

Zwerdling: So if I'm the madam for a bunch of geishas, I actually make sure that my geishas know what's going on in the world and read the newspapers so they can talk about it?

Cobb: Right.

Zwerdling: I would imagine that a lot of listeners right now are thinking, OK, Jodi Cobb, but you have not told us what also inevitably goes on. Sex, they're thinking, right? Aren't geishas basically, let's be crass about it, highly paid prostitutes?

Cobb: That's a conception in the West, and probably a misconception. The first thing most Japanese will tell you is that that's a misconception we have here in the West. They will tell you that if a geisha does provide sex, it is usually as part of an enduring relationship or purely at her discretion.

Zwerdling: Really? So at the typical party where geishas are present and they are strumming their samisens, and singing traditional songs, I cannot, as a guest there, expect that I can sleep with one of them if I want to?

Cobb: Oh, no. Absolutely not.

Zwerdling: On the other hand, you do have a picture in the book of a group of young men sitting on tatami mats. There are beer and sake glasses all over, and there's a geisha sitting next to them, strumming one of these traditional instruments, but all of the men are looking into another room, where they see a geisha kneeling on the floor at the feet of a very naked young man.

Cobb: Oh, that was just a game. That was a strip game, and the geisha never loses on those strip games because she's still pulling out hairpins, you know, by the time he's had his tie off and his shirt off. There's sort of five articles of clothing, and she's still pulling out hairpins.

Zwerdling: OK, so it's the end of the evening, everybody's about to go home. How much do the geishas get? How much do I pay for this evening?

Cobb: Well, a geisha party can cost about ten thousand dollars for maybe five guests.

Zwerdling: Who's getting rich? Is it the geishas?

Cobb: The cost of doing these is enormous. A kimono can cost twenty thousand dollars and up. A well-dressed geisha would have maybe twenty or more kimonos in her closet. It's a source of pride for her to be beautifully presented.

Zwerdling: So essentially what a geisha evening is for me, as a rich and powerful Japanese politician or businessman, is almost going back in time, right? I'm buying myself a little island of tranquillity and artfulness from the geishas.

Cobb: That's what their life is — selling dreams, creating this fantasy life, this fantasy world, for the men, to take them out of their own time and space, out of their daily grind, into this world of exclusivity and privacy and another century.

For the first time since the end of the war in Indochina, a Vietnamese ambassador represented his country in Washington in 1995. Ambassador LE VAN BANG set up diplomatic shop in an office building a few blocks from the White House. When Daniel Zwerdling dropped by a week after Bang's arrival, the new ambassador was greeting a delegation of Vietnamese Americans just in from California, the receptionist was fielding calls from Americans eager to do business in Vietnam, and Zwerdling and crew were ushered into a room with plush black leather couches where tea was served in white china cups. February 12, 1995

Bang: We, you know, just arrive here so everything is still, you know, in disorder, so please excuse us.

Zwerdling: But you've done a very nice job. You have all these arrangements of beautiful flowers.

Bang: Thank you.

Zwerdling: Who sent them?

Bang: Some of the companies and some Vietnamese Americans, you know, they send flowers every day now.

Zwerdling: When you first came here, what struck you about the United States?

Bang: The people. When you talk to Americans, I think that they are friendly, straightforward, you know, open-minded, so I love to talk to them that way.

Zwerdling: You found Americans are open-minded.

Bang: Yes, yes.

Zwerdling: And that surprised you.

Bang: Yes, yeah.

Zwerdling: Did you think Americans would be angry toward the Vietnamese because of the war?

Bang: Yes, that's it. But here I don't find it that way.

Zwerdling: What preconceptions do you think many Vietnamese people have about the United States still that you have found to be untrue?

Bang: If you talk about United States in Vietnam, you might talk more about the violence, the crime rate and the use of guns, the protests about abortion, about the gays, what is on the news every day in Vietnam, you know.

Zwerdling: So the Vietnamese, everybody seems to think that Americans are always shooting each other or having abortions, or that everyone's homosexual?

Bang: They don't have a balance of information, so they might think that way.

Zwerdling: As you know, over the past week there have been some small protests in front of this building by people who charge that the Vietnamese government has not been completely honest with the United States about what happened to some of the American soldiers who were missing in action or who were prisoners of war. And there still are quite a few Americans who feel a lot of anger about what happened during the Vietnam War. If we go to Vietnam, will we find that there are many Vietnamese who bear anger toward the United States because of what happened during the war?

Bang: I think that now if you are going to Vietnam, you can be welcome by Vietnamese anywhere, especially if you are telling them that you are Americans. Then you will be most welcome. So we change almost totally the attitude of the Vietnamese people.

Zwerdling: I have to say I find that hard to believe completely. Many Americans have family members who died in the Vietnam War, and so they still feel a lot of pain about the war.

Bang: I see.

Zwerdling: It's hard to imagine that in Vietnam that all the families that also lost family members do not still feel some bitterness or pain.

Bang: I must say that this is our history because of the two thousand or three thousand years of history of Vietnam and, you know, that in Vietnam we have wars with many countries — with China, with Thailand, with Cambodia, and lately we have a war with France, with the Japanese, and then with you and China again. So the war between Vietnam and United States is a short one, so we can easily forget and go on.

Zwerdling: Really? So you're saying in the Vietnamese psyche, the war with the United States was not that big a deal?

Bang: No, no, not a big one, not a big one.

Zwerdling: Although you did not fight in the war, I understand that your family did have members who fought who died.

Bang: Yes, I think that I have two relatives in my generation, by marriage. One lost a leg and he still gets around and I have to help him.

Zwerdling: Because he still is —

Bang: Yeah, he has, you know, difficulty in making a living.

Zwerdling: Because he lost his leg during the war?

Bang: That's it, that's it.

Zwerdling: And do you have any residue of bad feelings toward the United States about the war?

Bang: No, no, no, I have not, and my feeling is that I should go on to friendship between the two countries and have no residue of the bad feeling.

Zwerdling: Are you going to have any time to have fun in the United States? Are you going to see any movies, for example?

Bang: Yes, sometime I go to movie and go to opera in New York, you know?

Zwerdling: What's your favorite these days?

Bang: Movie, Clint Eastwood, my hero.

Zwerdling: Clint Eastwood is your hero?

Bang: Yes, yes, sure, I love him.

Chinese dissident and human rights activist HARRY WU spent more than nineteen years in China's prisons before escaping to the United States. In June 1995, Wu, then a naturalized U.S. citizen, made a daring trip back to China to document his claims of human rights abuses in Chinese labor camps. While there, he was found out, arrested, and incarcerated for more than two months until his release under diplomatic pressure from Washington. Daniel Zwerdling asked Harry Wu about his detention and about the psychological tactics his captors used. August 27, 1995

Wu: I was watched over by three police guards, twenty-four hours. The room is three-by-four square meters. So it means in the two meters distance I have police.

Zwerdling: You mean they weren't just looking at you through a window, but they were with you in the room?

Wu: No, with me, even when I go to shower. Even when I go to bathroom, even when I'm eating, even when I'm sleeping, twenty-four hours.

Zwerdling: I'm completely astonished that you somehow managed to keep a secret diary.

Wu: That's to confirm my nineteen years' experience. I do various more pieces and very secretly. They discover once. They took it away, but I still succeed. I got something.

Zwerdling: But did they see you writing things down?

Wu: Sometime as I'm writing, I pose like I'm study English and using the dictionary, you know. I know that they checking all my writing all the time.

Zwerdling: So you would be looking like you were reading, secretly scribbling.

Wu: Yes.

Zwerdling: And in what?

Wu: In the, you know, in the dictionary in the end of the paper is more places you can hidden over there, and mix my secret code in somewhere.

Zwerdling: Do you have that dictionary with you right now? Could you read something from it that you wrote in secret?

Wu: Yes. Hold on, I turn the page. This is page 710. That means, 710 mean July tenth.

Zwerdling: So you would pick pages based on the month and the date?

Wu: Yes. And this is the day they took away my marriage ring. [*reading*] "Afternoon — 3:15 to 3:45, a new officer come to question me. I ask to mail a family letter, but not allow."

Zwerdling: You asked to send a family letter, but you were not allowed.

Wu: Yeah. In the sixty-six days, I never receive anything from family.

Zwerdling: Speaking of your family, I've read that you forced yourself not to think about your family, not to think about your wife, and that surprised me because I would think that in prison one strategy for keeping sane would be to think about my family in great detail so that I could feel close to them.

Wu: No. For me is no. Because one thing that really can destroy me is if I fall into thinking my family, my wife, and then cause me crying. I don't want to let the police guard saw my tears running.

Zwerdling: So what did you focus on minute to minute?

Wu: I try to memorize my boyhood, my school time, all that. When I was a child and I was captain of the baseball team. The time I was in the labor camps, in for nineteen years, are small pieces played like a movie in front of me, one by one by one.

Zwerdling: So you lived in the past but not in the present?

Wu: Yes. Because I don't have future. I don't know what's going to happen to me.

Zwerdling: Now, this whole incident, your captivity and the way the U.S. and the Chinese officials responded, raises some interesting and, I think, some complicated questions about the nature of political protests and about the moral and ethical rules of protest. For instance, you have cheerfully acknowledged that you confessed to the Chinese, you basically told them what they wanted to hear, right? But you did not mean a word of it. You lied to them.

Wu: Yes. Let me tell you, OK? Why should I be honest with the liars? They lie to me. I have the right to lie to them. Deal with the men, deal with them, as they deal with you.

Zwerdling: This is a difficult question for me because I can't even imagine being in prison for a day. But what do you say to all those political dissidents throughout history who have endured torture, gone to their deaths in some cases because they insisted on telling only the truth. They said if you lie to your captors, you're stooping to their own level and then you become as morally tarnished as your captors are.

Wu: I think it's a very different situation, depend on different country, different culture. This is my way, particularly in Chinese, under Chinese communist power. They knew me. The police say, "I don't believe you, you will come back." They repeat many times, "I don't believe you, you will come back." And, yes, I will come back.

Zwerdling: So it's almost as if you're playing chess with each other and everybody knows what the rules are.

Wu: Yes.

Zwerdling: When you went back to China early last month, you knew that you were taking a big risk.

Wu: Yes.

Zwerdling: Your friends had even warned you not to go back because they were so sure you might be arrested. Were you frightened when you went back to China this time?

Wu: Of course I am frightened.

Zwerdling: Knowing, though, how risky a trip this was, how do you feel now about the fact that in fact this risky mission did end up badly, although not as badly as it might have because you're alive? But how do you feel about the fact that it did end up causing U.S. leaders so much time and trouble and might have even damaged relations between the two countries?

Wu: Well, I don't think my activities have damaged the relations. The relations between two countries depend on many, many things, OK? But basically the human rights violation is a serious problem in China, not only a single person or single case. "Shall we forget about it, only focus on one single person, Harry Wu?"

Zwerdling: You say you told your captors that you were going to go back to China. Are you really?

Wu: China is the place I born and I raise. In that piece of land, I have my tears, I have my blood, have my parents is grave over there. My former inmates, my people, is over there. This my land,

SHIMON PERES negotiated with the Palestinian leader Yasir Arafat as Israel's foreign minister before succeeding the assassinated Yitzhak Rabin as prime minister. In the United States to meet with U.S. officials and to discuss his memoir, Peres talked with Robert Siegel about, among other things, the lobbying campaign by the American supporters of his political opponents, the Likud party, to have Washington move the U.S. embassy in Israel from Tel Aviv to Jerusalem. All Israeli governments have insisted that Jerusalem, seat of the parliament, is the country's capital. Nearly all foreign governments have embassies in Tel Aviv and regard moving them to Jerusalem as a provocative act in the eyes of the Palestinians and other Arab governments. May 30, 1995

Peres: I think the Likud is committing a mistake. You can have a divided opinion back home, but you cannot have two foreign representatives abroad. I don't think that it is proper for the Likud to get itself involved, something which is not necessarily part of the Israeli foreign policy. They shouldn't approach senators or American members of the administration. As far as we are concerned, Jerusalem is the capital of Israel, no regret. Jerusalem as the capital of Israel is inviting everybody to build its embassies there. But we must be careful and responsible in the way we are handling our relations with such a friendly country like the United States of America.

Siegel: But what would be wrong? Is the government now, your own government, in the awkward position of saying that even though Israel has always insisted that Jerusalem is its capital, that actually you accept the idea that it would be considered provocative if, in fact, the U.S. were to move its embassy to Jerusalem?

Peres: No, we didn't say anything like it. What we are saying is that we are not going to become a party in the American debate concerning Jerusalem.

Siegel: To read your recollections of so many years of diplomacy on behalf of Israel, it's clear what we've always known, that you have a remarkable rapport and respect for King Hussein of Jordan. It's not at all clear that you hold Chairman Arafat of the PLO in any similar esteem. And I wonder right now how you would appraise Mr. Arafat's performance as leader of the Palestinian authority over the past year or so?

Peres: Well, clearly, I know King Hussein for a good many years. I know him actually since 1974. We have reached an agreement in London in 1987 that if it would be implemented the whole situation in the Middle East would be different. I think he's a man of grace, of responsibility, and I have much respect for him. I think he won over even the hearts of most of the Israeli people. Now, about Chairman Arafat, let me say one thing. In real political terms, you should never judge a person psychologically. I don't know if there's any measurement of an objective nature when it comes to psychology. You should judge a leader on his record. To be honest and straightforward, Arafat is the first Palestinian in this century that has decided to renounce violence and terror and attempts to destroy Israel and went over to negotiate in a dialogue peacefully. In all of those very long nights of negotiations we have had, he told me, "You know, I was admired like Muhammad. Now look what's happening to me because of you. They are throwing my pictures to pieces. I am no longer as popular." I told him, "Mr. Chairman, the Palestinian people in this century were led by two leaders. One was the grand mufti of Jerusalem, who led the Palestinians for forty-three years. You followed him, and you led your people for twenty-six years. In those years, you were popular because you were negative, because you said no on every subject, because you killed some people, and you raised admiration. Now tell me, what did you bring to your own people by your popularity? What did you win by their applause? They were thrown out of their places. Many were killed. Many became refugees. You are perfect when you say no. You become imperfect and controversial when you say yes. So maybe you lost your popularity, but your people gained. For the first time, they have a geographic address. They have a real authority. They have a hope. They return to history. So if really you want to serve your people, don't look just for applause, look for hard choices of a real nature."

Siegel: And what did Mr. Arafat say back to you after you told him that?

Peres: Oh, he says, "Democracy was invented. It is so tiring. You have to go from place to place and from meeting to meeting." I told him, "Well, it's tiring, but other alternatives are hopeless."

Siegel: How committed are you really to democracy for the Palestinians? If there is an election soon, it is at least conceivable that Arafat supporters could lose it and you could be dealing with somebody from Hamas, if not this year, a year or two down the road? Are you willing to do that?

Peres: We are willing, but why should Hamas go to elections if they want to destroy peace and they want to destroy Israel? Why should they be elected? What for? Now, if they will go for elections in order to be elected and conduct peace, then they will no longer be what they are today. It is either you use your ballot or you use your bullet. You cannot use both of them at the same time.

Siegel: I'd like to go back to just one other subject, 1987, which you mentioned earlier. As you said, in 1987 you negotiated a peace agreement with King Hussein of Jordan, actually in London at the home of a mutual friend.

Peres: Yes.

Siegel: You were foreign minister within a government of national unity, and in the end that agreement was rejected by Israel's prime minister, Yitzhak Shamir, who was of the other party.

Peres: Right.

Siegel: Now, you've had to do some explaining in that chapter of your memoir about how George Shultz, the U.S. secretary of state at the time, has recollected things differently. He seems to think that you were free-lancing as foreign minister and negotiating without the authority of your cabinet.

Peres: Well, you know, the national unity government was made up fifty-fifty, so I didn't have really to report to Shamir, though he was the prime minister.

Siegel: You mean, fifty percent of Labor, fifty of Likud.

Peres: Yes, and I had a full right to do what I was doing. Actually, before I flew secretly to meet the king, I informed Mr. Shamir. When I flew I didn't know that we would reach an agreement. The United States was fully in the picture. When I returned, I informed Mr. Shamir about the agreement we had reached, and he, without my knowledge, sent an envoy to Mr. Shultz to tell him not to intervene in what he called an internal problem of Israel. It was not an internal problem for Israel, it was a matter of death and life because if he would have really implemented the agreement at that time we would save hundreds of lives. We would have averted the Intifada and we would see already a different Middle East a long time ago.

Siegel: Do you really think that if such an agreement had been approved by Yitzhak Shamir and if the U.S. had stood up and tried to promote that agreement, that Israel could have avoided dealing altogether with the PLO and Yasir Arafat, or was it inevitable, that you would at some point have to confront the Palestinians through their own leadership?

Peres: You know, we would have peace with the Jordanians and, following that, peace with the Palestinians. I think it would be better for all parties to have it that way than to have it the way we are having now; namely, first with the Palestinians and then with the Jordanians. The fact is that the things that we have agreed in London in 1987 were realized right now and it produces wonders. Both parties are happy and content. So it is a theory that is being now tested in practice.

....

I n the midst of a ten-day visit to the United States, the
DALAI LAMA, the spiritual and political leader of Tibetan Buddhists, spoke with Robert Siegel about his people
and the quest for peace. The Dalai Lama has lived in exile in
India since 1959, when China occupied Tibet. Born in 1935,
he was identified at the age of two as the fourteenth incarnation of the Lord of Compassion. As a Buddhist monk, he
counsels nonviolence, a stance that earned him the Nobel
Peace Prize in 1989. As the leader of a nation subjected to
documented, systematic human rights abuses, he has sought
throughout his life to maintain and later restore some measure of autonomy, if not outright independence, for the Tibetan people. He visited Washington, in part, to talk with
members of Congress about relations with China, which he
says are at a turning point. September 11, 1995

Dalai Lama: My basic feeling is that China must enter mainstream of world community and mainstream of world democracy.
That is not only interest for world, but Chinese people themselves
want. So, now, in that respect I feel the close relationship between
U.S. and China is very essential.

Siegel: Some Americans will find it surprising to hear you, as the
leader of Tibetans, say that there should be a close relationship
between the United States and China. Many of those who are dis-
turbed by Chinese violations of human rights think now is the
time to say, "Let's not have such close relations with China."

Dalai Lama: Of course, at the emotional level sometimes we do
feel some more hostile attitude toward China. That is not realis-
tic. In real sense, that after all, my basic fundamental belief is
any human conflict or problem should be solved through negotiation and dialogue. In order to produce meaningful results through
dialogue, the two parties should have some kind of closer understanding.

Siegel: Many people are moved by the plight of the Tibetans, the violations of your people's human rights. But many don't know what to make of a system in which leadership is determined in the traditional Tibetan fashion. How do you reconcile a belief in democracy with a system of leadership that derives from a religious belief in the reincarnation of the Dalai Lama, the Panchen Lama, or other lamas? How do these two things make sense together?

Dalai Lama: The institution of the Dalai Lama as well as Panchen Lama is historically a purely spiritual or religious matter. The Dalai Lama is only since the fifth Dalai Lama now involved in political leadership.

Siegel: How long ago was that, when you say since the fifth Dalai Lama?

Dalai Lama: About three hundred years.

Siegel: Three hundred years.

Dalai Lama: Now, you see my position is that of the old system. Even as early as 1969 in one of my official statements, I stated whether the institution of Dalai Lama remains, continues, or not will be decided by the wishes of the Tibetan people. I state it. Then, about four years ago, I made one statement, official statement. In it I stated as soon as we return to Tibet with freedom, then I will set up an interim government. Then that government, I will hand it all my legitimate authority. Then I will no longer be head of Tibetan government.

Siegel: So in your incarnation you see radically reforming the way in which Tibet is governed. Your country is accused by the Chinese of being a feudal system. "Well, not anymore" is what I hear you say.

Dalai Lama: Right. I mean, times are always changing politically. In the Buddhist doctrine, the impermanence is one of the key philosophical factors. So, therefore, we have to act according to that philosophy. After all, I'm making the distinction — the institutional Dalai Lama may cease, but the Tibetan nation, Tibetan culture, Tibetan civilization, will remain.

Siegel: Well, I want to ask you just a bit before I go not about China or about your mission here, but about your sense of world peace and your sense of what lessons the world might learn right now that might enhance world peace.

Dalai Lama: Now, peace is everywhere, you see. We always we hear peace, peace, peace. Now, my thinking, we should have two programs. A long-term program and a temporary program. Now, for the immediate, the idea is demilitarization, step-by-step. We should aim for the complete ban of nuclear weapons. Then we should have some effective check on the arms trade and eventually we should abolish it. Then, long-term program, we must make every effort to promote human compassion, make clear the positive emotion is useful and negative emotion is harmful and destructive. So make clear and without touching religion, simply in order to create happy human family or happy human community or happy individual human being, compassionate attitude is, I feel, is the key factor. Once we double up or once we increase power of compassion, then many human conflicts suddenly will reduce.

Siegel: Some of my listeners, upon hearing you talk about demilitarization, will say, "Compassion, yes; but if Tibet had had a strong army, it might have prevented its takeover by China."

Dalai Lama: I think even if every Tibetan had been armed, the Chinese might could not be stopped. So, you see, basically under certain circumstances violent method could be justified, but as for long run the violent method is against the human nature. So, as a result, if you realize violence, although you may solve one problem, very often it creates another bigger problem. So the best way to solve any problem is negotiation, through human dialogue, on the basis of nonviolence. That is the human way; that is how I feel is the effective method. This is my feeling.

ANNIVERSARIES

On May 4, 1970, Ohio National Guard troops shot thirteen Kent State students on the fourth day of protests against the Vietnam War. On the twenty-fifth anniversary of that event, Noah Adams reported on what happened and how the people of Kent, Ohio, remembered it. Among those he interviewed were a national guardsman who was there that day and insisted on anonymity and SANDRA PERLMAN, who was married to a Kent State professor at the time. Perlman described her reaction upon hearing the news that students had been shot. May 4, 1995

Perlman: There was only one way into Kent that wasn't blocked. I came in the back route, and it was eerie, it was quiet, it was nothing. There was a helicopter following me. There was no one anywhere, and by the time I finally got into my house and finally saw my husband was all right and we started to really talk about what he had seen or not seen and started to get the news reports and then I think I, like many people, was glued to the television and saw this Dorothy Fuldheim, the woman up in Cleveland who sat there. Her face was so emotional, and she said, "There were murderers on the Kent State campus," and everyone else was, you know, picking and choosing words, but she used that word.

Adams: She was a newscaster, in fact.

Perlman: Yes, she was a newscaster, I don't know, definitely in her seventies, if not older.

Adams: Does it divide Kent, the town, over the twenty-five years depending on whether or not you thought there was justification for the guard to shoot? In other words, have people been on various sides of this, taken up various positions on this issue and kept those positions and, therefore, has the town been divided that way?

Perlman: Absolutely. It's still palpable, that feeling of "This had to be stopped." You know, law and order. It is a small town, and anarchy is always frightening to people, and I think many people did not see it as anything less than a direct threat to them. There was no doubt that weekend we had neighbors with guns in their windows. We all knew it.

National Guardsman: There was a mist of tear gas in the air. Our masks at times didn't fit well. And I must confess, I wear glasses, and with the gas masks, the glasses didn't fit. I didn't have my glasses on. There was sweat inside the gas masks. Very tunnel vision, the older-style masks. So we were given all that, but as we moved up the hill your vision was very limited. I was surprised to hear shots, I guess is what I could say. I was not surprised that a shooting would occur, let me put it that way. We were not trained in crowd control, riot control, if you will. We were trained combat soldiers. We weren't trained to be a touchy-feely group. We were trained in combat. We were taking a lot of abuse that I don't think we were ever trained for. Again, this is going back twenty-five years ago. Things have changed. People, evening before and the day before, urinating on us and throwing bags of fecal matter at us, and it was very tough and the tensions were very high. Keep in mind also, we had no personal protection equipment then other than a steel helmet. We had no face guards, no body armor, no gloves. We had an M-1 with a bayonet, and I think a lot of men were concerned for their own safety.

Adams: Do you recall any orders about firing, any standing orders?

National Guardsman: None whatsoever, none, no.

Adams: Was it ever discussed?

National Guardsman: Yes, it was discussed. It was discussed from the standpoint of, you know, do not fire, you know, but weapons were loaded at all times. I had an eight-round clip and an M-1 semiautomatic, and we were — as we used to say — a click away from a trigger pull. You just put the safety to fire and you're ready to go.

Adams: Did you ever feel that day that it would have been possible for you to fire?

National Guardsman: If I'd have been given the order to fire, I would have, certainly. That was what I was trained to do.

Adams: Yes. But did you get angry?

National Guardsman: Oh yes, yes. Very angry for a couple of days. This was my backyard, literally my backyard. I mean, I lived right across the street from the campus at the time. But literally in my backyard, with soldiers and helicopters and armored personnel carriers, people coming in my face yelling obscenities, spitting at me. I was very angry. The campus that I knew and the campus I were on were two different campuses.

Adams: And you were angry at the students?

National Guardsman: Yes. I was angry at a certain faction of students. It didn't take very long to pick out those students that were just bystanders and watching the action, so to speak, and those that were really involved in the action.

Adams: When you look back on it, do think that the shooting of the M-1 rifles was justified by the guard?

National Guardsman: Oh, I don't know. I've thought about it a lot of different ways, a lot of ways of justifying it. I hate to see anyone lose their life, I really do. But I think it came to a point where — just a boiling point, and I thought it was going to happen. I really did. I thought it was going to happen. Justified? I don't know. I know I've talked to some of the men that were involved in the shooting and they were very concerned, you know. They took some of their own countrymen's, so to speak, lives. It would be difficult — if I were standing up there. Quite truthfully, I probably would have fired, knowing the others were firing. And if I had a line of sight, a line of fire, I would have fired, just because others were firing. And I don't know how I would have justified that.

Just months before his death, Dr. JONAS SALK marked the fortieth anniversary of some of the best news in all history: the success of the Salk vaccine, a safe, effective, and potent prevention of the crippling disease, poliomyelitis. The announcement that the vaccine was to be made available to the public came in April 1955 at the University of Michigan. Forty years later, Dr. Salk was back in Ann Arbor and recalled the event in a conversation with Linda Wertheimer. April 12, 1995

Salk: It was a day of great excitement, needless to say. I felt myself, at that time, as if I was in the eye of a hurricane, but now that I'm back here and look back forty years ago and recognize what was accomplished in that time, it gives one a hopeful feeling about the future and what we might be able to do from here on.

Wertheimer: It was a very fast process, wasn't it, Dr. Salk? You thought you had the vaccine in 1953. There were trials in 1954, and then you released it to the public in 1955. That's very fast, isn't it?

Salk: Well, it was.

Wertheimer: Why was that?

Salk: Things were different at that time. Agencies that were involved in regulatory affairs were not as highly developed as they are now. Somehow, some way, it was in those pioneering days when there was much less structure in the organization of activities of this kind. There was less to do, you might say. Technology was not the way it is now, and one could and had to pursue ideas based upon imagination and exploration.

Wertheimer: Did you, do you, think that something that will be as important to as many people as that was can ever happen again?

Salk: Why not? If it happened once, it can happen again. Obviously, we're all anticipating the possibility that something of this same nature might happen as far as HIV and AIDS is concerned. There the problem was one of trying to prevent the infection, prevent the development of the paralysis. Now there are two problems, two challenges. One is to prevent the development of disease in those already infected and also, of course, to try to prevent the establishment of infection initially. It's a much more complex problem, a much more complex virus, but it can be solved.

Wertheimer: Dr. Salk, when you look back at the fact that you found a vaccine which saved the lives and changed the lives primarily of children, I wonder if that had an effect on the intense desire for a solution to be found.

Salk: Well, there's no doubt about that. At that time, one did not know from whence came the virus and hence the closing of swimming pools and parks and playgrounds and the attempted isolation of children in the summer months. And also, needless to say, the fact that it affected children had a profound influence on great concerns because parents as well as children's lives obviously were disrupted, and a great thing that I learned at that time was the importance of freedom from fear. And that's what I hear constantly. What a great relief it was and how it changed people's lives.

Wertheimer: To know that they didn't have to fear polio.

Salk: That's it. Yes, and on a day in which what is being quoted again and again is Franklin Roosevelt's statement "There's nothing to fear but fear itself," that's echoed in what did happen when the fear of polio could be lifted because we knew what we could do about it in order to avoid it.

Wertheimer: Let me just ask you one sort of foolish personal question, Dr. Salk.

Salk: Yes.

Wertheimer: You know that there are grown men and women walking around today who don't remember polio at all.

Salk: That's true.

Wertheimer: What do you think about that?

Salk: Well, it's wonderful. One less bad memory to have. However, I must confess that what we must do is learn lessons for the future from the successes of the past, just as, in a way, the immunization induces a memory, so that when at a later time a virus comes along that against which immunity has been induced, the immune system says, "I've seen you before," and reacts quickly and protects against it. And so it's useful to have both experiences of success and also use the challenges that still exist to try to improve life for all of us.

The fiftieth anniversary of the end of World War II occasioned many remembrances. For JAMES MILLS, the war's end meant liberation from a German POW camp. Mills was a first lieutenant in the U.S. Army, captured at Bastogne and held in various camps, the last at Moosburg in southern Germany. In late April 1945, elements of the Third Army, under the command of General George S. Patton, rolled up to the gates of the camp. Mills was one of tens of thousands of POWs who were freed then and there. He told the story of his life as a prisoner of war to Liane Hansen. April 30, 1995

Mills: We were captured by SS troops during the Battle of the Bulge, and we were really a division that was 106th Infantry Division. It was a green, completely green, division, put in right where the front of the German attack was going to take place.

Hansen: What prisoner of war camps were you taken to?

Mills: Well, we were put on the road and marched, and the first night we marched, we went to a factory, a cheese factory in Limburg, and if you like Limburger cheese, you'll never like it again, 'cause you have, maybe, a thousand men in that factory bedding down and not being allowed out. And the big thing on the march was that there was no water, and as you're marching at, say, eight miles an hour, which is pretty fast, and they wanted us to go fast. You wanted water, but there was no water. There was just snow, but the word came from the head of the column that if you eat the snow, your mouth will — your tongue will get large and you'll almost gag, and several men did have that happen and they fell out of line and they were shot.

Hansen: Where did you go after the Limburger factory?

Mills: After the Limburger factory, we were put on boxcars and sent to a place called Bad Orb. So we were on the boxcars. One of the interesting things on the boxcars was that we were there at Christmastime, on Christmas Eve and Christmas Day. On Christmas Eve, the marshaling yard where we were was pretty well bombed, and a lot of the cars were completely annihilated, with all the people inside of them. There were sixty men to a car. But we weren't hit, our end, and they started singing Christmas carols in the cars, and you could hear them start down below, and we joined in, and I was looking out the barbed wire window in the car, which is just an old cattle car with straw in it, and here were German guards out there singing right along with us.

Hansen: How long did you stay in Bad Orb?

Mills: We were there about a month, I think.

Hansen: And then you were moved on?

Mills: Then we moved on to Hammelburg, and in Hammelburg, there were about two thousand prisoners, and some of them were Serbian. They were mostly American officers, a few enlisted men, and there were some French.

Hansen: I understand you had what could be called some celebrity roommates in this prisoner of war camp.

Mills: Well, we did. We had Jack Hemingway, who was Ernest Hemingway's son, and then we also had, later on, a Colonel Waters, John Waters, who was General Patton's son-in-law and later became commandant of West Point.

Hansen: What was the morale like in the camp? You're not getting much to eat. You've been marched and carried on boxcars halfway across Germany. What was the morale like?

Mills: Well, when we arrived, we had a commanding officer who was not skilled in commanding troops, and our morale was low, and there were all sorts of problems, such as lice and other things. And we just weren't up to it, and, as I say, the morale was low. We were just existing. Nobody shaved. Everything was messy, and then a little bit before we were liberated, a colonel came in from Poland with a bunch of prisoners, and this is where John Waters came in, Patton's son-in-law, and Colonel Good, who had been a commander of a regiment in the First Division, and then of a regiment, I think, in the Twenty-ninth Division, and he was a seasoned commander. And when he came in, you just knew that something was going to happen, and he met with our colonel in the courtyard, and I was there at the time, and they compared West Point rings, and the man that had the lowest number, or who was there first at West Point, would be the commander, and Good won, and he told the other commander to clean out his barracks and that he would take over. And that night on the blackboard there was a big sign that said INSPECTION, and we couldn't believe that prisoners were going to be inspected by American officers, and so we all went back to our barracks and we did as best we could, but the barracks were dirty and we were messy, and we did the best we could. Anyway, they had the inspection. They didn't have white gloves, but they had everything else, and, in fact, they said to me, one of the inspecting officers said, "That's a button off your shirt." And I said, "Yes, sir." And he said, "Well, get that button put back on." I said, "I don't have a button. I don't have a thread and needle." He said, "I just said, 'Put the button back on your shirt.'" And I said, "Yes, sir." That was the kind of discipline, and it suddenly permeated the whole camp, and suddenly these men who had been very demoralized became, really, competent soldiers again, and the Germans looked at us and were afraid of us. I mean, we suddenly had come into our being, and from that time on the Germans gave us Red Cross parcels. They stopped harassing us. All the things that we disliked stopped, and we were ready for when the liberation came.

Hansen: Go back to your famous prisoner roommate, Colonel Waters. Go back and describe, then, the circumstances. What actually happened?

Mills: Well, we in camp had seen a plane fly over, and usually we didn't get planes that low. And they didn't even have time to run an air raid in Hammelburg, so we knew something was up, but we didn't know what. So about four o'clock, it was getting dusk 'cause this was March, and sure enough we heard the American armor, you could almost tell the difference between that and German armor.

Hansen: Just by the sound?

Mills: Just by the sound, yeah. German armor was heavier and it had a different, a less metallic sound than ours did, and a couple tanks came in to what's called Hull Defalade. You could just see the hull of the tank, the turret, and it had a star on it, and as soon as we saw the star, we just went bonko, I mean, that was it. They were there. They were right outside the wire, and then they broke through the wire, and that was just like the best birthday present you ever got.

Hansen: So this was, what, a break-off unit that decided to come down to the camp and rescue Patton's son-in-law?

Mills: Well, there was a lot of controversy about it. It's not so much controversy anymore. This was a task force, and Patton, in a story in the *Saturday Evening Post* said, "If I had it to do over, I would have sent a combat command. I wouldn't have sent a task force." And this task force was led by a Captain Abraham Baum, but then, after they had broken through the wire, Abe Baum said, "We have three alternatives for you. We think that we've been surrounded by SS panzer units and we don't know how we're going to get out of here, 'cause we don't have the armor to take off something like a panzer unit — "

Hansen: Oh!

Mills: "So you can get on the tanks and hope, you know, hang on to a gun, or get into a half-track," but mostly they had their own infantry in the half-track, so there wasn't much room for the prisoners. But he said, "Do what you can. The other alternative is to go back into the camp. And the third alternative — we've broken the wire. You can go through it and get on the countryside and try and get back." And he said, "We're located back by Frankfurt, it's about sixty kilometers, and those who want to go back into camp, go ahead. Those who want to get up on the tanks, go ahead," and Jack Hemingway and I took off cross-country, and about seventy-eight percent of the rest of them went back into the camp. And it's understandable that they went back because this was five weeks before the war was over, and we all sort of sensed it. We knew that the war was going to be over, and I think we were damn fools to take off. I mean, at this age of seventy-six, I think I wouldn't think twice. I'd go right back into the camp and sit on a box and wait.

Hansen: But you took off.

Mills: And we got as far as Main River in Gemünden, the same little town, and we were in the woods above the town, and we had acquired four or five other people, also stragglers from the camp, and we saw a roadblock along the Main River, and all we had to do was get over the Main River, but this roadblock was there, and we didn't know how to get to the boat that was on the other side of the roadblock, and Hemingway was a very accomplished French speaker — he had learned French in France — and so he said he would tell the Germans, in French, that we were French workers coming back from Poland, and we were on our way back to France. We had it all set up and rehearsed and everything else, and this one American came up and joined our group. We didn't know him.

He asked if he go with us, and we said, "Sure." And we got to the roadblock, and we all looked pretty miserable and looked like, maybe, workers from Poland. This one American got scared and he started to make a run for the river, the banks of the river, and they shot him, and then, of course, they asked us to put our hands up. So I was getting in the habit now of putting my hands over my head. So we were recaptured.

Hansen: And then, eventually, to Moosburg. April 29, 1945, the Allies come to liberate Moosburg. Given the experience you had had at Hammelburg, were you confident that this was it, that it was over finally?

Mills: Well, we didn't know the war was going to be over. We didn't know that much. One little interesting story was that Patton came into this camp, and by this time I had lost his son-in-law. I don't know what happened to Johnny Waters, but, anyway, he came into this camp and he had his twin pearl handles on and he has this jeep with the stars out in front and the stars on his helmet. He was quite a figure. And he came into the camp and he had two tanks ahead of him and two in the rear, and they did a complete 180 degrees, surrounded him, so he could come in in his jeep right in the center of the group, and he was giving, sort of, a good, patriotic speech, and meanwhile a Red Cross truck came in, and there were three girls on it, and very good looking young ladies, and they were passing out doughnuts, and if you could get a doughnut from a good-looking young lady as opposed to listening to Patton, there wasn't any question, so suddenly there was nobody listening to Patton, and he had some of his aides round up guys, "Get back," you know. "This is a photo opportunity," and stuff. So anyway, that was the end of it.

Hansen: You went back to Hammelburg.

Mills: Yeah, we went back in 1990. My wife, Barbara, and I went to revisit Hammelburg. The camp was, strangely enough, very much the same. It hadn't changed much. I couldn't understand it, in a way. I thought it would be — either it would have been torn down, like Moosburg, which is now just a beautiful farm community, there's no camp. But they hadn't, and they had put in the German infantry command, which was teaching in there. So I told them that I had been a prisoner there, in my German which is nonexistent, but anyway, he understood me enough. So he said OK,

On August 6, 1945, a thirteen-year-old schoolgirl named HIROKO TASAKA stood outdoors with some other students in Hiroshima, Japan. She and her friends were working on a project to clean up the rubble left by the aerial bombardment of Hiroshima. The U.S. bombing runs until that day had dropped conventional bombs on Japan. Until that day, the distinction between conventional bombs and other sorts was not understood. From her home in Japan, Hiroko Tasaka described her experience fifty years later to Daniel Zwerdling. She was standing less than a mile from where the atomic bomb fell. She remembered one of her friends suddenly calling out, excited. August 6, 1995

Tasaka: One turns to me, "Hiroko, look sky. It's B-29 there."

Zwerdling: One of the students said, "Look, there's a B-29 bomber flying overhead"?

Tasaka: Yes. So I look up. It was real different plane. Is very small, of course. It's because it's very high up, but it had a beautiful vapor. And then I got flash.

Zwerdling: Suddenly there was a flash?

Tasaka: Yes.

Zwerdling: Can you tell me more about what happened?

Tasaka: Oh, it was so hot. It was painful, and after that, I was unconscious. So I don't know how long, but when I wake up, I become myself. Then it was like a very heavy fog, foggy day. Do you understand me? So I get up and run to the river. I jump in because I was so hot myself. And I try to soak my body. All the people, all the students, were already in there. Because everybody burn so bad, you know?

Zwerdling: I take it that in the coming years — that in the coming weeks and months and years, that you developed, that you and the other survivors developed terrible radiation poisoning symptoms. Can you tell me about what — what happened to you?

Tasaka: I was on the bed for half a year. I could not get up.

Zwerdling: In 1955, when you came to the United States for treatment, a taxi driver living in Baltimore saw a photo of you in the newspaper, and he wrote to you.

Tasaka: He send me a letter, and he say, "I hope we — you have a nice time in the United States and conduct the operation."

Zwerdling: OK, and then what happened?

Tasaka: Then, in the Mount Sinai Hospital, he came and visit me. But I could not speak English at that time — nothing. So anyway we have an instructor there, and she told me what he said, and says back to him what I say. So a couple time after he came with his sister to visit me in the hospital. He asked me to get married, but after he came to see me.

Zwerdling: You say that this man asked you to marry him after meeting you only a couple times?

Tasaka: Yes, yes. And after that, he asked me, only he can give me happiness. So I said, "What is he talking, this man? I don't come here to get married. I came here plastic surgery."

Zwerdling: But after you moved back to Japan, the taxi driver in Baltimore continued to write.

Tasaka: I saw that this man has a warm heart, so after ten years, I go back to the United States to get married him.

Zwerdling: That's a very romantic story.

Tasaka: Yes, but he was a very nice man, you know?

Zwerdling: Your husband, I understand, died in 1989, and you moved back to Japan?

Tasaka: Yes.

Zwerdling: Did America do the right thing dropping the atomic bomb?

Tasaka: First time was wartime, you know? So I cannot say. This is government that decide to do, so I don't know nothing about. I was only thirteen years old, but fifty-nine years today still I am suffering, suffering so bad. So I wish nobody ever use again for nuclear bomb because it just destroy the people, and people like me have to suffer all the time until I die.

Zwerdling: Let me just ask you one more thing, please. You mentioned a moment ago that you are still suffering. Have you healed emotionally? Have you healed in your heart?

Tasaka: Yes, sir, I think that I have done many, many nice people — I meet many, many nice people in United States, and I'm fine myself. But nuclear bombs are not right, you know? Do you understand?

Zwerdling: What are you doing this fiftieth anniversary of the bomb?

Tasaka: A quiet peaceful day I would have.

Attempts to mark the fiftieth anniversary of the bombing of Hiroshima proved problematic. The Smithsonian Institution's Air and Space Museum prepared an exhibit on the *Enola Gay*, the plane that dropped the bomb. Veterans' groups objected strenuously to what they saw as the depiction of the Japanese as victims. Linda Wertheimer asked the historian PETER NOVICK of the University of Chicago about the Smithsonian's effort to interpret the recent past, and about the general problem of conflicting perspectives on controversial events. January 27, 1995

Novick: An historian tells a story, and shapes that story however he or she chooses, draws whatever morals, and the reader takes it or leaves it. That's life. An official museum necessarily, in some way or other, is presenting an official view and, therefore, that has got to be negotiated, and is responsible to constituencies which are very different from the historian in a private capacity.

Wertheimer: Is that a good thing?

Novick: That's life. When something is officially, semi-officially presented, it's reasonable for the people who pay the bills, whose collective voice in some way is being expressed, to want to have a say.

Wertheimer: The Smithsonian in its first script, setting up this exhibit of the *Enola Gay* and the dropping of the atomic bomb on Japan — the first take that veterans' groups had on that script was that it was too sympathetic to the Japanese.

Novick: I think in a way that's right, but there are all sorts of different alternatives, and all legitimate ways of framing the story of Hiroshima. You can frame it as the veterans appear to want, as the culmination of America's response to unprovoked Japanese aggression. You can frame it as a chapter in the history of white atrocities against nonwhites, as an episode in escalating barbarization of warfare in the twentieth century. You could talk about it as the opening of the terrifying age of potential nuclear devastation, and the notion that any one of these or others that one could conceive, has a kind of superiority, you know, inherent superiority or appropriateness. I think that's silly.

Wertheimer: Does being a veteran of the war give you a credential in terms of recounting history, beyond the history that you saw with your eyes, your personal history?

Novick: You're opening up a large and fascinating question because the notion that participants have a special authority and, in particular, the victims have a special authority is one that's been very current in recent years. Certainly, in the case of the Holocaust, we're familiar with the special privileged voice of the survivor, and we have this certainly in the case of black history, in the case of women's history, in the case of working-class history, the claim — and I'm not unsympathetic to the claim — that there is a particular kind of interpretive authority, moral authority, that goes along with being a victim. One among many ways of framing the current fuss is that a lot of the historians and the Smithsonian people had a kind of identification with the Japanese victims of the bombing at Hiroshima, whereas the veterans' perspective was that of potential victims, potential casualties in the invasion of Japan.

Wertheimer: Or the victims at Pearl Harbor.

Novick: Or the victims at Pearl Harbor, yeah, to be sure, so that in a peculiar kind of way, both sides are claiming a privilege for a different kind of victim status.

Wertheimer: The man who represented the American Legion in this debate and discussion at the Smithsonian was a man named Hubert Dagley who was the internal affairs director for the legion. He is quoted by the *Washington Post* as having said this debate started fifty years ago and has never been resolved. "It's not going to be resolved by the Smithsonian or the American Legion. I don't know if it ever will be." Do you think there's some sort of a time at which a debate like this could be resolved? Is there a distance at which we could see clearly, as we cannot now?

Novick: No, I don't think there's such a thing. What is true is that as the things on people's minds change, subjects once charged seem less relevant. But as of right now, as of 1995, some of the issues involved in Hiroshima are perhaps more alive than they were, what, twenty, twenty-five years ago. So it's not a straightforward matter of the passage of time dulling these issues.

Wertheimer: Two hundred years?

Victory over Japan brought joy to a war-weary country. That sense of joy was summed up by an image, a photograph, *The Kiss*, by Alfred Eisenstadt. It was on the cover of *Life* magazine, a nurse in a crisp, white uniform, a sailor in navy blue. He is planting a celebratory kiss on V-J Day in Times Square. It was only in 1980 that the nurse was identified as EDITH SHAIN, who now lives in Santa Monica, California. The sailor was not identified until 1995. He was CARL MUSCARELLO of Plantation, Florida. Linda Wertheimer spoke to them both by telephone on the fiftieth anniversary of V-J Day and of their famous embrace. August 14, 1995

Wertheimer: How did you come to be in Times Square that day, Edith Shain?

Shain: Oh, well, you know, I was working at the hospital, Doctor's Hospital, and I heard about the war ending and had to go celebrate and in New York that was going to Times Square. You know, New Year's Eve and any big celebration is Times Square. So I went down there. Took the subway for a nickel, got off at Forty-second Street, walked a small distance, and a sailor grabbed me.

Wertheimer: Just out of nowhere, huh?

Shain: Out of nowhere. That was a day when you could do that kind of thing, you know?

Wertheimer: Mr. Muscarello is speaking to us from his home in Plantation, Florida. Mr. Muscarello, did you on that day kiss very many girls?

Muscarello: Yes, I did.

Wertheimer: You did?

Muscarello: That's what I said.

Wertheimer: You mean you just grabbed them and smacked them?

Muscarello: Yes, sort of going through the crowd and if I saw an attractive lady I'd give her a kiss, even if she wasn't attractive. And

I suddenly stopped when I saw Edith. She stood out, as cute as she is today, with a little nurse's uniform on, and I just walked over and grabbed her and very gently planted a long, luscious kiss on her beautiful lips, and the kiss lasted for, God, over a minute, I would say, and when I was out of breath I just stepped back and I didn't say "Thank you," "Good-bye," or "See you," and I just drifted off into the crowed, ran off and kissed a few more ladies and got on the subway and went back to my home in Brooklyn.

Wertheimer: So how do you remember it, Edith Shain? Do you remember this as a pleasant experience? Sort of hard to tell in the picture.

Shain: Well, it's hard to tell, but he was someone who had, you know, fought for me and fought for all of us, and it was, you know, an exuberant moment for everyone, and everyone was sharing this moment.

Wertheimer: Did you realize when you saw the cover of *Life* magazine that that was you, Mrs. Shain?

Shain: Yes, I knew it was me.

Wertheimer: How did you know?

Shain: Well, if you look at the photograph you'll see the shoes that I wore with that kind of heel and my stockings. I knew, you know, what kind of stockings, and my slip is even showing. I knew exactly what I looked like from the back and from the front. And I also have my hair up. I used to wear my hair up because I was very short and I thought it gave me a, you know, feeling of being taller.

Wertheimer: You can just about see that you're holding your stockings up with garters here.

Shain: That's right. Everybody wore them. I mean, then it wasn't done for any other reason except that's all there was. There wasn't anything else.

Wertheimer: And your skirt is a wartime short skirt.

Shain: Right. It was the length then, right?

Wertheimer: Uh-huh, everything to the knee to save material.

Shain: Yeah, right.

Wertheimer: Mr. Muscarello, there was and still —

Muscarello: Linda, please call me Carl.

Wertheimer: OK. Carl, there was considerable confusion about who the guy was. Did you see your picture?

Muscarello: Well, this may be confusing, but I know I am that fellow in that particular picture kissing Edith. I did not know that the photograph was taken when it was taken. I did not become aware of it 'til about two or three months later. From there I went back to my base and I shipped out shortly thereafter, and about two or three months later my mother went to a doctor's office in Brooklyn and while she was in the waiting room she picked up a copy of *Life* magazine, and as she thumbed through the pages she saw this famous picture and she stopped, and said, "This is my boy."

Wertheimer: Edith, did you remember him?

Shain: No. I have no way of positively identifying the person because, you know, when he kissed me I closed my eyes. And when it was finished, he was gone.

Wertheimer: And you never saw him again?

Shain: No. But it was a great possibility that he was a sailor.

Wertheimer: Did it change your life to have this picture taken and have it become such a famous picture?

Shain: Yeah, maybe if I had told him earlier. It didn't change my life, but it did enrich my life.

Muscarello: Well, thank you, Edith. You thoroughly enriched mine, especially fifty years later when I had the pleasure, and I really mean this, the pleasure and the honor to meet Edith in person.

Shain: Well, Carl has a very open and warm personality and very adjustable, you know, so flexible, and that the fact, you know, it's hard to see that a policeman, New York policeman, of all things, would behave that way because I would imagine — of course, I don't know any New York policemen, but my assumption would be that they're, you know, on guard more or less.

Wertheimer: Well, now, let me just ask you that question: What did — what did you do after this picture was taken?

Shain: Maybe I was there another minute when a soldier came up and kissed me. So I thought it was time to leave because they were all just grabbing, you know. Those days, you know, that kind of thing wasn't my expectation.

Wertheimer: Did you stay at Doctor's Hospital for very much longer? I mean, what happened in your life?

Shain: Well, I was going to college then, and so I worked part-time at Doctor's Hospital, and I graduated a psychiatric nurse and I worked as a supervisor and an administrator at a psychiatric hospital. And then I decided to teach little children because I thought my psychiatric background would be, you know, valuable. And then I went to graduate school at UCLA and did some social work.

Wertheimer: Mr. Muscarello, what happened to you in your life?

Muscarello: I joined the police department shortly after I was discharged from the navy, and I was a policeman. I enjoyed it very, very much. I married a beautiful young lady from Montclair, New Jersey, and she gave me two beautiful children — a boy and a girl — and after I retired from the police department, I moved down to the state of Florida and went to work for the American Express company as an investigator. And I enjoyed that job very, very much. Unfortunately, my wife passed away with cancer in 1978, and I remained single for a long, long time. And three years ago, I married a lovely young lady who's a flight attendant for American Airlines. Her name is Shelly. She's a delightful person. She has two children and three grandchildren, and I have four grandchildren and we get along well.

O n the sixty-eighth anniversary of Charles Lindbergh's takeoff for his historic trans-Atlantic flight, Scott Simon interviewed an eyewitness. By the time Lindbergh landed at the end of the first solo flight from New York to Paris, crowds of cheering Parisians were on hand to watch. A far smaller group of spectators saw him off. Among them was a twelve-year-old girl, her brother, and parents. For ISA-BEL HAYNES, the memory remained vivid. May 20, 1995

Simon: How did you happen to be there that morning?

Haynes: We were very fascinated with the whole procedure at those airfields that spring. Everybody was there. Byrd was there. Chamberlain was there. They were all planning to take off. And out of the west came Captain Lindbergh. My father used to take us over there all the time to watch the planes and to hang around the hangars. And he bribed the night clerk at the Garden City Hotel, where Captain Lindbergh was staying, to please call us if Captain Lindbergh got up and got out early any one of these mornings. He was supposed to go any minute. The man kept his word. He called us. And at five in the morning, my father came and got me up and my brother and my mother and we piled into the car and we drove over to Roosevelt Field and there was the plane (it had already been towed over from the hangar at Curtis) and Captain Lindbergh was standing around, waiting to decide whether or not to take off. You have got to picture that this is not like La Guardia or anything like that. This is a muddy field with a very narrow track down to the road. And along the road are high telephone and electric-light wires on poles. He's trying to decide whether to go or not, and finally he gets in the plane. And the men start pushing it to help him get started, and he's rolling down the field and finally he's going fast enough so that the men drop off and he bounces (there were a couple of puddles) once or twice, and everybody's running down the field after the plane and holding their breath while they run, if that's possible. And he went up. And, my God, was he going to clear the wires?

Simon: Yeah.

Haynes: He did, by about twenty feet.

Simon: Were you cheering?

Haynes: Oh, you can't believe how excited we were. This was one of the highlights of my childhood.

Simon: It tops anything I can remember in mine, let me tell you. It was wet, real wet, that morning, though.

Haynes: Oh, it was wet and overcast and gray and miserable. But the low was supposed to be moving out, and he wanted to follow the low across the sea, as I recall.

Simon: So that was it. Because I was going to ask you what the concern was about the weather. He felt he could, in a sense, use it, by following it?

Haynes: By following it and hopefully getting a tailwind.

Simon: Did you follow the flight over those next thirty-three hours?

Haynes: Well, as much as we could. All we had was the radio, you know, and what reports came in. I stayed up as late as my parents would let me. I was up at the crack of dawn the next morning and by that time, we knew he had been reported over Nova Scotia. Well, you know, on the way to Ireland, he stopped. He went down almost to the surface of the ocean, where there were fishing boats, and he screamed, "Which way is Ireland?"

Simon: Yes. But it also helped them fix his position when word got back to New York.

Haynes: But I don't think the fishermen ever sent word back. It was when he was over Nova Scotia that word went back and then, when he hit Dingle Bay, word went back from Ireland.

Simon: Mrs. Haynes, looking back on it, and I know a lot of the legend gets mixed up in this, but can you say as a twelve-year-old youngster that you had a feeling that morning that you were looking at history one way or another, but that this man, Slim Lindbergh, would fly the *Spirit of Saint Louis* to Paris?

Haynes: Yes. I knew he would do it. I was sure he would do it. You're talking about a child, you know.

Simon: Mrs. Haynes, as you look back on it, can you help us to appreciate what a dangerous proposition that was?

Haynes: Do you realize how fragile that plane was? Do you realize the only way he could see his compass was in a mirror that he got from a girl, that was one of the standbys when he was getting ready to take off?

Simon: Right, right, her makeup mirror.

Haynes: Yeah.

Simon: And he put it up there with a wad of chewing gum.

Haynes: That was the only way he could see his compass.

Simon: And in those days, if he had gone off, say, three hundred miles into the ocean, it's not as if they would have known about it, not as if radar could have tracked it.

Haynes: He had no radio with him. He had no way to signal back. He did have a life raft. He didn't take a parachute.

Simon: Now this sounds strange, but that morning, sixty-eight years ago, did your eyes lock? Did he wave hello to any group of people that might have included you?

Haynes: No. He was very absorbed in what he was having to decide to do in making sure his plane was ready, and no, he never waved to me. I might have died on the spot if he had.

Simon: Well, I'm glad it didn't work out that way.

Haynes: I wish I'd been the girl with the mirror.

W hen Australia's favorite song turned one hundred, there was a celebration in the small northern town of Winton. "Waltzing Matilda" was first sung in public at a hotel in Winton exactly a century earlier, in April 1885. The song about a vagrant wandering in the Australian outback is special to Australians. Noah Adams called the Australian-born novelist THOMAS KENEALLY, the author of *Schindler's List*, to ask about Australians, their national song, and its popularity in other countries. April 6, 1995

Keneally: Well, I think [the song] indicates that Australian idiom is nearly impenetrable to anyone else, and I think Australians are perversely proud of that.

Adams: Are you given to singing the chorus from time to time? Could we entice you to a bit of patriotic —

Keneally: Oh, yeah. Well, my God — this could be — I could give up writing after this and become a singer, but let's see. [*sings*]

"Once a jolly swagman camped by a billabong,
[That's a sort of anabranch, or lagoon.]
Under the shade of a coolibah tree,
And he sang as he watched and waited 'til his billy boiled,
['til his quart pot boiled]
'You'll come a-waltzing Matilda with me.'"

Now, "waltzing Matilda" means carrying your swag around the countryside, looking for work. "Matilda" is the blanket that goes over the shoulder of an itinerant worker in the nineteenth and early twentieth century, and carrying that blanket was called, in slang terms, waltzing Matilda, and that's where the name of the song comes from. But it's still the unofficial anthem. We got rid of "God Save the Queen," thank God, because her gracious majesty is twelve thousand miles offshore, so she probably wouldn't hear the strains of that. There's another anthem called "Advance Australia Fair," but this anthem, unofficial as it is, has a strange magic over the Australian mind still.

Adams: Is it analogous to say it is sort of what an American Western song would be? It is about the outback of Australia.

Keneally: Yes. It is. It was written in Queensland by a balladist called Banjo Patterson, who was the same man who wrote "The Man from Snowy River," and it is a Wild West song. An American song that reminds of it is "The Streets of Laredo," and "The Streets of Laredo," like "Waltzing Matilda," derived from Celtic airs. I mean, the Celts make the best airs, and of course, Celtic songs always end in tragedy, and the ghost of the swagman is the tragedy with which "Waltzing Matilda" ends.

Adams: That's right: "You'll never catch me alive, said he."

Keneally: Yes. [*sings*]

"You'll never catch me alive, said he,
And his ghost may be heard as you pass by that billabong.
You'll come a-waltzing Matilda, with me."

Nearly forgot it. You've unleashed the thespian in me.

Adams: Now, as Australians gather worldwide tonight and lift a glass, how powerful is the emotion that comes with this song, or is it just simply some charming thing from your past?

Keneally: Well, it's something that's sung at times of national adversity. I remember being in London last October when the British rugby league team beat the Australian rugby league team unexpectedly, and to our great national chagrin, and it's at moments like that, of heroic collapse or threat, the we tend to sing "Waltzing Matilda." Of course, it also is a good song to sing, with its large, looping melody, while under the influence of substance abuse, and this is a national tendency all too common, and so it tends to be a drinking song also.

SPORTS

G EORGE FOREMAN is the patron saint of middle-aged men: a heavyweight boxing champion of the world in his late forties. As a grandfather, he reclaimed the title he had held as a younger man, becoming the oldest reigning heavyweight champ in history. When he came to NPR for a two-part interview with Bob Edwards, Foreman had published a new autobiography, *By George.* He talked about how, after winning the gold medal at the 1968 Olympic Games, where other black athletes raised clenched fists as a protest against racism, he waved a small American flag instead, and about his childhood on the tough streets of Houston during the 1950s and 1960s. June 14 and 15, 1995

Foreman: We called it the Bloody Fifth Ward because every weekend somebody would get bloody and die, and my role models were all troublemakers, guys that had been to jail and on their way to jail, and I wanted to be the best of all of them. I decided early on in life I wanted to be a tough guy, Band-Aid on the face, mugging, everything bad.

Edwards: You didn't take their money or anything like that, you just liked to see them go down?

Foreman: I'd go run down the street, robbing guys, and all that. As a matter of fact, that's what changed me because when you're growing up in poverty there's a lot of ignorance that goes along with it. You're robbing people and you don't even know it's a crime. Nobody's telling you any different, everybody's doing it. And one night, trying to escape the police, I ran under the house to hide from the dogs. I thought the dogs were going to sniff me out, and I had to cover myself with mud like criminals do in the movies, and that's when I realized, man, you are a criminal, and I stopped stealing at that point. But still I had this chip on my shoulder, trying to beat everybody. I just wasn't going to steal their money anymore.

Edwards: In 1965, when you were eighteen, you saw an ad for a new federal program and signed up for the Job Corps.

Foreman: They gave me a ticket to Grants Pass, Oregon. I had never seen streams and all the beautiful trees, and it changed my life. For the first time, I saw there was another part of the world. People cared about me. I was interested. I had gone through school just because I had to. At sixteen, I could legally drop out. I hadn't learned anything. Now here was a group of people trying to teach me to read, study, and learn. That was a help to me because books, life and knowledge, had started to destroy a lot of the rage, not all of it but some of it.

Edwards: And you were getting three squares.

Foreman: You better believe it. That's why I'll always be grateful. You're talking about patriotic. Patriotic means when you've had three squares from someone, thank them all the time. I grew up hungry, peeking through windows, seeing families with two kids. My mother raised about seven kids on twenty-six dollars a week, so in the neighborhood there would be families with one or two kids, and they'd leave food on the plate. I'd peep through the window and see it and think, Wow, why don't they invite me in? I was always hungry. There was never enough to eat, and it looked like I was the hungriest of all. And then in the Job Corps, they gave me three meals. I loved it, man. I just couldn't get used to it.

Edwards: They channeled that rage into boxing.

Foreman: One night there was a Cassius Clay fight and Floyd Patterson, and everybody looked at me, and we were listening to it on the radio in sixty-five. They said, "George, you're always fighting, why don't you be a boxer?" I took the challenge and I moved to Pleasanton, California, to another Job Corps center. I had met Doc Broadus, the boxing coach, and told him I wanted to be a boxer. He said, "Well, you're big enough, you're ugly enough, come on down to the gym." And I did go down. The first time, I didn't like boxing. I couldn't hit the guy, and when I tried to grab him, they said, "You can't do that." I wanted to bite him. I couldn't do anything because I was a street fighter, and I quit boxing. But finally he stayed on me and then really challenged me. He said, "Are you scared or what?" I said, "I'm not scared. I need shoes." He gave me shoes and told me to stick with it, stop fighting in the streets, and I could become an Olympic gold medalist. He was right. In Mexico City, when I won the gold medal against a Russian opponent. I never served in the armed forces. I never had a chance to wear the colors. This was my uniform. So I would bow to the judges as we do, showing how humble we were. This time I had the small American flag I had in my robe. I said, "Uh-huh, take this. Uh-huh, take that. We got you this time." I waved that flag. "America, United States, we got you."

Edwards: That wasn't the only demonstration at that Olympics, though.

Foreman: In 1968 there were two demonstrations. Black athletes were recruited to boycott the Olympics. Some did, but because nobody expected that much of boxers, especially an Olympian like me, well, they didn't even think I'd win. They bypassed me. After winning the gold medal, I had the ring around the flag, showing it off. Most people thought it was a protest, or antiprotest, against the other Olympians who had waved a small clenched fist and bowed their head during the national anthem and the flag. So I went back home, and people said, "How could you do that, George? Here you are, the brothers are out there doing their thing and you waving the flag. How could you do that?" That put a chip on my shoulder. From that point on, I would never allow people to get that close to me to rain on my parade again. How could I not wave a flag?

Edwards: You turned pro and you had this image of a mean guy, and you liked that image.

Foreman: I had a chip on my shoulder and it got greater. The rage got greater. I wanted to be heavyweight champion of the world and, after a while, started winning and staring people down. It became part of me, even after I beat Joe Frazier in seventy-three. People kept saying, "Oh, yeah, he beat Frazier, but he didn't beat anybody." I kept thinking, "I'm going to kill one of these fools. The only way I'm going to get respect is I'm going to kill somebody." So the rage even got greater because it was no longer anger, it was a desire to really take someone's life in that ring.

Edwards: Your fights were nasty, brutish, and short. You hit with frightening power and quickly decimated the heavyweight division, except for Muhammad Ali. You two met in Zaire in October 1974 in one of the greatest fights ever. Ali was considered too old at age thirty-two, and many feared for his life against you, the invincible Foreman.

Foreman: I thought it was going to be an easy fight, easy fight. I had knocked out Joe Frazier, who beat him. I had knocked out Kenny Norton, who broke his jaw and whipped him. So Muhammad was going to be my easiest fight. He was old. So I get in the ring and I hit this guy with everything I had. Until finally I could barely hold my hand up at about the last of the sixth round, and I heard "Sixth round," and he said, "George, is that all you got?" I started thinking, Yep, that's about it. Now you show me the exit, I'll get out of here. People ask me who do I think is the best fighter of all time? Joe Louis, no doubt about it. But Muhammad was bigger than boxing, this man was a hero. Boxing is too small to put him into that. He's bigger than boxing.

Edwards: You lost the heavyweight title to Muhammad Ali that day in Zaire and after losing the heavyweight title to Muhammad Ali in 1974, you spent the next three years trying to get a rematch. In 1977, after twelve grueling rounds in hundred-degree heat against Jimmy Young, you were defeated. In your dressing room, you underwent an experience that changed the course of your life.

Foreman: Just to cool off, I walked back and forward, trying to think. I was thinking, You got everything. You don't have to worry about this fight. Don't care about it. You could go home right now and retire to your ranch. Retire and die. For the first time I had heard that in my thoughts. I hadn't put it there and I tried to get it out. Finally it dominated my thoughts. You're going to die. I said, "Man, I know these weren't my thoughts." I said, "I'm going to make a bargain with this thought." I said, "I'm still George Foreman. I can box and give money to charity and to cancer." The voice answered me back, "I don't want your money, I want you." That's when I knew this wasn't anybody I knew. And I fought for my life that night. Everybody was looking at me, like you are now, you know? Nobody knew what I was thinking, that I was trying to save my life. I had heard about athletes dying after some events. I was about to die in a dirty old dressing room that didn't even have a hot shower, and I had homes all over the world, money set aside, safety deposit box. I had hid money from my wife, and I remember thinking, God, you know, I believe in you. I knew it was God then, but before I could say another word, I heard a voice say, "You believe in God. Why are you scared to die?"

Edwards: You survived that night, quit boxing, and began preaching back in Houston.

Foreman: I started to teach kids, telling them, "Just come and hang out with me. I'm not going to preach, I'm not going to tell you anything. I just care about you." I didn't want to lose any more kids because it seemed like nobody cared, and by 1986 I had run out of money. I didn't have any more money, and the parents would drop their kids off to me. "George, these are your kids." Every kid in the city was coming by sooner or later. I said, "I can't close it down." I went to do a speaking engagement, they give me a honorarium. One night in Georgia, they said, "Let's give George more. He's helping our kids." It sounded like I was begging for money. I said, "I will never do this again. I know how to get money. I'm going to be heavyweight champ of the world again." I was thirty-seven years old, 315 pounds, but I said I could do it because I needed to do it. I wasn't going to close that youth center down. In eighty-seven, I went back into boxing and, after ten years of absence, people laughed at me. They said, "This guy is too old. He's too fat." They got me upset, and one day I looked in the mirror, and said, "They're only saying it because it's true."

Edwards: You began the most improbable comeback in sports. Three years and twenty-four consecutive wins later, in April 1991 you got the fight you had long wanted.

Foreman: Evander Holyfield for the title. We went twelve rounds. I lost the decision, but I made a point. The age forty is not a death sentence for athletes. I didn't win the title, but I said to myself, I had a lot of money at this point. The youth center was OK, but I said I was going to be champ of the world. So I kept pursuing excellence. Finally I matched, almost four years later, with a guy who beat Evander Holyfield, Michael Moorer, and the crowd was saying, "This old guy is too old. He'll probably last a few rounds. We'll go out and cheer for him," but after ten rounds there's Michael Moorer on the canvas. I looked up to heaven, said, "A miracle." I got on my knees and thanked God, and the whole audience was screaming, "George, you did it! Now quit, so we can go about our business. We're tired of cheering for you, now quit. Now get out of the business before you get killed." But it was the happiest moment I've had as an athlete.

Edwards: Well, there was a fight since then.

Foreman: Axel Schultz.

Edwards: Yes, and some folks that thought maybe the judges kind of gave it to you.

Foreman: Look, I tell people right now in Las Vegas you have the best judges that money can buy, I don't care what anybody says. But they asked me, "George, how did you see the decision?" I tell them, "Man, my eye was shut, I couldn't see anything." I could barely see Axel Schultz, let alone the decision.

Edwards: What's next?

Foreman: Well, I hope to stay active. This is my final year to box. I will not be a boxer beyond 1995. I set a goal. I was going to be champ of the world and get some money for the youth center. Those goals are satisfied now.

Edwards: There are people who want to see you go up against Mike Tyson.

Foreman: Which is the only way reason I stayed around anyway this year. He said after I became champion, "I will get out of the jail today and fight George Foreman tomorrow." He got out of jail and I haven't seen him. I've been pleading for him. We could have made a hundred million dollars if he decided to fight me right now. He wouldn't need a promoter. All he'd need is to sign on the dotted line, take his money, and go hopping and a skipping down the street. They say, "Well, he'll whip you, George." Well, let it happen. They say, "Well, he needs a few tune-up fights." Hey, for a senior citizen? I am a grandfather. I have a grandchild. What do you need to tune up and warm up for an old man like me? You don't need any warm-ups. Fight me. I'm too old for you to be talking about warming up, but it tells you the story about the quality of life in the United States. I'm in that demographic forty-five through fifty-five, and the toughest guy on the planet needs a warm-up before he fights a granddaddy? It's fact.

Edwards: Along the way, the mean George disappeared. Since your comeback, we have a new George. You've gone from this mean killer to this cuddly grandfather who's doing commercials for Kentucky Fried, Doritos, and who knows what else.

Foreman: You name it, I've done it. It's strange. There I am dying in San Juan, Puerto Rico, and the last thing I could remember was I didn't say good-bye to my mother, I never told my kids, "I love you." I was given a second chance to live, and this time I'm not trying to make people love me, I'm trying to love people. Who knows when I'll go again, and I don't want that to be on my mind. I didn't say good-bye to my loved ones, so it changes you. I didn't even know how to box again because the rage, the killer instinct,

There's a famous photograph of Y. A. TITTLE taken in 1964, his last year as quarterback for the New York Giants. Tittle was thirty-eight. Football had broken his bones, age and asthma had stolen his wind. The camera captured him, kneeling on the turf, helmet off, bloodied and exhausted, a onetime boy wonder at the end of a brilliant career. Yelberton Abraham Tittle had come to New York just three years before. He was the oldest quarterback in the game and the best, a man who could throw a football with stunning accuracy. He learned to play football the way it used to be played before sophisticated coaching staffs with wireless telephones moved players around the field like chess pieces. The quarterback used to call the plays. Once during his playing days at Louisiana State University in the 1940s, Tittle made a seemingly brilliant call against Texas A&M that was, in fact, anything but brilliant. In an interview with Robert Siegel, he recounted the story. December 8, 1995

Tittle: In those days, you could not get any kind of coaching from the sideline. If you received any information, a hand signal or any of that nature, you would get a fifteen-yard penalty. If a receiver came into the game and brought in a play and told you what to do, it was a fifteen-yard penalty. The referee would actually stick his head in the huddle to make sure he wouldn't talk to you. But we sort of cheated a little bit. The water boy would come in with the jugs of water and my jug would be a different color. It might be fourth down and one, so I'd open up the jug, and inside the top it would say, as an example, punt. Then I'd put the jug — put it back on, and that would constitute a fifteen-yard penalty if they could catch us. But I would go in the huddle and call a punt. When we were playing Texas A&M, the score is six to nothing, and about a minute to go in the ball game, and we're behind, and do I call time out? And here came Lang, the water boy. I opened up my little top and it said punt. I said why would we punt with less than a minute to go and we're behind. Well, he forgot to take the top off from the time before and — but still, I was going to follow orders like I'm supposed to do. So I got in the huddle and called a quick kick, and of course we had a revolution in the huddle with ten other ball players saying I had to be stupidest guy in the world with fifty seconds left in the game and behind, so we're gonna kick the ball away. But I did it, and the ball went dead on the one-yard line and then the first down, Texas A&M ran off tackle, fumbled, we covered it, and then I threw a winning touchdown pass with about twenty seconds to go to Jim Cason, and we won seven to six. The papers came out the next day and said it was the most brilliant call that any eighteen-year-old quarterback had ever made in the history of the game, and Coach Moore said that he knew that we could never win without a break and he took the chance and did it. The only reason we did it, because I got our illegal signals mixed up.

Tittle tells that story in his daughter DIANNE TITTLE DE LAET's book, *Giants and Heroes: A Daughter's Memories of Y. A. Tittle.* The famous photograph of her battered quarterback father is on the back cover. Many Giant fans saw Y. A. Tittle as a mythic character, the "Bald Eagle." None saw him that way more so than his daughter, of whom he is immensely proud. A poet and harpist who sets classic verse to music, she discussed her own art and father's career.

De Laet: I just gave a performance last week at Stanford of the lyrics of Sappho and some selections from Euripides' *Trojan Women.* That's the program I did the first, and it's the one I think I love the most.

Tittle: I was just thinking, Mr. Siegel, don't you think that maybe the doctors got mixed up and we got the wrong baby in the hospital forty-some-odd years ago? That my daughter is a harpist and a poet and talks about Sappho and the only Sappho I ever heard of was a linebacker for the Packers or something like that?

De Laet: You're more related than you realize. Maybe not to Sappho but to some of the other characters. Hector. Hector, in fact, you know, being dragged around the walls of Troy three times. I mean you could say you had a strange variation on that theme.

Tittle: I know they made a switch at the hospital. I know they did.

Siegel: There's a passage in your book, Dianne, when your father was made the second-string quarterback for the San Francisco 49ers, having been a great T-formation quarterback. I guess you were made second string because they went to a shotgun formation? Is that what happened, Mr. Tittle?

Tittle: That was in 1960, I think.

Siegel: Dianne, I wonder if you can read from your book describing your feelings as a young girl then?

De Laet: Let's see. [*reading*] "Personally, I felt very lucky when Red Hickey decided to go with the shotgun formation and a younger quarterback, because in 1960 I had had a hero in Perseus for nearly half of my life. It happened in kindergarten that I had opened a book before I could read and found a picture of a man holding a ghastly trophy. Like sports, the picture had its share of violence. But the severed head of the Gorgon was only a part of the picture, and what was even more amazing than the head of snakes was the peace and contentment of the man leaning on one hip as if to say that he was not surprised in the least by what had to be the most bizarre and fantastic moment of his life, because victory, in spite of its strange and sometimes startling shapes, was not only his, but humanity's true element.

"And so it was that I began to wonder about the hero. And it was a good thing, too, because when the going got tough for my father in 1960, there were a multitude of Greek heroes I had come across in books who had it a lot tougher than he did. These people who faced nine-headed hydras, clashing rocks, three-headed dogs, were like exotic candles being lit, one by one, inside my own dark and brutal world."

Tittle: I want you to read the book to me, Dianne. I love this. When I read it, it doesn't come out like that.

Siegel: Well, there's the connection you see between the Greek heroes of the ancient world and your career as a quarterback in the National Football League. You still think she was switched at birth is what I hear?

Tittle: I definitely think so. Anyone who could write these beautiful words like that.

Siegel: Dianne, you quote Seneca, "In the morning they throw men to the lions and bears. At noon they throw them to the spectators," when you write about a game, which — well, even for me, as a sixteen-year-old New York Giants fan at the time — was heartbreaking. There was no Super Bowl yet — the championship game of the National Football League between the New York Giants, with Y. A. Tittle at the helm, and the Chicago Bears. Y. A. Tittle, when you think back on that game, what are your memories of it?

Tittle: I was disappointed because for so many years I chased the whale. I had never really won the championship game. We won our district championship when I was in high school. We went and we lost in a crucial game later. I didn't go as far as we could've gone. I did go on to college. We played in the championship game. In the Cotton Bowl, we tied with Arkansas. We were a much better football team than Arkansas that year, but we caught a snowstorm there. The same thing seemed to follow me all my life, never ever really winning the big game, and I think Dianne's book has been built around this. It's the quest of really winning that I never did win. But I did win really in the long run because I have four wonderful children and grandchildren, and Dianne has written this book and she's written it with good taste. She's praised her father while I think telling a lot of truth about the people in sports that I played with. Mr. Siegel, I've loved football ever since the day I played with a stuffed Lindbergh cap, I guess, back in East Texas and to the very last day of thirty-eight years old when I threw a ball in the last practice with the Giants. I almost wish I could do it all over again because it was a wonderful experience and a wonderful ride.

Siegel: Do you remember watching that game, Dianne, the 1963 championship?

De Laet: I would say out of my entire childhood, that is the moment, that is the one thing that I remember more than anything. In particular, the last ten minutes or so of the game when my father threw an interception. That game stands out in my mind as sort of as perplexing a riddle as Perseus was for me when I found him in the book and that's why I chose to make this game the subject of my victory ode in a sense. I feel that at least for me, there was a victory that was shared by my father and maybe me too because I think he did show his excellence that day even though it was the worst day of his career. I came away from that game with something that I needed to keep in mind as I continued to grow and explore my own art and go and run down the field with my own ball, so to speak.

P HIL JACKSON coached the Chicago Bulls to three NBA
championships, but it was not always clear that he
would succeed as a basketball coach. Noah Adams talked
with Jackson about his coaching career shortly after the publication of Jackson's book, *Sacred Hoops: Spiritual Lessons
of the Hardwood Warrior*. After playing for the New York
Knickerbockers, Jackson took a job with the Albany Pa-
troons of the Continental Basketball League. It was a far cry
from Madison Square Garden and the limelight of national
television coverage. November 9, 1995

Jackson: When I first came in the league, all travel was done
by van. So sometimes you would get in your van in Albany, New
York, and drive to Detroit, Michigan, where there was a team in the
inner city.

Adams: You just put everybody, all the players, in an old Dodge
van and go?

Jackson: Yes, in a Ram van, and you would have ten guys with
yourself and maybe a trainer. You would drive out — and try to do
it in one day — and bust it out and play a game and maybe hit a
team on the way back like Rochester, New York, and finish up the
trip. What players were looking for was the opportunity to get their
talent shown and get to the NBA.

Adams: These guys were in their early twenties for the most part,
and any night there could be an NBA scout in the stands.

Jackson: It's still that way in the CBA.

Adams: So that's quite a challenge for a coach because these guys
want to go right out there and show what they can do immediately.
The idea of team play is kind of gone, right?

Jackson: It really is, and I was fortunate when I came to Albany to
have an expansion team. They were players that had come off of
other CBA teams or were just new in the league, and I convinced
them to share the money together at the same pay rather than one
guy getting $375 a week and one guy $300 or whatever. Let's all
share $325 a week. It kind of made a community project out of it.

Adams: Everybody being paid the same salary?

Jackson: Yes, and then we all shared time. The first unit played eight minutes. The second unit played eight, the third played the third eight minutes of the half. The first unit would go back on the floor if they were playing well. So everybody got time. There was nobody that was going to sit and not play, and I wanted to make that emphasis.

Adams: This is in the early eighties. Looking back on it, do you think you were sort of a hippie basketball coach? You were living in Woodstock, New York, making the drive to Albany to coach. What was your life like then?

Jackson: Well, at that time I had four children between the ages of three and seven. Twins were my youngest. I had another child from another marriage that was a fourteen-year-old, but I had four living at home. My wife had been saddled with those kids while I was in the NBA. I shouldn't say saddled, but she had been run pretty ragged with having four kids within that age proximity, and it was an opportunity for me to do a little bit of househusbanding while she went to graduate school and worked and got out of the house. So the basketball season in the CBA really didn't start till Thanksgiving. So that was kind of a part-time job for me, and the coaching aspect was interesting. It was interesting to live in Woodstock because it was a missed opportunity, perhaps, to experience the seventies that I had missed. I could do some personal things I had always wanted to do like Rolfing, which makes everybody's eyebrows go up, and intense therapy and massage therapy. For a guy who had a spinal fusion, that was real nice to have. I could go to a men's group, something I had missed out on as a basketball player. I had that. I had a fraternity of people and a circle of friends to live with. I could drive forty-five miles and be in Albany at work, take care of business up there, and then come back to kind of a sequestered life in the Catskills.

Adams: You were trying to figure out, indeed, if you wanted to be a coach and if you could be a coach for your career.

Jackson: Well. That's a good assessment. I said, "Well, I'll go into this and if I succeed I'll stay in it three or four years, and if somebody likes what I do maybe I'll get a chance in the NBA."

Adams: Now, something happened there that is very timely to talk about. You traded for Dennis Rodman last year. When he played for San Antonio, he came out of a game, sat down and took his shoes off on the sidelines, and it was a big controversy. You had a player in Albany named Frankie J. Sanders — the J. stood for "jump shot" — and Mr. Sanders did exactly the same thing and you had to suspend him.

Jackson: I did. The situation was that we were in a play-off game, and Frankie had not had a good game. I had gone with his backup in the later stages of the ball game. With about two minutes to go in the ball game, I wanted him to go back in and finish up the game. We weren't doing well. He refused to go in and had his shoes off and went down to the locker room. I suspended him. It turned out to be a situation in which there was a tug-of-war between the owner and myself, actually the commissioner of the county, which was at that time the managing partner of that basketball team. He wanted the ballplayer reinstated on the team with an apology. I allowed it to happen perhaps against my better judgment.

Adams: And, of course, he goes out and scores thirty-five points the next game, right?

Jackson: He sure does. He goes out and single-handedly wins the ball game for us. I learned a little bit of a lesson. Now, hopefully, Dennis is not going to present the same problem, Noah, because Dennis actually does have ingrown toenails and some foot problems, but he always seems to get those shoes back on when the time-out is over and it's time to get back into the game.

Adams: You say that the rules of basketball always are fulfilled, perhaps not right away and perhaps not in the way you expect them to be, but they always work somehow.

Jackson: Yes. This kind of goes in hand with that statement, "The dice of God roll pretty even over a course of time," and that karma kind of thing that keeps going round will find its way back to players, too.

Adams: Back in Montana when you were growing up, your father was a Pentecostal preacher and your mother was an evangelist and you had leanings in that direction. How close is coaching basketball to being a minister?

Jackson: It's real close. I always tell my mother that my ministry may be just to twelve players, but then Jesus Christ had twelve disciples. You can't go too far wrong with that, but that's a little blasphemy when I say something like that to her because she is very serious about that topic. In reality, there is a lot of convincing that we do and there's a lot of spiritual work that we do with ballplayers. You're always healing egos. You're always melding talents together, and you do have a voice. I think that more often than not, the voice of our teams and how they play reach the community to their heart and soul.

Adams: You seem to be a settled down and measured person. There is a lot about Zen meditation and visualization in the book, but I wonder if during any given week there isn't a moment when you completely lose it on the basektball court. Does this still happen to you?

Jackson: Oh, yeah. All you have to do is have a goaltending call not called, or an illegal defense because of an errant defensive player standing in the lane, and I'll be upset, like most coaches. The thing about it is, and I tell my players this when I give them some of the training and teachings that I have gone through, my only stat that I have that is significant in the NBA was I led the league in fouls one year and also that year led the league in technicals. So I know what it is like to have an errant temper, to have a loose trigger, and I have been able to corral it a little bit and find control.

L abor troubles struck major league baseball in 1995. During spring training, the players were still on strike and the owners threatened to open the season with replacements (the regular major leaguers thought of them as scab labor). In the end, the strike was settled just before opening day, the players returned to the majors, and their replacements returned to their real-life jobs. When CHRIS WALPOLE spoke to Noah Adams, spring training was about to begin and he was about to make his debut as the New York Mets's third baseman. Walpole is a six-foot-two, 205-pound twenty-six-year-old, who makes his living teaching autistic children in the Bronx. March 1, 1995

Walpole: My college coach gave me a call and asked if I would be interested in going, you know? So I thought about it for a couple of days, and I said, "Hey, why not?" Something I always wanted to do.

Adams: Now, when you came out of college, did you have a chance to go the pros in any form? Semipro ball?

Walpole: Well, yeah. A couple of people told me that they were going to take a look at me out of college, and nothing really panned out. That was a big disappointment because that was something that I was kind of working toward, you know?

Adams: Right.

Walpole: And I went to tryouts after that, and nothing came back from that, so there I just basically said, "I'm just going to play, you know, because I love to play, and the game is still great. The system maybe was bad to me, but I still play."

Adams: Play a lot of sandlot ball?

Walpole: Yeah. The semipro league up in Westchester. We're in a couple of leagues. We play about an eighty-game schedule and tournaments, and we play a lot of games.

Adams: Now, you told the Mets that you had played with the Thunder Bay Whiskey Jacks in Ontario in 1993?

Walpole: Right.

Adams: Professional team?

Walpole: Right.

Adams: But that really wasn't true?

Walpole: Yeah, it wasn't.

Adams: Yeah?

Walpole: Well, you know, I just wanted to play, and they wanted pro experience. I had none, and so I basically said that. It might have been a mistake, but I really wanted to play. I really wanted to have a chance.

Adams: Had you ever heard of the Thunder Bay Whiskey Jacks?

Walpole: I have. A couple of friends of mine played in the league.

Adams: Ah, OK. So they didn't check you out, and you're in Florida. How are you doing?

Walpole: I'm doing pretty good. I think that all of us are doing better than people expected us to do. I mean, they're really working us hard, and we've been doing the drills of second minor leaguers, and hanging with them. Nobody's embarrassed himself. You get your injuries here and there, but I guess that's to be expected when some guys are a little older than the young guys. I don't think that the coaches really thought that replacement players would hang as well as they did, but we did OK. There was a lot of soreness and aches and pains, but you work your way through that, I guess.

Adams: You going for the Advil at night?

Walpole: Oh, yeah. There's been a lot of Advils taken down here. I think the Advil market is definitely on the upswing in southern Florida. This is a good time to have stock in Advil down there, no question. And ice.

Adams: Ice?

Walpole: Ice is another big item. It's on the rise down here.

Adams: You know, is it not possible that, in the first exhibition game you have coming up this weekend, that you could go four-for-four with a home run and a double and two singles, and you could be a great hitter and nobody had known that, and you could play in the major leagues? That is possible, isn't it?

Walpole: Well, I guess anything is possible, you know? But I think the attitude down here on the whole is, once this is all settled and the strike is over, that we're going to return to, basically, our old lives as they were.

Adams: How have you been treated by the Mets coaching staff?

Walpole: Not bad. It really is putting up with a bad situation, you know? I mean, they'd rather be coaching the major league team, I'm sure. But, due to the situation, they've been pretty good about it.

Adams: They haven't been mean to you?

Walpole: No, nobody really has.

Adams: How have you been handling, in your own mind, the union situation here? There is a strike going on, you're coming into it as a replacement player.

Walpole: Right.

Adams: How do you work that out?

Walpole: I don't really have any allegiance to any union, any baseball union or anything like that. It's an opportunity for myself, and I can't see it from their view. I've never made the kind of money they make. I see it down here right now and I'm not making really any money and I'm enjoying myself. So how could you strike making that kind of money?

Adams: Do you have a teachers' union in your school?

Walpole: Yeah.

Adams: So if you folks decided there was an issue worth striking about and you had a replacement teacher come in —

Walpole: Well, I don't want to get into that, really. It's different. We're not taking anybody's job down here. When these guys come back, they come back, and they step right back into what they were doing, and so nobody's down here taking a job.

Adams: But the owners say they could go ahead and have a season with replacement players.

Walpole: Well, that would be great from our standpoint.

Off the coast of San Diego in the America's Cup competition, one of the Australian boats cracked in two and sank in three minutes. The boat appeared to fold like a sheet of cardboard. The seventeen crew members were quickly picked up, unhurt. Noah Adams spoke with one of the competing designers, GERRY MILGRAM, who designed *Mighty Mary* for the America Cubed team. Milgram explained why the other boat sank the day before. March 6, 1995

Milgram: The wind was an average of eighteen knots, some puffs to twenty and some puffs to twenty-three, which is not really all that windy. It's windy for San Diego, but in general terms it's not all that windy. There were some short, deep waves that the boats would occasionally fall off and slam quite hard. *Mighty Mary* lost her main halyard at the beginning of the second weather leg. Fortunately for us, the other boat was unable to hoist its mainsail and was quite far behind, and then we were able to go on and finish the race after we lost the main halyard falling off a wave. One of the frames came loose in the boat structure. That particular frame is not an essential one and not a major one and so we were able to finish the race.

Adams: Now you sound very calm about all this. Were you, in fact, quite worried about your brand-new boat?

Milgram: I wasn't worried about our boat. I've seen these conditions before, and twice during racing I've predicted a mast will come down in advance. One was the first race of the world championship in 1991 when the Japanese lost their rig. I predicted a rig would come down yesterday too, but I certainly didn't predict a boat would sink.

Adams: Did you at any time think the weather was too rough for this kind of sailing yesterday?

Milgram: No, not at all. In any other part of the world, these are relatively ordinary conditions.

Adams: Well, what, then, do you figure happened to *oneAustralia*?

Milgram: Well, from my observations, and of course I don't know for sure, but I saw the complete video footage, and it looked to me like classic longitudinal failure. In other words, collapse due to longitudinal bending movement. The upper part of the topsides and perhaps the very small deck of midships, or perhaps slightly forward of midships, buckled, and the hull lost its longitudinal stiffness and folded up. This happens to big ships too in bad conditions when they're inadequately designed, and this boat was either inadequately designed or inadequately constructed for the conditions that we had.

Adams: Is there a situation, though, where a designer has to walk a pretty narrow line between structural integrity and speed? Is there a compromise that you have to build into these boats to make them competitive?

Milgram: Well, to a point. In this case, you always want to make the boat light, but we made our boat quite strong and stiff. You gain something in sailing from the stiffness; you lose something from the weight. But we put quite a lot of material in our boat in the area where *Australia II* failed. I should say that the way these boats have evolved leads to a shape which is more conducive to this kind of a problem than a more traditional sailing vessel shape. What's happened is, the boats have become narrower and the cockpits have become wider. Those two conspire to make the decks along the sides of the boat extremely narrow. I mean, I always used to say if you design a boat so strong that it never breaks, you can never win. So you have to break some things sometime, but within that context you don't design them so that breakage includes something so severe that you sink.

Adams: How disastrous is an event like this? Seventeen crew members were rescued, but they could have been in bad trouble. The boat is gone.

Milgram: Maybe and maybe not. There are a lot of chase boats very nearby and assuming that they can swim and that nobody gets injured, the only real danger, then, is to anybody that's below, should that person be trapped. In this case, they got the one person below up on deck in a big hurry.

Adams: As a designer, when you hear of something like this happening, is this your worst fear?

Milgram: It's not something I really consider. It's not my worst

ALISON HARGREAVES was thirty-three years old, from Scotland, a wife, a mother of two, and a mountain climber, when she stood by herself on the summit of Mount Everest. She climbed the north face of the tallest mountain in the world, 29,028 feet, without oxygen supplies. Only one other climber in history had done that. Shortly after Noah Adams talked with Alison Hargreaves about conquering Mount Everest, she was killed in an avalanche while attempting to climb K2. May 22, 1995

Adams: Have you had any dreams of being on the mountain?

Hargreaves: No, strangely enough, I haven't had dreams. I mean, I think about it because people ask me about the summit, and I can still visualize it. It's so very, very vivid in my memory, but I don't actually dream about it.

Adams: Now when you think back on what it looked like, describe that for us, please. Did you have good weather on the summit?

Hargreaves: Oh, it was absolutely unbelievable. As I approached the summit, I got onto what is like the final summit ridge, which is a bit of curving arc of snow, and I could actually see the summit, and it really did look like an enormous egg-white meringue because it was huge, a great white cornice, and there were prayer flags all over it. It was sort of white snow, contrasted against the really bright red and yellow and orange prayer flags, and as soon as I saw that, I just burst into tears because I knew I was going to reach the summit at that point, but also it was just so beautiful. It really was. I've been to the top of a lot of mountains, and it wasn't just the fact that it was Everest and it was the highest. It was just a beautiful summit. It was such perfect weather. There wasn't actually a cloud in the valley. All the valley bottoms were totally filled with clouds. It was like cotton wool, totally filling the whole of the world. It really was incredible.

Adams: What sort of physical shape were you in at this point? You had made what amounted to a dash to the summit without oxygen.

Hargreaves: At that actual point, I was actually in very, very good physical shape. There's two reasons why. Obviously, I was very excited mentally. So obviously, there was the adrenaline dose, if you like, and the euphoria of going to the summit. It's very difficult because obviously if you're aiming for the summit, you really aim for the summit. It's very difficult to keep something in reserve, but I think I've been climbing long enough to know that if you go to the summit, you've still got to get down again, and I was very conscious of that. But even so, basically going for the summit, I really did have so much adrenaline inside me and so much excitement that I felt I could keep going forever almost.

Adams: What is the danger, what is the complication, of doing it without oxygen?

Hargreaves: The danger is that, really, your body cannot cope without lots of oxygen, and if you're at that sort of altitude for more than one or two days. People call it the "death stone." People say above eight thousand meters, it's the death stone. It really is because your body is dying, literally dying. It can't recuperate in any way, and if you end up having to bivouac and spend a night out and really sort of sleep, at that altitude, for more than one night, you are really not doing your body any good at all. I mean, that's one of the reasons that when I got back down to my high camp, where I spent the night before, which is eighty-three hundred meters, I picked up my tent, I stuffed it in my rucksack, and even though this is already evening time, and I actually went down lower, just to get lower, so I could sleep, because it's so important to your body.

Adams: Was it a gamble, in many ways, what you did?

Hargreaves: It wasn't so much a gamble as the fact that I had a very, very slim chance of success. People kept saying to me, "How likely is it you'll get to the top?" I told people that if I had a ten percent chance of getting to the summit, I was lucky. And the reason for that is the weather. I'd already been on Everest in the autumn of last year, and I knew that if it was very cold and it wasn't a good day, that I would start to get frostbite, and I wasn't prepared to risk losing fingers and toes going to the summit. So many people climb eight-thousand meter peaks and they come back with no fingers and no toes, and I wasn't prepared to do that. So as far as I was concerned, my chances of success was very, very slim. They really were.

Adams: Did you have any altitude sickness at all? Any symptoms?

Hargreaves: In a word, no, I didn't. I really do find it absolutely incredible. I've seen people literally dying from altitude sickness on this trip. Sherpas being taken out with very severe altitude sickness, and I can honestly say I have not even had a headache. It is just so unbelievable, it's amazing. The only thing I've had was when I came down to my camp at seventy-seven hundred meters, I was so exhausted I physically couldn't actually accept the liquid. I melted some snow. I melted a liter of liquid, and tried to drink it, and I immediately brought it straight back up, and obviously that's partly the altitude, but also it was partly being the exhaustion.

Adams: It was said that you intend to climb K2, there fairly nearby, in the middle of June, after a visit back home to Scotland. Do you still intend to follow that schedule?

Hargreaves: Yes, as far as I'm concerned, I fly home to the U.K. on Friday, and I have two weeks with the children, and then I go off again to Pakistan to try and climb K2. There's no reason why I shouldn't try and do that. And again, God willing, if I get good weather, then hopefully I'll get to the summit.

WASHINGTON

When he began his book tour for *My American Journey*, General COLIN POWELL was the favorite of many Americans to be president of the United States. The book, written with the biographer and historian Joseph Persico, only amplified Powell's popularity. It tells the story of how a kid from a poor immigrant family in New York, a young person with no obvious gifts, found his calling in the army, worked hard, rose high, and became the chairman of the Joint Chiefs of Staff. Powell was close to three presidents and allied himself politically with the liberal wing of the Republican party. As he weighed the possibility of running for president, he spoke with Linda Wertheimer about leadership and about getting things done, especially in the current political atmosphere. September 18, 1995

Powell: There's a heck of a lot of fighting going on right now, and we have seen a revolutionary change since November 1994, when the Republicans took over. And the Republicans, I think, have really shaken things up. I mean, we are going to change. We are going to deal with these incompatible positions and we're going to cut government. And so we have seen in the last couple of years where the people watched this drift in the early nineties and the post–cold war period, and they have decided to turn loose these Republican revolutionaries for a while and let's see what happens. And they're watching it carefully. As I've said in my book, and I kid with audiences around the country, the American people are channel surfing, like on TV. They watched the presidential election in ninety-two, said, "Well, I don't think I like that," so they gave President Clinton a chance, and then they watched ninety-four and they didn't like the way the Democrats were operating. Well, we'll watch that for a while. And they're going to ask for something different in ninety-six if they're not satisfied with the results.

Wertheimer: I wonder how you would feel if somebody like, say, for example, Sam Nunn or Phil Gramm, somebody who has supported military force in this country for a long time, were to, if such a thing were legal, wish to be appointed chairman of the Joint Chiefs? In other words, to go to the top of your profession having never actually had anything to do with your profession except for being near it, involved in it, knowing about it. That's essentially what people are talking about for you.

Powell: Well, that's quite a comparison. I'm thinking rapidly here to see if there is anything in the Constitution or in law that would prevent Sam Nunn from becoming chairman of the Joint Chiefs of Staff and at the moment I can't think of anything. That's shocking. Obviously, there is no such route up for them, and I understand what you're saying here. But the wonderful thing about our democratic system is that anybody can jump in regardless of qualifications and present himself or herself to the American people, whether you are a former general, a former politician, a fool, or whatever. That's what small-d democracy is all about.

Wertheimer: And the notion of a neophyte politician taking on the biggest job?

Powell: I don't know that there's anything in the Constitution or in experience that suggests a career politician is that much more qualified to be president then a neophyte politician. I can give you examples throughout the course of our history where some neophyte politicians did exceptionally well. Think of George Washington, for openers, and Dwight Eisenhower is another comparison. And I can think of situations of career politicians who have spent their whole life who were not terribly effective, and I can think of some who were terribly effective.

Wertheimer: One of my personal theories about people who have been in the presence of presidents is that they tend to think being president is not as impossible a dream as all that if this person with all their flaws got there. I wanted to ask you about the presidents you served under because in the book you do talk about their flaws, as well as their strengths — Ronald Reagan as a leader, but very detached — and you clearly think that at some points he doesn't know whatever it is you're trying to tell him. And yet you say you feel that your relationship with him is a loving relationship.

Powell: I think Ronald Reagan is a remarkable man. It's the term I've used in the book. He did not have a total grasp of all detail, and if you ever got into an arms control agreement with President Reagan, you would rapidly exhaust his knowledge on the subject. But what he had which was so valuable was a sense of self, who he was. He understood the American people. He knew that they were looking for inspiration and leadership and he had several consistent themes — taxes are bad, the commies are bad, we need a strong defense, we are a shining city on a hill. And for his time, he was right, and he was elected twice. And the only reason he didn't run a third time is the Constitution prohibited it, and he would fuss about that from time to time.

Wertheimer: George Bush you thought a very able president.

Powell: I thought he was a very, very able president. I think he was a great commander in chief. He performed that role very, very well. But in the last two years of his administration, the end of the cold war and the end of the Gulf War, the American people turned away from those two, and said, "Well, that's fine, that's behind us," and started looking inward. And when they looked inward, they didn't like what they saw. The economy wasn't rebounding, at least they didn't think as quickly as it should. They were troubled by violence and crime and drugs. And President Bush wasn't able to convey a message that persuaded the American people to stick with him for another four years. And as I've noted in the book, I don't know this, I'm not a medical person, but I don't think he was quite himself as a result of the illnesses he had.

Wertheimer: President Clinton you talk about as holding college bull sessions.

Powell: Yes. It's his preferred style. And this was known before he became president. I mean, he's a master of gathering in huge amounts of detail.

Wertheimer: This got on your nerves big time, though.

Powell: It got on my nerves, but it doesn't make any difference whether it got on my nerves or not. I learned from working for three presidents that you do it the president's way. And the president has to use that process or system which has worked for him over the years and which he finds successful, as long as it brings him success.

Wertheimer: You said Reagan and Bush were insensitive to race, you felt. They were insensitive to problems they didn't understand.

Powell: I had trouble with this section of the book because they never treated me in anything but the most straightforward, equal way, and they did not ignore the fact that I was black. I didn't look white to them. They knew I was black. And I never did anything to suggest that I was anything different. People would say, "Well, nobody sees that you're black." Wrong. That's wrong. But at the same time I feel that the Republican party during that period was not sufficiently sensitive to the struggles that were taking place in the inner cities, to the lack of opportunity that existed among African Americans and other minorities. Not that they were totally ignorant of it, but they just weren't able to connect with that community.

Wertheimer: Do you think white people in this country, the sort of average white voter, at this moment before people have necessarily read or heard the five thousand interviews with you that they're about to hear, do you think white people view you as a black man in the same sense that they view Jesse Jackson, who's a black man?

Powell: I suspect some do, some don't. You know, I don't think there's a single answer to that. If you want to know what I think white people should see in me is an American first, somebody who deeply loves this country and has served it for many years and hopes to serve it in some way in the future. But while they're looking at me, don't ignore my color, don't ignore my kinky hair, my somewhat flat nose. I am a black person, and I don't want anyone to forget it. I've never forgotten it, and I've had occasion over the years where people have not let me forget it. So let's not forget it now.

Wertheimer: What about black people?

Powell: Black people certainly know I'm black. I mean, I don't think there's any question there. But there's mixed feelings there because I am not a black official or public person or celebrity that has come up through the traditional civil rights movement. And so I'm somewhat strange and different compared to Reverend Jackson, who was, you know, a leader of the movement for many, many years and many others like that. So I'm in a sort of a unique position here because I came up through national security and defense routes that are not that well known to black Americans because it didn't deal with the great concerns that black Americans have. And we'll see what happens now that I'm speaking out on other subjects.

Wertheimer: Your friend Stu Spencer, who's a Republican political consultant, has said to you, "Powell, you're a Democrat. If you run, you should run as a Democrat." If I were to make one of those lists you're so famous for making, pro-con, and just make a column, under the Republican side I would say "loyalty given should be returned." Reagan was loyal to you; Bush was loyal to you. And then on the other side, your friends in the black establishment are almost all Democrats. You are not talking about the black intellectual conservatives. I think you mentioned one black Republican in your book.

Powell: I don't owe anything to anyone with respect to this choice. And that isn't the way you would make such a decision. I would make a decision to enter politics and wherever I end up on the spectrum because I thought I could lead at that end of the spectrum and I could do it better than someone else, and that I thought the American people were looking for this kind of leadership and they'd support it.

Wertheimer: George Bush was criticized by lots of people for having run for president because he wanted to be president, not because he had a vision for the country, as Ronald Reagan certainly did, but because it was time for him to be president.

Powell: I think that's unfair. I think President Bush had a vision for the country. I think he wanted to continue the Reagan-Bush revolution that he was part of for eight years. He sometimes had trouble communicating that vision, and he lost connection with the American people.

Wertheimer: Do you have a vision?

Powell: I don't have a political vision yet. I have a vision of an America I want to see. I have a vision of an America that is starting to think again as a family. I have a vision of America where the extremes are not batting at each other, where while we create wealth and while we create jobs and while we make it easier to get into business and make money we don't do it in a way that fails to try to do the best we can for those of our fellow citizens who are not enjoying the best of America.

I have a vision for putting families back together. I have a vision for youngsters growing up in two-parent families with their little bright-eyed, bushy-tailed selves coming into school systems at the age of six, school systems that are prepared to teach them and train them for jobs that are waiting for them at the end. I have a vision of reinstilling faith in all these young people.

So I have many visions for America, and some of them are often dismissed as, gee, this is all pie-eyed rhetoric, and you know, it's not serious politics. But that's the kind of vision I have.

The first one hundred days are a traditional time for taking stock of new presidents. In 1995, it was a point to take stock of the new Congress, whose arrival in Washington had signaled as much of a rupture with the past as a change of parties at the White House. Three freshmen in the House of Representatives who had discussed their hopes for the 104th Congress in November came to discuss their experiences in April. J. C. WATTS, a Republican from Oklahoma, is a former football hero who spoke at the time of his election about wanting to cut taxes and reform welfare. FRED HEINEMAN was a chief of police in North Carolina before winning a Republican seat in Congress. He had spoken of strengthening national defense. ZOE LOFGREN, a Democrat from California, had said she wanted to protect children and give them opportunities to become productive adults. One hundred days into their first term, Linda Wertheimer sat down with them at the Capitol. Watts and Heineman said they had accomplished most of what they promised to do in the first hundred days; Lofgren said she tried but had generally been outvoted. Wertheimer asked if they ever felt like imposters, surprised to find themselves really serving in Congress. April 6, 1995

Watts: I recall when I was at the State of the Union, it dawned on me that at one time President Lincoln had stood behind that microphone and had given his State of the Union address, and I'm quite an Abraham Lincoln fan. And after the State of the Union address, we went to a press conference. They asked me about the president's speech. I said, "I can't tell you. I really didn't pay attention to it. I was caught up in the history of the moment." I'd seen this on TV many times, and I was actually there. So it's a special place.

Heineman: I went through that. Probably four months before I got elected, and I came to a realization that there were, and still are,

535 people in this world, and only 535, that make the decisions not only for this country and the future of this country, but in a large part, for the whole world, and that I was going to be one of those 535 people. And the enormity of that realization and the responsibility, that was awesome. And compared to that realization, everything else was an anticlimax.

Lofgren: I haven't had exactly that experience, but one memory I have — I was standing in back of the president of the United States and he was speaking, and I was supposed to speak at this press conference, and I had, momentarily, I felt almost kind of dizzy. I thought, This is the president of the United States who is standing in front of me and who knows my name, and it just seemed totally bizarre and — but there I was, and I pulled myself together and made my talk.

Wertheimer: And said your piece.

Lofgren: Yes.

Wertheimer: What about serving so far back in the minority — I mean, a freshman member of a much-diminished minority? Is there anything more obscure than you are in this Congress? How has that been?

Lofgren: Well, I don't have any other experience to compare it to in the Congress, but I guess, you know, from what I've heard and what I really believe, the Congress of last year did need to change, and obviously I think the change that we had is too extreme, it's gone too far, but to the extent it got a wake-up call and a shake-up, I am very free to do what I think is right, to speak my piece, and no one has ever told me, "You can't do this" or "You've got to do this," and if they did, I wouldn't do it anyhow. But it's a very open, democratic process, and I don't know if that's true when, you know, the Speaker is on your side of the aisle and they're pressing you for votes, and I suspect not.

Wertheimer: Congressman Watts, you're a considerable celebrity in this Congress. You've been on TV all the time, you're constantly being called on for your views. Reporters interview you a lot and so on. I know that you're used to being famous from the time you were playing football, but how's that been? How's it been to be singled out?

Watts: Well, I have had some experience with that before, and I can do with or without it. I hadn't asked for the attention. I've tried to go about my business and do what I felt like was important to the people of the Fourth District of Oklahoma. I guess the national press, they do think it's a bit of a novelty to be black and to be Republican. You know, we've tried to stay focused on what our responsibilities are and what our mission is, and I think we've done a fairly decent job of doing that.

Wertheimer: You have been pretty much going down the line with the leadership, voting with Mr. Gingrich. Are there issues that are coming up where you can see that now that the first hundred days are over that you may have to take a different path from time to time?

Watts: Well, I like to think that Mr. Gingrich voted with me. Like I told Newt when he came to the district to campaign for me, I said, "I've been talking about these issues for the last five or six years. I'm glad the Republican party finally caught on and they're joining the team," but I like to think that I voted with my district more than I did Newt Gingrich, and that's the way I approached it.

Wertheimer: Affirmative action is going to be a big issue in the near future, I believe, and as the presidential campaign heats up. Is that going to be a problem for you? I know what your own views are, but I just wonder if your constituents, if you and your constituents part company there?

Watts: Well, just like President Clinton said and just like Bob Dole said, it needs to be reviewed. It's interesting that that question has been directed at J. C. Watts. I think it's important that we ask everybody, Republicans, Democrats, white, black, "What's your views on affirmative action?" Forty-six percent of the black community say they disagree with affirmative action, so I think there's some room for improvement and there's some room for scrutiny.

Wertheimer: Mr. Heineman, what about you? Do you feel that anything is likely to be headed your way in which you will just have to say to the Speaker, "Newt, I'm sorry. This time I've got to go another way."

Heineman: No, I don't see that. I don't really see the leadership imposing themselves on us to think other than the way we think. I've always been independent. We have voted, for the most part, with the leadership in the Republican party, but we have almost exclusively addressed ourselves to the Contract. We signed the Contract with the people. We didn't sign the Contract with the leadership. Like J.C., I think the leadership voted with me, and I've said that several times, and I was glad to hear J.C. say that. But I don't expect leadership to put pressure on any votes. I'm only up here three months. But I've always stood my grounds on where I was coming from, and certainly the media back home had us five freshman Republicans marching in lockstep with the leadership. Well, perhaps they didn't look far enough to realize that we also signed on to a contract and we've done what we signed on to do. We said we were going to do it, and we did it.

Wertheimer: But it sounds like you're feeling a little tiny bit burned by those columnists that say that you've been marching in lockstep.

Heineman: Well, I don't like having someone try to characterize me as a clone. I've never been a clone, and I'm not one here. I may have voted the right way on all those bills, but I have not been part of any coalitions. I call them as I see them, and I let the chips fall where they may, and I've got a lot of scar tissue on my hind part to prove that. It's worked for me in the past, and I'm going to stay with the winning team, with the winning game.

Wertheimer: Let me just, to go back for a minute to the personal side of serving in Congress and to one of the promises that the Speaker made, which was that this would be a family-friendly Congress. Mr. Heineman, how about that promise?

Heineman: Well, it depends on whether you live in North Carolina or California. I feel very privileged to be forty-five minutes, by air, from my district. I think you'll see more frustration from the western part of this country than you do from the eastern part, but nevertheless, I feel privileged. I got the best side of any schedule we have, but family-friendly, yes. I would like to spend more time back in my district because they're the people that elected me and they're the people I pledged to serve.

Wertheimer: Representative Lofgren, is your family friendly to the Congress after sending you here?

Lofgren: My children are not feeling especially warm toward Newt Gingrich, no. I have been home every weekend also, and that's out to California. And, you know, it's been rigorous. The sad thing is that the pace of it has been too fast. I mean, it doesn't have to be as slow as it used to be, for sure. I mean, that was way too slow. But I think the haste with which we have acted has led to what I have said on the floor is the unalterable law of unintended consequences, where you find out later that things are written in such a way that no one wanted to do that and it's not a good process. And that's not because it's family-unfriendly. It leads to shoddy work 'cause there's not enough time to do it right.

Wertheimer: What do you think, J. C. Watts?

Watts: It has been a very brutal pace, but I don't think there was anyone that signed the Contract with America — Now, of course, you know, Congresswoman Lofgren didn't sign it, but I did, and when I came up here, I had some kind of idea, or they had fore-warned us that we would be working very long hours in the first hundred days. So I hope that if anyone comes up with any contract ideas again, I hope they'll make it a hundred fifty days rather than a hundred because it has been a very brutal pace. But I think it's been a pace that's provided some good things for America to get us back on the right track.

The House of Representatives debated welfare reform: a rancorous, cantankerous discussion, mostly about children and how the changes foreseen by the Republican Contract with America would affect them. Among the reforms advocated were capping benefits for families on welfare and refusing benefits to babies of mothers under eighteen. The Conference of Catholic Bishops opposed those reforms, arguing that they would encourage abortion. Moreover, the bishops insisted that the government has a responsibility to help the poor and the hungry, as Bishop JOHN RICARD, the chairman of the Domestic Policy Committee of the Conference, told Linda Wertheimer. March 23, 1995

Ricard: I live in an inner-city neighborhood in Baltimore, and I can tell you firsthand that I can experience an escalating need on the part of many people to go from month-to-month simply to feed themselves. And I'm not speaking of people who would be driving Cadillacs or people who would spend their money on something other than food. I'm talking about a very genuine need. I see many, many children who are going to school and having their first meal of the day at the school, and having perhaps their only substantial meal at a school setting. If we were to talk about a welfare program and an approach to the poor in our country that denies or significantly cuts back on some of the programs we're offering now, we're going to have a lot of people suffering.

Wertheimer: Many Americans have votes in the 1994 election, basing them on concerns about moral values, concerns about family values, and the fact that there seem to be no longer moral absolutes in this country. All sorts of concerns that they seem to feel that voting for another group of politicians might, in some way, address. Are you telling us, with your opposition to this bill, that that is just not happening, it's not the case?

Ricard: Well, there's no question that people are concerned, as you very well stated, with the direction this country's going in moral values. There's a premise that if we cut back significantly on some of the resources that we're providing to mothers who have children who are out of wedlock, that we're going to see a reduction in this. There's no evidence that would support this, first of all, whatsoever. Secondly, we feel that it would be wrong to punish children when we're trying to correct the behaviors of adults. We've met with people in Congress. We feel that they're strongly convicted people, that they're very sincere about what they're doing. But we feel, to look at this without an adequate understanding of its human consequences and dimensions, is morally wrong.

Wertheimer: One of the things that the Speaker of the House has suggested is that charities, like the Catholic Charities, can help to strengthen the safety net, can pick up some of the slack if the government moves out of some of these programs. What do you think of that as an alternative, a positive alternative to the federal government's involvement in welfare?

Ricard: Well, we've made it clear in our letters to Congress that we feel very strongly that the federal government has a role in providing for people who cannot provide for themselves. There is no way our Catholic Charities agencies, our soup kitchens, which are sponsored by our parishes — there's no way that our shelters can handle the responsibility of the federal government or of the state government. Our charities, our programs, right now are at their limit. The reason why the federal government became involved in the first place is the private charities couldn't handle them. And we're going to regress considerably, as a country, as a society, if we think this is going to happen again.

The Emory University historian DAN CARTER located the source of contemporary conservatism in the legacy of George Wallace, who ran for president as an independent in 1968. In his biography of the segregationist Alabama governor, Carter calls George Wallace the most influential loser in twentieth-century American politics. Wallace captured the rage of white voters against integration, against Washington, against liberals, libertines, and intellectuals. As Carter told Robert Siegel, echoes of Wallace's angry populism can be heard in the Reaganite assault on big government, in Rush Limbaugh's demonization of liberals, in the Contract with America. November 1, 1995

Carter: Wallace understood that there were millions of Americans who felt in some way or another betrayed, betrayed by what they saw as the decline in American culture, in values, moral values, and frightened. The war in Vietnam, riots, the rise in crime, all of these things we now associate with the sixties, but Wallace saw them coming in every case.

Siegel: George Wallace became known to everybody in the country in the years following the Supreme Court rulings on desegregation when he was a man standing in the schoolhouse door blocking desegregation of Alabama's schools. This is what we heard him say in those days.

Wallace: [*excerpt from archival tape*] I stand here today as governor of this sovereign state and refuse to willingly submit to the illegal usurpation of power by the central government. I claim today for all the people of the state of Alabama those rights reserved to them under the Constitution of the United States, among those powers so reserved and claimed is a right of state authority in the operation of the public schools, colleges, and universities. My action does not constitute disobedience to legislative and constitutional provisions. It is not defiance for defiance's sake but for the purpose of raising basic and fundamental constitutional questions.

My action is a call for strict adherence to the Constitution of the United States as it was written for a cessation of usurpation and abuses. My action seeks to avoid having state sovereignty sacrificed on the altar of political expediency.

Siegel: The argument he makes there is all about states' rights. Did he believe in states' rights?

Carter: My favorite Wallace story is from one of his associates who told a very long and involved story about George Wallace. If he had been suddenly parachuted into Albania, he would describe the steps by which Wallace would have ended up being head of the Soviet Union within about three years. As he said, George Wallace can believe whatever he needs to believe. And that was true throughout his career. He could believe whatever he needed to believe. And in the 1960s he believed in states' rights. That speech that you just played is an interesting kind of transitional speech because on the one level it's the same old defense of Southern sovereignty going back to John C. Calhoun, whatever that means after the Civil War. But there's another element and tone. The constant references to the central government and to the overbearing central government. There in that speech, that very early speech by Wallace, you can see the seeds of what becomes a major theme of his attack upon the national state.

Siegel: George Wallace was one of those people who pioneered what we would now consider to be the social issues, one of them being crime. And here's what he had to say about crime in his 1972 primary campaign as a Democrat.

Wallace: [*excerpt from archival tape*] And so, my friends, today law and order is an issue. And, as I used to say, if someone knocks you in the head when you walk out of this building tonight, the person that knocks you in the head is out of jail before you get to the hospital and on Monday they'll try a policeman about the matter.

[*cheers and applause*]

Siegel: This is a line he repeated very, very often.

Carter: Well, he was saying it even earlier. Obviously, there were other candidates who talked about the crime issue, but Wallace, again, it has to do with his effectiveness as an orator. What he does is he takes the crime issue and he personalizes it. It's not some vague abstract issue, it's what's going to happen to you — you're going to be hit over the head, you're going to end up in the hospital. And then he loads onto that this anger and rage over what is seen as the way in which the criminal is not sufficiently punished. And when he puts this together, it becomes one of his greatest crowd pleasers, really, beginning certainly as early as 1968.

Siegel: You try to sort out and establish whether indeed Wallace actually said something after he was defeated for governor of Alabama in 1958, which is often cited as the turning point in George Wallace's political career. It was an election in which he had, in fact, talked a good deal about roads and schools and fairly conventional things that an Alabama politician would pledge.

Carter: Well, that's the famous "out-niggered" statement, pardon my quotation here. The gist of it was "I'll never be out-niggered again," after he lost in 1958.

Siegel: That he would never find himself running against a candidate who took a harder line on race than he did.

Carter: Exactly.

Siegel: And won votes at his expense.

Carter: And he later insisted that he hadn't said it. I think he did. Unless you were there, there's no way to be sure. I've talked to two people who were present, one of whom says he doesn't remember; that's his old press secretary. Another newsman who was there says he definitely remembers it. It's something he'd never forget. In any case, it's totally consistent with what he told other people at the time and later on. One of my favorite accounts is actually by the editor of a north Alabama newspaper who liked Wallace, supported Wallace, and was angry at him for retreating into racism. And when he scolded Wallace about it, Wallace responded, "I started off talking about schools and highways and prisons and taxes, and I couldn't make them listen. And then I began talking about niggers and they stomped the floor." Well, the essence of it was the same. Wallace realized that there was no place for middle-of-the-road politicians in Alabama on race in 1958, and he made the choice to turn hard right on race.

Siegel: The last chapter in George Wallace's public life was that round of apologies when some black leaders agreed to appear with him, and he apologized for what he had said earlier. Was that a sincere move on Wallace's part?

Carter: Oh, I don't have any doubts that it's sincere. I don't evade that question, but to me it's not as important as the consequences of his actions. Ellen Goodman once talked about people who have abusive fathers. And I don't mean sexually abusive, I mean just people who mistreat them or whatever. And when they're old and they see the end of their lives, the fathers come back to the child, and they say, "Please forgive me." And the child, now the adult, forgives him, but there's still the person that was made by that abuse. And I think in many ways, we can all say, yes, we forgive George Wallace, but we can't forget what he did to this country and it was not very positive when you weigh it on the scales of history.

Another former independent candidate for president was JOHN ANDERSON, the ten-term Illinois Republican congressman who ran in 1980. He received about six percent of the vote, which is enough to receive matching federal campaign funds, but he carried not a single state. As people looked ahead to the 1996 presidential election, memories of Ross Perot's candidacy were fresh, President Clinton was at that time an unpopular incumbent, and the field of Republican prospects was lackluster. Scott Simon asked Anderson, then a law professor, about recent political developments, including the retirement announcement of New Jersey Democratic Senator Bill Bradley, who appeared to leave open the possibility of his involvement in a third party. August 19, 1995

Simon: How do you read Bill Bradley's announcement? Both his retirement and any further political interests?

Anderson: Well, I think his comments are entirely consistent with the fact that I believe today that there is an astonishing level of disillusionment with the political process; there is a kind of attenuation of party loyalties to the point where you are no longer looked at as somewhat peculiar when you talk about the possibility of a third party competing for the presidency in 1996.

Simon: Now, this is interesting. I covered your campaign in 1980. It is often said by the pollsters that you would have done much better if people had made an individual decision, but as it got closer to the election, people decided "I don't want to waste my vote on a third-party candidate," so they make do with either of the major-party candidates. Do you think that's changing?

Anderson: It is. And you're quite correct that the most disenchanting part of any press conference that I ever held was the fact that they always concentrated on my standing in the polls, and then the question came: Don't you believe that when push comes to shove, people aren't really going to want to waste a vote? This

time I believe people are sufficiently upset with the two-party system that they would not consider that they wasted a vote, they
would consider it a valid political expression.

Simon: What effect do you see Senator Bradley's announcement
having on that parochial institution, the Democratic party?

Anderson: Oh, I think it shows that really the Democratic party
is in very, very deep trouble. It's too much at this point to say
it's coming apart at the seams, but certainly this almost diffident
way in which a very prominent Democratic senator would indicate
that, yes, he's not necessarily bound by the hidebound tradition
that you support the incumbent president of your party; that the
situation is extreme and grave enough to consider a run as an independent. Coming from a prominent member of the Democratic
establishment, I think it shows that the party is in real trouble and
that President Clinton's leadership of that party is very tenuous.

Simon: Are a lot of the independent third- and fourth-party candidates that get explored, in reality, personality vehicles?

Anderson: Well, to some extent I suppose they are. But up to this
point, the mystery of the attractiveness of all of these people as
possible alternatives to a Republican or a Democrat is that it is still
so diffuse and people haven't formed ranks and joined to follow
someone because they are promoting a flat tax, or because they are
promoting some other specific program. It is the general feeling
that our political leadership is vapid, that it is vacuous, that it is
self-interested and that political reform at a very basic level has got
to be the number-one item on the agenda. I think any successful
candidate is going to have to start out with pledging that he will not
allow the factor that wealth now plays in determining who's going
to be nominated, who's going to be elected. I think that bothers an
awful lot of people in our country. And a lot of work has been done
to substantiate the fact that, to a very real extent, it is something
that is literally poisoning the well.

Simon: Senator Lugar of Indiana, for example, began his candidacy this year, and he was asked, inevitably, "Can you raise the
twenty million dollars to run?" And he said, "Well, I don't intend
to and I don't think the American people want me to raise or anyone to raise that kind of money to run." A widely admired comment, and so far it hasn't seemed to necessarily redound to his
benefit in the polls.

Anderson: Well, I think you've got to go beyond saying that I'm not going to spend this specific sum. You've got to demonstrate a willingness to endorse a specific program of campaign spending reform. And, heaven knows, there are plenty of them around. I introduced legislation with former Congressman Mo Udall way back in 1973, more than twenty years ago. And other legislation since that time repeatedly has been introduced and reintroduced. So I think you've got to get a candidate who really doesn't talk simply in terms of "Well, I'm not going to take all that much money." What is he going to do to shut off the valves that are pumping all of this money into the political system?

Simon: Mr. Anderson, were you a man ahead of your time?

Anderson: Well, in a sense I was because even though we achieved a level of support, I think people were still back in that frame of mind that, well, the two-party system, like it or not, it's almost a part of the Constitution, which it isn't. But nevertheless, today, I think all bets are off. There is the weakening, almost the dissolution, of the old loyalties that people felt to a party system that now seems to be malfunctioning.

Former Tennessee governor LAMAR ALEXANDER sought the Republican presidential nomination until he failed to achieve any victories in the 1996 primaries. As his campaign got under way, Alexander set out to raise twenty million dollars, more than two million at a single political fund-raising event at the Grand Ole Opry in Nashville. Alexander told Linda Wertheimer that his campaign was about sending authority for government programs from Washington to the states. March 6, 1995

Alexander: We're not too stupid to make decisions about school lunches in Nashville. We're not too stupid to decide what the third-grade curriculum ought to be. And we're not too stupid to see someone who needs help and help them. And we've gotten, in this country, into the idea that somehow just because you take a plane to Washington on Mondays that you suddenly have all this great wisdom. We Republicans are even guilty of that. I mean, look at the welfare and crime bills right now. The welfare bill would tell us in Tennessee what the welfare benefits ought to be. "Cut them off after two years," they say in Washington. We don't need their advice on that. And we keep building and building and building these decision-making entities in Washington until it's become an arrogant empire, and people are fed up with it. Not just Republicans, but a lot of people who normally think of themselves as Republicans feel that way.

Wertheimer: Now, I know if I were to ask you about tort reform, you'd say the same thing, and if I were to ask you about any number of other issues you'd say the same thing, so why do you want to be president and go to Washington?

Alexander: You know, I think that shows better than anything how far we've gone the wrong way in Washington. I want to be president of the entire United States, not of Washington, D.C. I mean, I don't want to be president of Washington and tell everybody what to do. I want to be president of the whole country and help give people in their own communities, families, and neighborhoods the freedom to do things for themselves. I mean, that's the single biggest fight we have. That's why a president would really help right now. It's very hard for the Republican Congress to lead the country. It's almost an unnatural act for a legislative body to be leading the country as it now is. It needs a Republican president to go with it, and then we might get something more done.

Wertheimer: Tell me about running for president as a Southerner. You'll be running against, if you get the nomination, a southern president. To get the nomination, you'll be running against Senator Gramm, who is, if anything, more of a conservative, more of a sort of good ole boy type candidate than you are. How did we just suddenly move our whole politics into the South?

Alexander: Well, the South — you're right in the center of it when you're in Nashville. I mean, the values of America, the music of America, the temperament of America, a lot of it comes right out of here. I mean, people are very comfortable, I think, with what we do here in Nashville. This is more of an all-American view than it might be from somewhere else. We've shifted the population center down this direction, and that's where a lot of America is. Plus the South has changed. We're more a part of the whole country, and we're big.

Wertheimer: Your state voted for a lot of Republicans this year. Many of the people we've talked to in Nashville say, "We were sick of what was going on in Washington so we voted for a new bunch." And I asked, "How long do you give them to fix it?" And they say, "Two years."

Alexander: Well, that's longer than I thought. This is a very impatient country, and this is a very independent state. We've run about fifty statewide races since 1964, and we've only won seven of them — we Republicans — up until this past year, and Senator Baker and I won five of those seven, so the Super Bowl win we had in ninety-four with all these Republican wins was unusual. And I think it's true. Unless we turn that anger into hope, unless we can dredge up out of our lives and music and feelings here a picture of America's future, then they'll turn back to somebody else.

Wertheimer: What do you think about running, essentially running with Newt Gingrich? Newt Gingrich is the nominal leader of this new movement. Do you think he really is the leader of the people that voted Republican in Tennessee last time?

Alexander: I think the answer to that's yes. Newt is doing the best job on the national scene of painting a picture of where he'd like to take the country. He helped that when he announced early that he wouldn't be a candidate for president because that seemed to be a principled stand. I mean, he seemed to be saying, "Well, I have a job to do. I believe in what I'm doing, so I'm going to stay here and try to do it." I think people like that. Now, he's taken a lot of hits. Any time you're in charge on the Hill, you're going to take some hits, but I think Newt's providing the ideas and, in the long run, people will respect ideas. I would like to present ideas. I'd like to be the ideas candidate in ninety-six. I have a little different personality than Newt.

Wertheimer: Can you imagine circumstances in which you and Newt might get in each other's way here? There's some very difficult issues that are immediately coming up in the Congress.

Alexander: I would love working with Newt Gingrich. I mean, I like working with strong people. I think our Republican Congress is doing a good job. I just think a Republican president has a different role, and I'm going to try to persuade the people that my background and the fact that I live here, that I'm from outside Washington, adds a dimension to our leadership that will serve us very well in October of ninety-six. By October of ninety-six, the Democrats are going to be after us. They're going to be painting us as extremists. They're going to have a lot of ammunition. The better we do, in a way, the more trouble we'll be in. And I think a good, strong Republican candidate from Nashville painting a picture of the future may be just what we want by that time.

AMERICA TALKING

....

In April, we measured the progress of the 104th Congress, which arrived in Washington with new Republican majorities in both houses, and as much acclaim as a new chief executive. Linda Wertheimer visited several suburbs of Kansas City and asked different groups of voters what they made of the new Republican Congress. In Gladstone, Missouri, a mostly middle-class community north of the Missouri River, she met a few of the parents who were paying for their four-year-olds to spend three days a week at a special preschool: MIKE DUNN, an engineer at a TV station who moonlights as a disc jockey; his wife, JEANNIE DUNN, who tends bar part-time; DEBBIE YATES, who stays home with her two children; LUCY SMITH, who works part-time for the Kansas City school system; and KEVIN BOLAND, a sales representative who has a wife and small daughter. They had not closely followed the Republicans' work on the Contract with America, although they broadly approved of giving more authority to the states and lowering taxes. They began by explaining why they live in Gladstone. April 3, 1995

Boland: Nothing drew me here. I was born here. My parents, when I was born, built a house in Gladstone, so I've lived here all my life.

Mike Dunn: I was born in St. Louis. My wife is from Kansas City, around here. But we like it because it's family-oriented.

Jeannie Dunn: We chose to move to Gladstone. I lived in Independence, south of the river, all my life. But we like the area up here, so we moved up here just recently, about, well, five years ago.

Mike Dunn: Well, we just bought a house.

Smith: One of my reasons, I was looking for was the resale value of your house. You know, it will climb; it won't go down.

Wertheimer: So, Lucy Smith, are you thinking that you would like to, at some point, trade up?

Smith: Oh yes, because we just bought a house in June, a starter home.

Mike Dunn: Basic starter home. Mid-fifties.

Wertheimer: What is a basic starter home in Gladstone?

Mike Dunn: Well, I would call it a ranch-type house. Maybe two or three bedrooms, you know.

Wertheimer: Two-car garage?

Jeannie Dunn: One car.

Wertheimer: Do you find you are working harder to raise young children and keep one parent at home?

Boland: I am working harder. When I say harder, I mean longer hours. I'm working harder for less money now.

Wertheimer: Anybody else have that feeling?

Mike Dunn: Oh yes, I have. I think I've progressed. I work two jobs, you know. One in the evening, one on the weekend. But they're basically career-oriented goals. I guess I'm looking to increase certain positions within my career. So it's not really a money factor as much as it is just attaining experience and working my way up that way. My wife is staying home with the children instead of taking them to a full-time, eight-hour-a-day day care center.

Jeannie Dunn: That's why I work part-time, kind of supplements our income.

Wertheimer: What about you, Debbie Yates?

Yates: I just couldn't see a stranger taking the best care of my child.

Boland: My wife and I have done the same thing. She worked for Southwestern Bell for thirteen years, and when we had Caroline, we decided that she would stay home, and we probably would have moved up a step to a bigger house by now but we haven't. You know, our vacations are to the lake instead of the coast, and we don't go out to eat every weekend. But it's definitely worth it.

Mike Dunn: I do feel we need some help from Uncle Sam as far as taxes for the middle class, especially when you have kids. I believe in added deductions for families with children because so much is going into the care of the child.

Wertheimer: One of the tax breaks that is being contemplated by the Congress in the original plan was a five-hundred-dollar deduction per child given to people who have up to two hundred thousand dollars in taxable income.

Mike Dunn: Is that what they call middle class? Up to two hundred thousand dollars a year annual income? I think I'm still the working poor, then, I guess.

Wertheimer: Do you have any feeling that taxes are too high, too low, about right?

Smith: Oh, I think they're too high, but you know, they say they want to do one thing, and all these people gripe about it, and you know, I don't see how anybody could do anything in Washington. It's a farce.

Wertheimer: Do you feel optimistic about your future?

Jeannie Dunn: Future looks bright, although it isn't as bright for us as it was for people maybe thirty years ago, you know. I think that here we see quite a bit of people maybe working part-time, whereas before you would see the traditional family — husband working, mother at home. The mother didn't work part-time, the father didn't work part-time. But now you see a lot of that. For that same type of lifestyle, I think we're having to work harder.

Wertheimer: Are you bitter about that?

Jeannie Dunn: I think it's just a sign of the times. I think you can't be bitter about it. You just have to work through it.

Wertheimer: Kevin, you expressed something like that at the beginning of the conversation, about feeling that you were working harder to stay in the same place. How do you feel about the future?

Boland: Well, I think it's getting harder. I think it's harder for me to achieve some of the goals that I want to get to than it was for, say, my father, or even somebody that's ten years older than me. My parents bought a house for a certain price and sold it twenty years later for six, eight, maybe ten times what they paid for it. I don't think that's going to happen with me. I'm not trying to be pessimistic, but I think it's rougher now. Definitely.

Another Kansas City suburb, Overland Park, Kansas, is one of the wealthiest communities in the nation and a source of strong support for the Republicans, particularly the former Kansas senator Robert Dole. At a prayer breakfast hosted by the mayor and attended by hundreds of people, Linda Wertheimer heard assessments of the Republicans' first hundred days in control of Congress from CHRIS ILIFF, a lawyer who works in the insurance business; his brother-in-law STEVE HUGHES, a golf course appraiser; RAY MATTIX, a contractor; DAVE WEBB, an auctioneer; BILL ELWOOD, a banker; and RICK GUINN, an assistant district attorney for Johnson County, Kansas. These men, most barely in their forties, were generally prosperous, content, and indifferent to events in Washington. April 6, 1995

Webb: I look at politics as affecting about ten percent of my life, and if we have effective, good politics, maybe that's going to have an eleven percent effect on my life versus nine or eight. In my daily life I really don't know what's going on in Washington, D.C. I don't pay too much attention. I couldn't tell you the basic points of the Contract with America. I do like the idea of accountability, and I do like the idea of politicians saying, "This is what we intend to do." And being able to measure that, have some kind of a yardstick. I like the principle. I don't feel a lot of direct effect myself, personally.

Wertheimer: Chris Iliff, do you think that what is going on in Washington now, with the Republicans in power and the changes that are being attempted, is this going to be good for you and people you care about or not?

Iliff: I think, generally speaking, the drift back toward conservatism is a good thing for the financial community in the United States. I have a fairly strongly held belief that when the financial community prospers, that the entire country benefits from that. A lot of people have made fun of trickle-down economics. But, in fact, trickle-down does have beneficial effects throughout the entire economy, including that some people who couldn't enter the marketplace before will have their first opportunities.

Wertheimer: Has anything happened in the Congress so far that you didn't expect or that surprised you or startled you in any way?

Iliff: First of all, I would agree that I like what's happened so far, generally speaking. In terms of more fiscal responsibility, one of the things that surprised me and concerns me is that if the change is legitimate and everybody's sincere about it, why are we talking about a tax cut, when we still have a deficit that seems to be causing so much trouble? That surprised me, that the Republicans would take that approach when we have the deficit that we've got.

Wertheimer: Might be good politics. I mean, it might not be good budgeting, but it might be good politics.

Iliff: That's what concerns me. The first hundred days to me, I feel are maybe less politics and more reality. And this seemed to get back into the mode of too much politics.

Wertheimer: Anybody else, anything that you've seen that you particularly like or don't like?

Hughes: I like the idea of bringing many of these budgets and these programs to the table to be reviewed and to be held accountable that in the past have always just been granted and reviewed. They all should be held accountable and they all should be made accountable for their actions and what they do. And I think the review is good for the system.

Wertheimer: Do politicians who speak about values make sense to you?

Guinn: Among my circle of acquaintances, I think a lot of people have recognized that politics fails us when it comes to the essentials of life. The meaning of life doesn't come from the political processes. It comes from the things we do day to day, our families, our work, our lives and our churches. And the way we deal with our friends and neighbors. Mostly I want politicians to stay out of that matter. And my prayer today is that politicians will refrain from doing things that hinder the things that really give meaning to life.

Wertheimer: Mr. Elwood, is there any particular thing that you would like politicians to get into or stay out of? I mean, how do your concerns about politicians getting in your way express themselves?

Elwood: Right now, I have three young children. I think the school system is very important. I want to have the primary responsibility and I want to be involved in decisions when it comes to curriculum for my children. I don't want the government to make those decisions for me or my wife, my family.

Wertheimer: How do you feel about prayer in school?

Elwood: That's a tough question. Prayer is a very active part of my life and my child's life. I happen to know that my children do pray at school and they feel that they can. If something would happen that they wouldn't be able to do that at some point in the future, I wouldn't be happy about that. And I might have to look to some type of a private school. At this point, my children are in public school.

Wertheimer: What do you think of the leader of the Republican revolution in the Congress, Speaker of the House Newt Gingrich?

Mattix: I think he's doing great. I'm proud of him for sticking in there to follow through with what he believes and what he's trying to do in the face of really tremendous pressure from news media and political opponents. And I'm real proud of him. I hope he hangs in there.

Iliff: I agree with most of the things he does. I wish he would bite his tongue more often.

Hughes: I characterize him as a mover and a shaker, and I think the system needed somebody like him, just to shake things up. I tend to agree with Chris that he could control what he has to say a little bit better and maybe that's just his true feelings coming out, or maybe it's the Rush Limbaugh in him. I don't know. But, at times, I wish he'd tone it down a little bit.

Webb: I think it takes a very strong character to do what he's attempting to do. As the old saying goes, "A shy salesman has skinny kids" and you have to be pretty aggressive, I think, to get the ball rolling.

Elwood: For years we've had politicians and we don't know exactly where they stand, and with Newt, you know where he stands. I appreciate that.

M any Americans were fascinated with the double murder trial of O. J. Simpson and held strong opinions about it. The photographer GREGG SEGAL confirmed as much on assignment for the *Los Angeles Reader*. His photographs, reprinted in *Harper's Magazine,* were called "O.J.: The People Have Spoken." Segal captured people advertising their thoughts about the case. For example, in a trailer park, a child looks straight ahead through binoculars; behind him, a man is seated holding a sign that reads WHY WOULD HE RUN? The photographer talked about his assignment with Robert Siegel. August 4, 1995

Segal: I didn't want to point my camera where all the other cameras were pointed. That didn't seem to be very interesting. I was really more interested in talking to the nun in Hollywood, the dressmaker in Silver Lake, the Marines downtown, the Punjabi Sikhs in North Hollywood, the full spectrum of people you find in L.A.

Siegel: There were really two parts of this. You wanted to talk to them, to hear what they thought about the trial, and also to photograph them.

Segal: Right. The trial has been much maligned and criticized for the tremendous coverage it has gotten, but I think that we fail to see one of the good sides of this whole trial, that it's an opportunity for discourse. So the challenge was really to turn this discourse into a photographic work.

Siegel: And the device that you settled on was to take one comment from a subject in a photograph and make a caption sign out of that.

Segal: Right. I chose one statement, often the statement that was least obvious, the one that had been shaded so that the subjects weren't making themselves controversial. They wanted to avoid controversy. Those statements tended to be more interesting, I think.

Siegel: So the result is a series of pictures in which we see some people, one of whom is holding up a sign. For example, a visiting fourth-grade schoolgirl from Ohio is in a mini-golf course, holding up a sign in one hand that says, HE WAS CRYING AT THE BEGINNING OF THE TRIAL. YOU KNOW WHAT THAT MEANS.

Segal: And that can be interpreted, I guess, in two ways. It's not really clear to the viewer. It's more interesting because it opens the imagination. Does she mean that he's crying because he feels guilty, or is he crying because he feels saddened by the death of his wife?

Siegel: Tell me about your photo of Metro subway workers on Hollywood Boulevard.

Segal: I stopped and asked them if they had been watching the trial. They had, as everyone seems to have been in L.A., and Detective Mark Fuhrman had just been testifying the day before.

Siegel: So the result is this very casual group scene, a bunch of guys in hard hats, and this little sign in the middle saying, FUHRMAN PLANTED THE GLOVE.

Segal: Right.

Siegel: Did any people, when you approached them, simply say to you, "I don't know anything about the O. J. Simpson trial"?

Segal: No. Everybody had something to say. I went up to an ice cream vendor who spoke very little English, and I had to ask a little boy who was playing on a Little League team to translate for me from Spanish. People who you would think have no connection to American culture were aware of the trial.

Siegel: My favorite photo is of dressmaker Susa Sales. Could you describe that picture?

Segal: In that photograph there is an El Salvadoran dressmaker who is standing beside a group of mannequins who are also kind of looking into the camera. Maybe there's a cultural idenfication here. Her statement says, ROSA LOPEZ WAS TELLING THE TRUTH. A lot of people tended to believe that Rosa Lopez was not telling the truth, that she was evasive. I think a lot of that is, perhaps, cultural in the way that questions are answered. People from different cultures approach answering questions differently.

W hen the lawyer Johnnie Cochran made his closing argument for O. J. Simpson, the issue of racism was elevated from a defense case to a social cause. Cochran used such phrases as "genocidal racist" and "another Adolf Hitler" to describe the Los Angeles police detective Mark Fuhrman. When Cochran appealed to jurors to defeat racism by acquitting his client, Robert Siegel asked several African Americans who have written about racism for their reactions. KAREN GRIGSBY BATES is a Los Angeles journalist and *All Things Considered* commentator. GLENN LOURY is an essayist and professor of Economics at Boston University. ROGER WILKINS is a professor of history at George Mason University. September 29, 1995

Wilkins: There are times when playing the race card is absolutely abominable, as when Congressman Mel Reynolds, a convicted sex criminal, stood up, and said, "When you take me away in shackles, as you took my ancestors in shackles, you won't bow my head," and it defiles the humanity and the strength of all of our ancestors. The O. J. Simpson case is not as clear. Surely, I think that Johnnie Cochran went too far. But if you are black and you have had contact with the LAPD, as I have on a number of occasions, you do have to wonder about the veracity of the department.

Siegel: But is that an invitation, then, to black jurors, when confronted with white detectives and a black defendant in Los Angeles, to say, "We should acquit because this is a police force with very many racist cops on it"?

Wilkins: No, no. It seems to me, you go over the top when you say these people are racist and, therefore, he's innocent.

Siegel: And as for Johnnie Cochran likening Mark Fuhrman to Adolf Hitler?

Wilkins: I found it deeply offensive, and I think it is an offense to anybody who cares deeply about the history of Hitler to say that one racist cop is like Hitler, simply in an effort to get your client off.

Loury: I think it's entirely predictable and very lamentable. I think a lawyer is going to defend his client with any tools that are at hand, and race is certainly at hand, readily so. But I think that when one steps back from it and looks at the two dead bodies on the ground, the passions, the violence, and all the rest, this is not a trial about race at all. I say that notwithstanding Mr. Mark Fuhrman. It's a trial about all too familiar phenomena in human experience, and that it should be made to turn one way or the other on the emotions and loyalties that jurors may feel by virtue of being black or white is really too bad.

Siegel: I can imagine an argument that an acquittal of O. J. Simpson in this case would possibly create a squeaky clean police force in Los Angeles, one that would not only make sure that no racist officers were tolerated, but even clean up the police lab and make sure that things weren't done sloppily, that it is, in effect, a civic act to acquit. That seemed to be a theme of Mr. Cochran's.

Loury: Frankly, I find that absurd. That is, both the claim that there's some causal relation between the verdict in this case and the behavior of the LAPD and then the inference that if that relation were there, someone otherwise thought to be a murderer should be allowed to go free so as to bring about that effect. It's a monstrosity, isn't it, that a brutal crime of this sort should be forgiven in the interests of some abstract goal of advancing the social cause?

Bates: The fact that this was an interracial marriage, I think, has kept a lot of interest focused on it, and the fact that how what's happened has been viewed through a racial prism, on all sides, has contributed to a general upping of the ante in the tension department, in this city anyway. It's a way for the press to talk about race without really having to talk about it.

Siegel: What did you think, though, of what seemed to be the message to the jurors from Johnnie Cochran that they have almost a potential civic duty here to uproot racism in the police department by acquitting O. J. Simpson, that it would be a notorious violation of civil rights for Mr. Simpson to be convicted?

Bates: I think juries are a lot smarter than lawyers usually give them credit for being. I also think that the jury is looking at this as each of these sides are doing their job. You know, it's the defense attorney's job to fight tooth and nail for his client. It's the prosecutor's job to plunge ahead with absolute zeal to bring the accused to justice. And I think the people are looking at it that way.

Siegel: And you think, for example, in the black neighborhood that you live in, when Johnnie Cochran is seen screaming that this "genocidal racist" of a cop was the messenger so you can't believe the message, that Mr. Cochran is seen as doing his job, saying what he's paid to say?

Bates: What I heard was, "Hmm, Johnnie's taking 'em to church. You know, he's making them remember that yes, two people are dead in all of this and that there is a person who is accused of doing it and the way they are trying to convict him has relied heavily on people in their own ranks that have been suspect." He's reminding them, as Marvin Gaye said in "I Heard It through the Grapevine," believe half of what you see and none of what you hear.

The verdict of the jury to acquit O. J. Simpson was announced live on national radio and television and was heard or viewed by millions. *All Things Considered* telephoned four African Americans who had followed the trial and watched the verdict. Noah Adams spoke with TY FLEMING, who charters fishing boats in Orange Beach, Alabama, and LOUIS SMITH, a shoe salesman in south Chicago. Linda Wertheimer spoke with MALIK KEY, a warehouse manager, and ANGELA JONES. They watched the verdict at Mary's Hair Gallery on Harlem's 125th Street. October 3, 1995

Jones: I was devastated. I'm still devastated.

Wertheimer: Why?

Jones: Because he was definitely guilty. You know this whole thing was about O.J., not about Nicole and Ron.

Wertheimer: You identified with the victims, then?

Jones: Of course.

Wertheimer: What was it that made you sure that O. J. Simpson was guilty?

Jones: The blood, the DNA, the fact that he was not there where the limousine driver was looking for him. He changed his — I don't know — excuse, shall I say. It wasn't an alibi. He changed his excuse several times about where he was, what he was doing, how he got cut. I think the fact that there was mostly black on the jury and female. I think women are very meek, and he's charming, and you know, what we have seen of O.J. for years. I mean, I met O.J., and we dined in the same restaurant, the Dakota, and when he would come in, he would put on his charm, and men and women wanted to meet him. I think the fact that he got off is because of who he is and the jury was mostly black and Fuhrman was a racist.

Wertheimer: In the end, race was the reason?

Jones: Yes, and who he is.

Wertheimer: Malik Key, could you tell me what you think of the jury's decision?

Key: I think that they made a good decision, although I think that some of them were pressured into that decision.

Wertheimer: What do you mean?

Key: The jury was mostly black and most of them live in black neighborhoods, and a lot of black people felt like that O. J. Simpson was not guilty. So how could they go back to their neighborhoods, their own neighborhoods, and tell those people that they found him guilty? I mean it would create a lot of problems for some of them.

Wertheimer: Did you follow the trial closely?

Key: I followed every day. I even taped it while I was at work, you know.

Wertheimer: So did you come to any conclusion?

Key: On my own, I feel like he's guilty, but I have to honestly say that, if I was on the jury, I would have said "Not guilty."

Wertheimer: Why?

Key: Because people don't want to deal with the pressure. I know I would not want to go back to Harlem, OK, and tell the guys on my corner at the corner store that I found O.J. guilty. I might not be able to go to that store anymore.

Fleming: What I saw, what I heard on television, I thought he might have been probably guilty, but I could see his reasons for doing what he was doing if he did do it. Not too many people like their wives running around with other fellas, but that don't mean it was right to do it.

Adams: So you think he was guilty, even though he was acquitted?

Fleming: Oh, yes, sir. I'm pretty sure he was guilty, but the thing is in America, we've got a system where you're supposed to be innocent until proven guilty in court. Doesn't matter what anybody thinks — me or you or anybody else. And they just didn't prove him guilty.

Adams: Now, if you had been on the jury, did you see anything watching television or reading about it that would have convinced you of that guilt in court?

Fleming: No. No, I sure didn't. I saw a couple things that might have convinced me if they'd have turned out to be true, but they didn't turn out to be true, and that left reasonable doubt, and they didn't have a choice but to turn him loose.

Adams: What did you think about the yearlong trial, the televised trial, all the attention paid to it, all the money spent on it?

Fleming: Well, I think if it had been me, the trial would have been a hell of a lot shorter. I haven't got the money that Mr. Simpson has, but all in all, I think it came out about right like it should have.

Smith: Well, I'm going to be honest with you. I was with O.J. from day one, but first I'd like to say I'm sorry for the lives that was lost. I'm sorry for their families, but I always feel as though O.J. was innocent from the chauffeur driver because I feel as though if he would have did it, if anybody should have seen any blood, it should have been the chauffeur.

Adams: The fellow who took him to the airport?

Smith: Yes, the fellow that took him to the airport. If he was guilty in any way, I think he would have seen the guiltiness in him. I respect the jury's verdict. I like the way they did it, and I like the swiftness that they did it in.

Adams: Have you tried to put yourself in that jury room?

Smith: A thousand times. A thousand times.

Adams: When you get down to the end of a whole year of this situation, what's the big question you still have about this case?

Smith: What's my big question?

Adams: Yes.

Smith: Do he know who did it?

Adams: Does O. J. Simpson know who did it?

Smith: Does O. J. Simpson know who did it? See, I've been telling my friend the prosecution was trying O. J. Simpson for the murder that they were saying that he did it hisself. But I think they went in the wrong direction. I think O.J. know who did it. I'm not going to be the first person to say that he had it done, but I'm quite sure he have a strong belief on who did it.

Adams: OK, Mr. Smith, thank you for your time, sir.

Smith: But I can tell you this — I think if it was an all-white jury, I think he would have been found guilty.

Adams: You do?

Smith: I really do.

Robert McNamara, secretary of defense under Presidents Kennedy and Johnson, later president of the World Bank, broke his public silence on the war in Vietnam in 1995. An architect of the U.S. war policy in the 1960s, McNamara wrote twenty years after the war's end that it had been a misguided effort, that he had concluded as early as 1963 that the U.S. effort was doomed to failure, and that U.S. policymakers had improvised for years with no successful strategy in mind. Noah Adams sought the reactions of four Americans with different experiences of the Vietnam War: DAVID HARRIS, who had been an antiwar acivist; JAMES WEBB, the novelist and former navy secretary who had commanded a marine rifle platoon in Vietnam; JOSEPH GALLOWAY, who covered the war for ten years as a journalist; and EDITH MEEKS, who served in Vietnam as a nurse. April 14, 1995

Meeks: My immediate reaction was almost as if your husband would come home and tell you that he's been having an affair, and tell you all of the graphic details of the affair, and he'd go away feeling great and you'd feel terrible. And then he'd decide to write a book about this and tell all the graphic details and make money, and you'd still feel terrible and not have a cent. And I think the most appalling thing for me is that he's going to be making money off us again.

Harris: Well, I suppose, better late than never. It was nice to have McNamara finally come up and say what everybody had rumored he felt. But I was amazed at the paucity of his moral reasoning. I mean, he wanted to just say, "OK, it was a mistake. Sorry about that, guys." And leave it at that, which is impossible. I mean, what are the implications of having wasted the lives that we wasted? And what are the implications of him having sat on this information for almost thirty years?

Adams: James Webb, your thoughts when you heard, read the news about Robert McNamara's statements?

Webb: Well, I thought basically it was old news. I think everyone knew how McNamara felt. I think that's one of the reasons that he remained silent as long as he did. For me, it has been interesting more to watch the reaction of people, particularly those who were opposed to the war, as they seem to have grabbed ahold of this. There certainly hasn't been anything after the conclusion of the war in Vietnam in 1975 that's happened over there, that has given any justification to how strongly people felt against the war.

Adams: Joseph Galloway, tell us, please, your first response when you heard this about Robert McNamara?

Galloway: Not surprised. He was making statements throughout 1965, counting the beans, if you will, in the wake of the Ya Drang battle, and coming up with pretty good forecasts of what was likely to happen. He gave the president two options. One, let's cut our losses and get out of here, or two, we give General Westmoreland what he is asking for, in which case by 1967 early, there'll be 550,000 Americans in Vietnam. They will be dying at the rate of 1,000 a month, and all we can possibly achieve is a military stalemate at a much higher level of violence. The question to me is, having counted the beans that accurately and presented them to President Johnson, the wise men sat down at the White House on December 16, 1965, and they considered these options. They didn't consider option one very long. Option two, after a day and a half of chitchat, they voted unanimously to pursue. President Johnson began that conference by looking at Secretary McNamara, and saying, "Bob, is what you're saying that no matter what I do, I can't win?" And Secretary McNamara said, "Yes, that's right." Now, that to me, is one of the stranger moments in American history.

Adams: Well, you must feel, then, do you, that Secretary McNamara should have said something about this earlier, that lives indeed could have been saved had he said something publicly, had he disagreed with President Kennedy in public, with President Johnson, with President Nixon after he left the Pentagon. Do you think he should have talked out earlier?

Galloway: I certainly do. I think, in fact, if he came to this conclusion that early in the game, I would have a great deal more respect for what he says in his book, if he had said it in 1967.

Adams: Mr. McNamara says that in a cabinet position, one does

not do that while serving or after serving. James Webb, you re-
signed as secretary of the navy in a bit of protest. Do you agree with
Robert McNamara saying that a secretary of defense should not
criticize a president, any president?

Webb: No. I don't agree with that. And I think what Joe is saying
here is correct, that if he felt strongly that the policy that he was
responsible for formulating was not going to work, then he should
have said something. That is separate from the fact, in my view, of
whether we should have been attempting to do something in Vietnam. We were executing this strategy in a way that was accomplishing exactly what they wanted. It was the wrong strategy. That
doesn't mean that you couldn't have had a better strategy. In fact,
people criticize Richard Nixon, but I was there. I watched the Viet-
namization policy begin to take effect in the area that I was in in
Vietnam. And if it had been done earlier, I think it would have been
successful.

Harris: The issue of "for what?" sits out there. You know, the
problem was not simply a strategic one. The problem was the policy was sicker than that, sick down to its roots.

Webb: You certainly had your say on that issue during the war
and got a lot of media attention for it. But the South Vietnamese
people wanted to live under a different system and they still do. All
the Vietnamese people do.

Harris: Why didn't they fight for it?

Webb: They did fight for it.

Harris: The South Vietnamese troops were notoriously unreli-
able throughout the war.

Webb: Were you ever in Vietnam during the war? Did you ever
see them fight?

Harris: No, I didn't.

Webb: They're probably the most maligned military in history.
I've had friends who are down to —

Meeks: Gentlemen. Gentlemen, I don't particularly care about
the Vietnamese. The thing that I feel so sad about is our own guys
and our own gals. And it wasn't only those that died or those that
were physically injured. But there were hundreds of thousands that
were maimed emotionally and spiritually. And this man thinks
that he can have peace just by writing a book and making money.
And all the rest of these people are sitting there still in pain.

Adams: David Harris, let me ask you a question along those lines. What do you think now is going to be the attitude of people who protested against this war? Have you used the word *vindication* in conversation this week?

Harris: Well, I don't think it's Robert McNamara's role to vindicate me or anybody else that was against the war. I don't think that's the proper alignment of forces here. I think it certainly shined a light on the fact that the government understood as well as we did the paucity of the policy they were pursuing.

Adams: Mr. Webb, let me ask you about the dedication of your book, *Fields of Fire*. It says, "For the 100,000 marines who became casualties, dead and wounded, in Vietnam and for the others who became casualties upon their return." I'd like to ask this question of Joe Galloway and also of Edith Meeks. If you are a returning Vietnam veteran coming back to a country that, in many cases, did not welcome your actions in Vietnam, does this information from Robert McNamara change the way you perceive what you've done?

Webb: For me it doesn't. And I think this is where I disagree with Mr. Harris and other people, that if you look at what happened in Southeast Asia and look honestly at that, from 1975 forward, you will see the reasons that we were attempting to help an incipient democracy there, however flawed the strategy was. Unlike Ms. Meeks, I feel very strongly about the Vietnamese people. That's why I was there. I have spent a good part of my life working to help Vietnam veterans. I was the first Vietnam veteran on the House Veterans Committee to work as a counsel. These were not draftees for the most part. Two-thirds of the people who went over there were volunteers. The most reliable surveys that we have done on them show that ninety-one percent were glad they served their country. Two out of three said they would do that again, even with the end result. More than seventy percent said they did not feel that the government was taking advantage of them. They disagreed with that question. The problem has been that this age group was so split and so torn up because of the draft policies during the war, where principally the elites did not go, and they made it so extremely difficult for the people who came back to re-enter society, that this is where so many of the psychological problems the Vietnam veterans had. That's where they came from.

Meeks: When I came back, we were told by incoming nurses that as soon as we got stateside, we should take our uniforms off because of the negative reaction to the uniform. This was in 1969 when I returned. Which I did. For many years, I was not proud that I was an army nurse. And, for us, it was the hardest thing because we never saw any of the successes. We never saw them take a hill. We just got the leftovers, whether they won or lost the battle, we got whatever was hit.

Adams: Joseph Galloway, do you know veterans, men who you were with in the central highlands and throughout the ten years, who will now have their attitudes changed by what Secretary McNamara is saying? If it seems to me if you went and you've had doubts about what you were doing, and then your secretary of defense says, "Well, we could have been out of there in 1963 and 1965 and 1967," it might confuse you about what happened.

Galloway: I don't think there's any confusion. I think among some that I know and have talked to, there's a great deal of anger. There's anger and a feeling of betrayal. McNamara said, "They called it McNamara's War, and I was proud that they did at the time." He was the secretary of defense. He built the policies, the failed policies.

Adams: This brings up something that Secretary McNamara said about the issue of what is called "unleashing the military." He said the war was not winnable, short of genocidal bombing of North Vietnam, and that would have risked a nuclear confrontation with the Soviets or the Chinese. He says, "I know of no thoughtful analysis of the war that says we would have won if we had unleashed our military. The military scholars don't say it." Mr. Webb, you're suggesting the war was winnable. Mr. Galloway, do you think it was?

Galloway: I have no doubt that the war could have been won. It's the cost of it, not just in terms of lives lost, but the weapons that you would have had to use, the measures that you would have had to take, which would have made us a pariah in the world, I suppose.

Webb: I have a totally different take on this. You will recall in 1961, that when John Kennedy put the first troops into Vietnam, the communists were assassinating eleven government officials a day in South Vietnam. Their violence was very specific, very tightly controlled. We went in with a totally wrong strategy. We could not have won the war with McNamara's strategy. That I will agree with. We could have won the war with far less people, with far less bombing, by focusing on the political elements and the political assassinations and using military forces only as a holding action.

Adams: When you read the beginning of Robert McNamara's book, you become a bit discouraged about government. He says there was no senior policy group working on Vietnam. Very few people in the State Department had any experience there. There was not a great deal of expertise being applied to this problem. You're suggesting that had there been much earlier, many lives could have been saved and it could have been winnable?

Webb: I believe so.

Harris: I would take issue with the notion of a winnable war from two angles. First, what do we win, the right to dictate governments to people around the world? I mean, on some deeper level, the goal of our policy was not something that we wanted to accomplish. The second thing is, I have real problems with this notion of hands having been tied behind our back. I understand in relative military operations that ours was not a total war. On the other hand, we dropped 250 pounds of high explosives for every single living human being on the entire Southeast Asian subcontinent. This is not something that happened because people had one hand behind their back.

Meeks: I would like to just put something in here from a person who is not a professional in this. I was just a nurse in the army for two years and then I went and got married. And I have two children that are in college now. And I have to say that I do not trust my government, especially when it comes to using my children. My criteria for a draft would be that all of the children of the congressmen and of the president would have to go first for me to see that this was important enough for them to use up my children.

Webb: You know, I agree with you. It may surprise you after what I've been saying today, that I was opposed to the Gulf War, for a number of reasons which made it distinct from the way that I feel about Vietnam.

Adams: Secretary McNamara brings up the issue of cynicism. He says he wants to address this problem in the country. Some could argue that seeing, hearing, reading, his admissions would make an American more cynical.

Galloway: Hardly inspires trust, does it?

Adams: What do you think, Mr. Harris, Mr. Webb, Ms. Meeks, Mr. Galloway, about the role of the military, the role of the citizen in the wars that are to come?

Harris: I think the obvious lesson of Vietnam is that you cannot grant the government a blank check on the nation's manpower. They got us into that situation with such a blank check and it was the existence of that blank check that allowed them to continue it. I think that clearly, the military ought to be an instrument of American policy. But American policy has to be grounded in the values that we want to characterize our society. It has to be subject to public debate. It has to be subject to a kind of public political process before anybody is sent anywhere.

Meeks: I think too we need to remember that every person that is drafted or goes over, that I took care of, those were people. Now, to the generals they may just move lumps of people, and it's ten thousand here and ten thousand there. These are people, and that our government would think that we're dispensable, that is horrifying. Then, that our government would not take care of us after the war because they were ashamed of the war.

Galloway: You'll not find me defending the Veterans Administration on this or any other venue. As to the military, we have a very professional military now, very fine soldiers, very great leaders. In fact, one of the good things that came out of Vietnam was a generation of lieutenants and captains and majors who, once they left there, sure as hell knew how not to fight a war. They had learned the hard way, and those are the people who lead the uniformed services today. My question is, who serves in those uniform services? Once again, it's not the children of the elite. An army should mirror the society that it defends.

Webb: I don't think, in terms of whether this increases or decreases someone's trust in their government, that this really adds anything. I think that the years of the war, and then through the Watergate era and all that, caused so much turmoil that all this does really, is show us how raw the wounds of Vietnam still are. That, when McNamara can resurface after twenty-seven years and say anything, it's going to be the great Rorschach test. People are looking at it and they're pulling off their own emotions and their own memories and everything gets going. It shows us how we have not resolved it. I would suggest that the way to resolve this issue is for us to reconnect with Vietnam in a positive way. When I first went back to Vietnam in ninety-one and especially in ninety-two, when I was back there, I had some pretty tough times with the communists because every time I go to Vietnam, I still articulate the concerns of the people who believed in us and trusted in us and have suffered. If this is an important country and if the issue is important, we need to come together on it and move forward, instead of just talking about what happened in 1967.

JENNIFER DUNN and PAMELA DUNN are not related. Jennifer is a Republican member of Congress from Washington State; Pamela is a single mother who, until she found a job shortly before this interview, was on welfare. The two women met in an experimental program called Walk a Mile in Your Sister's Shoes. The program tried to clarify the problems of welfare by pairing welfare mothers with female legislators. The Dunns talked about the program with Daniel Zwerdling after they exchanged news with each other. September 16, 1995

Pamela: Bree started first grade.

Jennifer: How does she like it?

Pamela: Oh, she's doing OK. You know kids and school. Summer's over, and "Well, I'm not so sure I really want to — "

Zwerdling: Excuse me, Jennifer Dunn and Pamela Dunn, forgive me for eavesdropping on your conversation. You sound like you're actually friends.

Jennifer: Well, I think we are. We also have the last name that's the same. Isn't that ironic?

Zwerdling: Let me start with you, Jennifer Dunn. I'm curious about what intrigued you about the program, and why did you decide to sign up for it?

Jennifer: Well, when I first heard about the program, I was right in the middle of welfare reform, which is the first responsibility of the brand-new committee that I sit on as a sophomore in the Congress. And I didn't know a lot about welfare. I had been a working mother myself, but I had not been a welfare mother. I wanted to understand everything I could about it, and I really wanted to see it firsthand.

Zwerdling: Were you a little nervous about getting to know a welfare mother? Be brutally honest now. If I had asked you on the day you signed up for this program, "What is your image of a typical welfare mother?" what would you have told me?

Jennifer: I didn't have any qualms about meeting a welfare mother. I've met a lot of welfare mothers. But I'd never really sat down and studied it from an issues point of view, where I'm focusing on it and asking questions that are going to be important that I'm going to have to put a lot of thought into, as we put it into legislative language. This is a big deal.

Zwerdling: Let's get back to that in just a minute. Let me go to Pamela Dunn for a minute. Pamela, when you heard that you were going to be paired with Jennifer Dunn, what was your image of her? What was your image of a Republican congresswoman?

Pamela: Well, I'm afraid I can't be as gracious as Jennifer. My image was a little harsher. I really was expecting someone who would be just very coldhearted and not be listening to me and basically her own agenda and just be doing this, I guess, because it might look good.

Zwerdling: So, Representative Dunn, what have you and Pamela done together?

Jennifer: What have the Dunns done? Well, we've talked on the phone and we've gone to Bree's school.

Pamela: My daughter goes to an elementary school. She was in kindergarten.

Zwerdling: Was there a moment that you can remember when you really felt you got over what must have been sort of awkward niceties, and really started to click and somehow communicate?

Jennifer: I liked hearing about Pamela's daughter, Bree, because I have kids, too. It's interesting that we have a lot in common. I never went the welfare route, but still, when you have been a single mother on your own, there is just very tough stuff you go through.

Zwerdling: So talking about your children together, that sort of helped you bond?

Jennifer: Well, I think women can do that a little more easily.

Pamela: I agree. I think that in some cases women can more easily bond over things like family and children.

Zwerdling: Let me ask about a couple of the ways, perhaps, you haven't bonded. Pamela, you told my colleague the other day that you and Jennifer still have had some disagreements, big disagreements about specific issues on welfare reform. Jennifer Dunn has been supporting strict provisions that would cut people off welfare if they don't get a job after a certain amount of time. Do you think she's been way too tough on them?

Pamela: Well, yes I do. I mean, it's wonderful to say, "OK, we're giving you two years' time and in that amount of time you should be able to find a job." But we know jobs that pay a wage that will support a family are becoming more and more scarce. Everyone says, "Go get a job." But nobody's doing anything to say, "Here's jobs that you can live on and support your family on."

Jennifer: I understand what Pamela's saying. And I think that if things went on the way they are going now, that would be a major, major problem. What we want to do is create incentives for them to be able to get out and get jobs, the way Pamela's done, and eventually get off that system. I think Pamela would tell you that she doesn't want to be on welfare. She's a very bright woman and she's in the working market now. But she also needs some help. For example, she needs some help with child care on occasion.

Zwerdling: But has there been any way in which Pamela has convinced you, even if in a small way, to soften your stands on welfare reform? Has she persuaded you?

Jennifer: Yes, she has done that on EITCs, the Earned Income Tax Credit through which you get a credit from the government, depending on your income level. I had looked at that program earlier, and I had thought, We need to cut that out. But when Pamela started explaining to me that the thirty dollars or so she gets every month from this helps her pay her transportation costs, I started homing in on that and we literally put that program back in the budget, made it specific to people like Pamela, who have one or more children. That program is going to increase and not be done away with. So I think that's really important.

Zwerdling: So you're not just being gracious to Pamela on this? She really helped changed your mind?

Jennifer: Gracious isn't part of this whole thing. When you're working with two bright people who have a different type of experience, but share some experience, when you start listening to each other, you can always come up with some changed attitudes.

Zwerdling: Pamela, on the other hand, you sent us a note the other day, saying that despite your disagreements with Representative Dunn, that you have found her to be "one of the most gracious people I have ever met."

Pamela: This is true.

Zwerdling: How exactly?

Pamela: Well, I think just from listening to her and I talk, you can see for yourself that Jennifer is a very gracious person, that she listens when you talk to her and is just, you know, very easy to talk to and makes you feel like you're on her level.

Zwerdling: So what do you think you have gotten out of this program?

Pamela: For me, I think that we have been listening too much to the rhetoric that pits us against them and if people who live in my situation lose that fear of their own legislators and understand that those people are supposed to be there to represent them, and that while you may differ on opinion, you have a right to your opinion and you can express that opinion to your representative, I think we could go a whole lot further than we have. And I think that's what Walk a Mile has actually done on a very small basis.

I n a small park in Mott Haven, a section of the South Bronx where drug dealers once staked out their territories, the writer JONATHAN KOZOL talked about children raised in urban poverty, the children who are the subject of his book, *Amazing Grace: The Lives of Children and the Conscience of a Nation.* Mott Haven is in the poorest congressional district in the nation; its impoverished population of forty-eight thousand is roughly one-third African American, two-thirds Hispanic. Among its afflictions are a thriving traffic in heroin and its associated violence, as well as high rates of HIV infection and childhood asthma. Kozol, a writer long devoted to the problems of childhood, poverty, and racism discussed this neighborhood with Noah Adams. The park has been cleaned up and has new benches and grassy areas. October 22, 1995

Kozol: The city calls this a defensible park. The press will say, "Oh, well, that's very nice in the South Bronx. Now look. It's very pretty. They have a defensible park." I call it the vision of the perfectible ghetto, as though some day we will have it under control. Well, maybe we will someday, but to me that isn't the dream that Dr. King died for.

Adams: At a distance from the South Bronx, it would be easy to ask the question or to make the observation that the people who live here are doing what they want to do, specifically drugs.

Kozol: If you take away everything that makes life endurable, if you take away the jobs that once gave dignity to poor men of limited education, if you take away physical cleanliness, if you take away beauty, if you take away flowers and replace it by crumbling cement, if you take away the sense of being loved or valued by your society and you lock people into a place of pain, it's inevitable that many people are going to look for ways to medicate their pain. And that is the way I've often heard people here describe the use of drugs. If I had to live here for two years, I'm sure I would either be using drugs or alcohol to try to kill myself.

Adams: You talked with a minister about the fourth verse of "Amazing Grace," one that you weren't familiar with.

Kozol: The fourth verse of "Amazing Grace" ends with the words "And grace will lead us home," and I find an awful lot of people I meet here who sing that song in church have a longing for the afterlife, for heaven, for being united with relatives they've lost. Some of the people here I know tell me that when they pray, they feel they're talking to their brothers and mothers and children who have died. When the pain of life becomes unbearable, it's inevitable that people are going to turn their thoughts toward afterlife. That's why I found myself, for the first time, being drawn back to thinking of theology during these two years. I hadn't thought about heaven since I was a child. Suddenly, since I've been writing and walking the streets here in the South Bronx, I find myself thinking of heaven all the time, especially when children speak of heaven. I really want to believe there is a heaven and that every one of these children will end up there. It just seems unbearable not to believe there is a heaven. It seems unbearable to think that there won't be something else more wonderful for them after they die because the shriveled lives we give them here just aren't enough to justify existence. There's just not enough, not in America, not in a country like this. That's what's so upsetting because there's so much that's beautiful in our country. It seems like a tragedy that we won't share it.

By the end of 1995, the race for the Republican presidential nomination was under way with polls showing President Clinton narrowly favored for re-election, and the Republican Congress far less popular than it had been at the start of the year. Linda Wertheimer went to Michigan, one of the states that was seen as a likely political battleground in 1996. She interviewed several people who work at American Axle and Manufacturing, a company with five assembly plants and a forge plant in Hamtramck, on the edge of Detroit. The people she interviewed, about national politics, the state's popular Republican governor, John Engler, and welfare reform, ranged from assembly-line workers to the president and CEO. December 13, 1995

John Bilotti, Manager, Forge Plant: I don't know if you would call it the Republican philosophy versus the Democratic philosophy, but do the things that will help people to help themselves and then the country is going to prosper from that. And I think that's behind a lot of what Governor Engler is trying to do. Personally, I get very frustrated with politics. I think they focus too much on people and personalities and not on problems and issues. It just seems like they can never bring an issue to closure and turn it into an action.

Ray Pagliese, Metallurgical Manager: Some of the things that I saw that went through when the government shut down for days because they're in a bickering match, holding a lot of people's lives at stake just because you don't feel you were treated right, I don't think that's the right way to run the government. They didn't take into mind what was best for the people. They did what they felt was best for them.

Jerry Glenn, Purchasing Manager: It seems like the issues are the same from one administration to another, you know, then it turns around and people who were supporting a similar type of activity months before will do everything they can to roadblock it and — even though everyone agrees in principle that's the right thing to do. All we do is seem to argue and carry on like kids in the back-yard, that nothing gets accomplished. The game's over and every-one goes home.

Karen Owen, Quality Control Manager: To be honest, Clinton is looking better and better, and I'm a Republican. The last election I was shocked how the Republican party swayed, and I think that they lost a lot of voters and I think female voters. They're extremist right now.

Willy James Reese, Press Operator: Some [welfare recipients] maybe go to work. Some of them can't work, you know. But when they just have babies to stay on welfare, that's when it should be cut off.

Theresa Barber, Assembler: If you're working in an assembly line, and you're sweating your butt off and you're out here doing it every day, you start getting this attitude, Well, wait, you know, I earn this money. Why do I have to give it to all these people just because I made it? If I earned it, it should be mine.

Howard Tubb, Union Trainer: The economy in this country is coming almost to the point where you have the rich and you have the poor, and the middle class is getting eliminated. You're either — you're going back or you're moving ahead.

Frank Franklin, Job Setter: I'm probably one of the youngest peo-ple in here. I just turned twenty-one, so this is probably my first major job. And the money's great. I've been working here for about a year and two months. Since then, I've bought a new car, I've moved out, you know, I'm starting to save for a house.

Wertheimer: You moved out of your parents' house?

Franklin: Yeah. I mean, just the possibilities are infinite.

Wertheimer: Tom Jones, what about you? You've been through a few of the swings that the auto industry has taken here in Detroit.

Tom Jones, Union Representative: Well, the opportunity now is great; business is good. But that don't mean it's going to be good this time next year. The young people have to understand that if you don't set something aside now while you're working good, that when bad times come upon you, sometimes some people don't know how to cope with that.

Wertheimer: You remember what John Kennedy said about the rising tide lifts all the boats? Good economic times are good for everybody. Do you think that's still true? The tide is certainly rising in Detroit. Is it good for everybody?

Julius Osteen, Machinery Repairs: I would say it's about fifty-fifty. Seems like to me those who have it continue to have it, and those that don't, don't have it.

Wertheimer: Yvette Rhodes, you're nodding.

Yvette Rhodes, Customer Service: I'm in agreement. There's always people who just seem to kind of be kind of lost in the shuffle regardless of what the economic climate is. You'll see people that are making progress in their lives and things are changing for them and things are getting better. But there's a core of people that live here in this city that things just don't change for them.

Wertheimer: We're in the middle of what people are talking about as a revolution. You know, the Republicans in Congress are talking about how we're having a revolution. How's it going over?

Rhodes: I think that there's a tendency not only by Newt Gingrich, but people that go to Washington, they kind of lose sight of the people that they represent. What they're talking about accomplishing are things that are important to all of us. We all want the country to be economically sound and we know that a balanced budget will contribute to that. But they're also talking about taking people off of Medicare and everything and making it harder for them to be able to get medical care and making welfare reform, and it seems as though they don't have a concern for people who have a genuine need to be on welfare.

Wertheimer: Welfare reform is a big issue. What do you guys think about welfare?

Daniel Marcey, Machinist: Well, I think that there are people out there that really do need it. When I was a kid growing up, my mother was raising four kids on her own and we were on welfare. And my mother didn't just sit back and just raise the kids and let welfare happen. She went out and she tried to work. She got part-time work, and she did a real good job. But I'd made up my mind when I was a teenager that this was not the lifestyle I was going after. I was going to put my nose to the grindstone and I was going to work and make sure that my family did better than I did.

Wertheimer: What about welfare reform?

Sam Sanders, Human Resources Representative: I see a lot of young mothers, and they really want to work. They want jobs. They feel like they're doing what their mother did or their grandmother did. Same thing. They're like in a vicious cycle, and they want out.

Wertheimer: What do you think about the governor? The governor is setting out to reform welfare in the state of Michigan at the same time that the whole national program is working out. The governor has got his own revolution going, and by all accounts it's fairly popular. He was re-elected. What do you think about him, about the governor? He's a popular guy.

Jones: I think people in the state of Michigan, all the rich, when if the poor folks start coming up to their houses, knocking on the doors and telling what they got, then that's not going to go over too good with the voters. We got to solve the problem. This to me is a quick fix, and it's not going to go over.

Wertheimer: It's a whole year away, of course, but it looks like what we're headed for is President Clinton running for re-election against Senator Bob Dole of Kansas. What do you think about your choices, about the quality of your choices? Do you like having these two to choose among?

Osteen: Yeah, I do. Clinton.

Wertheimer: So it's easy for you?

Osteen: Yes.

Wertheimer: Sam?

Sanders: I would — I would say Clinton's a pretty good choice, you know? I'm the type of person, you know, I know that it takes more than four years to complete what he wants to do. And I will make my main choice after the next four years.

Wertheimer: What about the notion of having somebody else out there? For a while it looked like we might have Colin Powell, and then it looked like we might have Ross Perot. I mean, is there anybody out there that you look at, and you say, "Now, there, you know. If that person were to get into politics I could get excited"?

Sanders: Well, Colin Powell, of course, was one because he was a fresh face and he seemed to be a real honorable man. And he seemed to have the American people at heart rather than maybe special interest groups. I guess he had to back out because he wasn't willing to go into all the dirt slinging and mudslinging that would have to be involved in that. But I thought he would be a good choice for a president. He would've had my vote for sure.

Wertheimer: If he ran as a Republican?

Sanders: Even as a Republican, he would have had my vote because he represented something kind of pure.

Wertheimer: Do you feel like that's missing in politics generally?

Sanders: Oh, definitely.

Wertheimer: I see a lot of nods. What about you, Dan?

Marcey: I think Colin Powell definitely seems like a much more honest person than all the politicians we have out there. On the other hand, I think Clinton is doing well. I think they should leave his personal life out of it, and let's deal with politics up front and stop all the mudslinging and backstabbing, and let's hear what you've got to say.

Although writers campaign on behalf of a dizzying variety of causes, the subject of DAVID MASUMOTO's book was unusual. *Epitaph for a Peach* was the farmer-writer's tribute to the Suncrest, a type of the fruit so juicy and fragile that supermarkets rejected it, reasoning that its very delicacy promises a short shelf life. Masumuto, ever the missionary for his favorite peach, extolled its virtues in a talk with Daniel Zwerdling. May 13, 1995

Masumoto: The Suncrest is a wonderful-tasting peach. It's the type of peach that your fingers instinctively search for the gushy side because you want to find that rich side to sink your teeth into. When you bite into it, the juices dribble down your chin and the nectar explodes in your mouth and you sense the fragrance of the peach because it smells like a peach, a real rich peach that many people remember from their childhood. The color of the peach is this kind of golden amber harvest color. It's not a lipstick red color like many of the other peaches. And that's why it always has a problem in the marketplace because so many people tend to buy with their eyes as opposed to thinking about the flavor of the peach.

Zwerdling: Now, your father, as I understand it, planted these trees twenty or thirty years ago?

Masumoto: About thirty years ago, and I remember when he planted them because he was very proud of this orchard and he, just as I do, kept his fingers crossed that the harvest would be good because this was going to pay for our college education.

Zwerdling: So at the time when he planted them, these were considered —

Masumoto: Oh, they were state of the art at the time.

Zwerdling: When did you first start hearing people in the marketplace saying, "Suncrest, we don't want to carry these"?

Masumoto: About fifteen years ago, there was the first signs when the movement, as they call it, in the industry was slow for Suncrest because a new variety was introduced. Then about ten years ago, more new varieties were introduced, and a lot of these brokers would say, "Do you really want to keep these Suncrests?" and they outright recommended I yank them out. Then, a few years ago, was the final straw. I could not sell these peaches, and I had to basically dump them. A twenty-three-pound box was selling for a dollar. That's when I actually began writing about it.

Zwerdling: And the writing about it was your catharsis I guess.

Masumoto: Exactly. At least I could express my frustrations and anger at the same time and also re-examine why am I farming and what are the important things? Some of the important things, I wanted to believe in and they were things such as taste and value and character in produce.

Zwerdling: Over the years, as I understand it, you have ripped out a bunch of the Suncrest trees that your father planted. In fact, you've ripped out most of them.

Masumoto: There was originally about fifteen acres that I had and we're down to four acres. I wanted to save this last four-acre block because it was just something that was just very important to me and maybe the rest of the farm could be trying to balance this economic issue more. But these four acres, they're special for me. I'm going to try to see how I can make them work.

Zwerdling: But now, let's talk about the rest of the farm. Have you planted this sort of hard, tasteless, shiny red peach that the supermarkets want these days?

Masumoto: Yes, pretty much on the rest of the farm, and also I have a lot of grapes too that I make into raisins.

Zwerdling: And these other peaches, they're selling well?

Masumoto: They're selling fine.

Zwerdling: On those acres where you're raising those supermarket peaches, which have almost no flavor these days, I'm wondering if you feel at all like a sellout? I mean, you're a writer, and I take it that you would not write something that you think is a lousy read. Right?

Masumoto: Mm-hmm.

Zwerdling: So how do you feel about selling peaches that you think taste lousy?

Masumoto: Farming is an art of compromises. You can never control everything. I can't control the marketplace. But I can contribute the best I can.

Zwerdling: So you're compromising on most of the farm in order to support that last four acres of, well, peach purity.

Masumoto: Or idealism. You might call it that. I mean, maybe one way of looking at it is we're all idealistic in many ways. In some issues, we make more of a stand. In others, we realize that life is an art of compromise.

Zwerdling: The title of your latest book is *Epitaph for a Peach*, a somber title, but in truth you are not ready to write the epitaph yet.

Masumoto: No. At many times it has crossed my mind because I was going to get rid of them. A bulldozer came for my neighbor, who had Suncrest peaches too. The bulldozer stopped, and said, "Which field do you want me to do?" I pointed to my neighbor, and said, "Can you give me a few more hours to think about this?" He yanked out my neighbor's field, came over to mine. I said, "Why don't you let us think about it for a few more months. Maybe I'll give you a call in a few months." And then he left. And then I thought about it and decided to keep these peaches.

ENDERS

D r. NANCY KALISH calculates that about ten percent of the population experiences rekindled love, falling for someone they have not seen for at least five years. A psychology professor at California State University at Sacramento, Dr. Kalish has made a study of the phenomenon, directing the Lost Love Project. Her discussion with Alex Chadwick was both academic and confessional. May 12, 1995

Chadwick: Surprisingly few of the rekindled love stories start at old class reunions.

Kalish: In my sample, only two percent of the people connected like that worldwide.

Chadwick: Really?

Kalish: Yes. They're not passive people. They don't wait for their reunion. If they want to see somebody, they call the person's relative who often still lives in the town, and they pick up the phone or they write a letter and they reconnect.

Chadwick: And why is it, do you think, people go back to look for that first love?

Kalish: Well, it's possible that that person, being the first, serves as a model for all the others. You certainly don't have your cynicism yet from dating many people. I think even more than that, there is a similarity to ourselves in the people that we date when we're younger. If we're seventeen or younger, the person is probably going to our school, that's how we met them, in high school, maybe grammar school in some cases, and they know each other's family, the parents, the siblings. They're part of the community together, and that's a very strong basis for a relationship. And the number-one reason for the initial breakup is parents disapproved.

Chadwick: I'm sorry? The reason that people broke up was their parents disapproved?

Kalish: Yes. These were good kids. If their parents didn't like the person, it broke 'em up.

Chadwick: And then years later they will go back to that person?

Kalish: Yes.

Chadwick: What, after mom and dad are gone?

Kalish: Sometimes, or at least they don't care anymore.

Chadwick: There is a widely held view that first love is apt to be nothing more than a foolish infatuation. You get over it and you're the better for getting over it and going on to maturity and what you should be doing.

Kalish: Right. That's the parents' viewpoint: it's just puppy love and another one comes along every ten minutes. That is not true. When we are young we think we have a lot of partners out there waiting for us, but as we get older we realize that there are just a small number, perhaps, that we can connect with.

Chadwick: Dr. Kalish, did this study develop out of any kind of personal experience?

Kalish: Yes, it did.

Chadwick: What happened?

Kalish: A lot of people in my life I reconnected with, and the only person that I hadn't really reconnected with or found out anything about was my college boyfriend from when I was twenty. We had dated for a year, gotten engaged, and three days later he backed out. There was some parental disapproval because we were young. So twenty-five years later, I wrote a letter, which the alumni association forwarded, and I got a letter back, "Please call." So I did, and he had just separated from his wife, and we started a long-distance commute from New York to Sacramento and got engaged again in a fairy-tale romance with stays at the Essex House and rides through Central Park in the carriage.

Chadwick: Oh, Dr. Kalish, I hear violins.

Kalish: Oh, yes, there were violins, absolutely, and a gorgeous ring and the whole thing, and three weeks later he backed out again. So I went back to Sacramento heartbroken and was grieving until he called six weeks later. So I packed up and moved to New York for my sabbatical semester. Fortunately I didn't quit my job. I stayed with him for seventeen days, and then he left me stranded in a blizzard with my daughter while he went off to Florida.

Chadwick: Dr. Kalish?

Kalish: Yes?

Chadwick: Are you getting the message on this guy?

Kalish: Absolutely. But I wanted to see what happened to other people. I mean, this was the best of times and the worst of times. It's not like we didn't work. He didn't work. I don't know.

In our further explorations of cyberspace, the journalist DANELLE MORTON of Los Angeles told Daniel Zwerdling how she and her former husband negotiated their own divorce by computer electronic mail, E-mail. Morton says when they first agreed to get a divorce, she consulted a lawyer who suggested smearing her husband to squeeze more money out of him. With hopes of preserving "the thimbleful of goodwill" they still enjoyed, they attempted negotiating directly, by telephone. Talking to her husband, Morton said, proved a disaster. February 4, 1995

Morton: I would start getting emotional and then we would get insulting and then I would start crying and it would end up being humiliating and put me in the incredible position of calling him a few days later to open up the discussion again because I couldn't remember what we had decided. I was so focused on the emotional content of what was going on, it was really hard for me to get the factual part right.

Zwerdling: I've read that your husband, in fact, is a professional negotiator, right?

Morton: He is a professional negotiator, and those skills that make him a good negotiator made me feel like he was calculating. He was disciplined. He was logical. He was nonemotional.

Zwerdling: I take it that the tone of voice, something about your husband's voice, or former husband's voice now, really, you know, would push your buttons, drive you nuts.

Morton: I don't think I'm unique in that.

Zwerdling: Even the way you just sighed to me, I could interpret, if I were very insecure, that you were thinking, What a silly question this guy just asked.

Morton: Exactly.

Zwerdling: So you can see what happens at a divorce negotiation.

Morton: Right, when you have real stuff on the table to talk about. So in February of last year we discovered that we both had E-mail, and I thought, This is perfect. You send the message and it gets there within an hour, and then he can read it, respond to it, and come back to me. So the back-and-forth of negotiations can take place, but then, the beauty of it was that writing is easy for me and it allows me a chance to go over the document a few times and cut out all the completely gratuitous insults, so the ones that were really meant to sting will stand out. I could comb the tone carefully and make sure that it hit exactly where I wanted to while still making it an honest reflection of how I felt. So that worked really well. And I am living proof that if love can bloom over E-mail, it can also die over E-mail because it allowed us to maintain the kind of tone that allowed for negotiations but didn't allow for a lot of hysteria. And then you also have a written record of your exchanges, which you'd never have in voice. So if things started to get too heated, then you could go back over the record and find out what you had exactly said. One time I was getting a little testy with him and he wrote me a note that said I had said we should maintain a respectful tone with one another. I had called his E-mail message gibberish and accused him of being a liar. When I received this message, I said, "Did I actually call him a liar? Did I say that he had written gibberish?" As I was receiving the message, I couldn't remember that heated exchange. So I went back over the record, which was a lovely thing to do, and being able to have that record really meant that I could say, "I'm sorry. I am really deeply sorry. And I won't do it again."

Zwerdling: You were saying that when you actually tried to talk with your husband, almost everything he would say and the way he would change his tone of voice would drive you crazy. I'm wondering if, now that you negotiated by E-mail, whether you found yourself surprisingly feeling a little bit tender toward him sometimes?

Morton: Well, we had a lovely exchange recently because we still communicate on E-mail, although we're actually progressing from that to the point where we can speak voice to voice, where I sent him a message. He sent me a message that said he appreciated what a good job I was doing raising our two children by myself. I sent him another message back that didn't say "It's all your fault" or anything like that, "Why aren't you here?" But it said, "I know how hard it must be to communicate with the kids and maintain a relationship just on the telephone." Then he sent me another mes-

The police in Santa Cruz, California, cracked down on one CORY McDONALD, a.k.a. Mister Twister, professional clown. Twister, twenty-six, plays parties and corporate functions to earn his nut, and just to stay sharp, he works days clowning curbside at the main downtown shopping mall. His problem was that in addition to making small change doing extra work, he also dispensed it, in parking meters. It is against local law to place a dime in a meter where someone else is parked, sparing him the risk of parking tickets. That was Mr. Twister's offense. October 10, 1995

McDonald: It's not so much paying for their parking as trying to be a good Samaritan for quite a number of years. People would park behind me and then ask me after the parking attendant would go by and give them a ticket, "Why didn't you do that for me?" Well, when I started doing that for them, people would get out of their cars and hand me money and say thank you, or they would give me money back from the time that I saved them a few days ago. And it just kind of kept going on from there.

Siegel: How big a coin would you typically put in the meter in that case?

McDonald: Usually anything from a nickel to a quarter, and when people park there and I see the guys coming, I'll try to give them an extra five minutes so hopefully he can get back before she comes back again, which is a lot quicker than you'd think.

Siegel: Now, this is actually against the law in Santa Cruz. You may not put that nickel in the meter if it's not your car?

McDonald: Yes.

Siegel: And you've been waging a campaign of civil disobedience against this law?

McDonald: Yes, you see, most of the time people hand me a dollar or so for, say, making them a balloon. In return I take some of the change and give back the goodwill to the city. That's also creating revenue for the city itself by putting the coins in the meters, which is the legal form of creating revenue, not by giving out parking tickets and circling the place like a shark looking for every single one that pops or goes up.

Siegel: Now, when you started doing this, playing the good Samaritan, putting coins in other people's parking meters —

McDonald: I did it one hundred percent anonymously until I was actually threatened with a citation for it.

Siegel: But you say "anonymously." You were appearing as Cory McDonald, or as Mr. Twister?

McDonald: Just as a clown.

Siegel: Just as a clown. You were anonymous, but, shall we say, not inconspicuous.

McDonald: Not inconspicuous but pretty much just anonymous.

Siegel: Now, is it true, though, that more recently you were doing this not in your clown suit, but wearing street clothes?

McDonald: Wearing street clothes because I was accused of hiding behind the clown suit to draw publicity for my clown persona. So I decided to get out the suit and go do it. I had over seventy-five dollars' worth of coins donated to me the first day after a newspaper story ran, and then the next day I ended up with thirty-five dollars, and ever since then people have been walking up and down the street and just handing me money.

Siegel: Now that you have actually been cited, first warned and then given a citation for violating this law that you can't put coins in someone else's parking meter, what are you going to do? Are you going to continue?

McDonald: Being kind to other people is a basic professional trademark for a clown. I will still help out my fellow man by putting coins in his meter to keep them in these hard times that I don't think anybody can afford twelve dollars for a parking meter for coming downtown and shopping and doing business in our area. Now, these are not only their customers, but mine as well.

A comparative study of helpfulness in thirty-six American cities employed one conventional criterion, the level of local contributions to the United Way, and five unconventional tests, such as the Blind Pedestrian Experiment. A researcher would pretend to be blind: wear dark glasses, walk with a white cane up to a traffic light, and wait for help crossing the street. In another, a researcher would approach the locals to get change for a quarter. The study was conducted by Professor ROBERT LEVINE, chairman of the Psychology Department at California State University, Fresno, and a native of Brooklyn, New York, where he says one learned early in life that a prudent response to strangers was to avoid them, to step around them, to ignore them. One of Professor Levine's tests of helpfulness was the Lost Letter Experiment. January 30, 1995

Levine: What we would do is leave an envelope addressed to myself with a stamp on it. We would put them on cars, actually, with a note on top of the envelope that would say, "Excuse me, we found this letter next to your car." We would simply count the percentage of the letters that came back to my house here in Fresno.

Siegel: Now, of the thirty-six cities where you conducted the experiments, tell us how your native New York fared.

Levine: Well, my native New York, to nobody's surprise, ended up last in helping behavior. Actually, depending on how we calculated the data as to how much weight we gave to the type of helping, occasionally it would flip-flop with its neighbor Patterson, New Jersey, but for the most part New York City was the least helpful.

Siegel: Tell us about the cities that scored the highest, where you found people were most helpful.

Levine: Rochester, New York, was the one that ended up scoring the most helpful on the overall index when we put all six of the measures together. Other cities that came out very high, which didn't seem to surprise anybody, were the Tennessee cities of Nashville, Memphis, Chattanooga, and Knoxville.

Siegel: You noted that merely helping a person in one of these experiments might not be the most thorough description of what they did because, for example, in sending the lost letter there were ways of being helpful in a civil manner and helpful in an uncivil manner.

Levine: The most curious was a letter back from New York City, where the whole side was torn open and on top of that written in Spanish, actually, was what my Hispanic colleagues tell me was really an awful insult, calling me an irresponsible something and calling me a whole lot of other things. To think about this person who is somehow still compelled to help, a person walking to the mailbox, and what was going through this person's mind. He despised me at that time, but was still compelled to help. You know, if I can make another comment about the distinction between civility and helping, we filmed some of those episodes in Rochester and in New York City, and what we saw was quite often when people helped in Rochester it was with a smile. It was with a have-a-nice-day kind of an attitude. With, for example, the blind person crossing the street, quite often the pedestrian standing next to that person would walk up, and say, "Excuse me, can I help you?" and then ask some questions along the way. "Can I be of further help?" And they almost were expecting or hoping for a thank-you. It almost made their day. It was a wonderful experience for them. What we saw among the helpers in New York when we watched them is typically they wouldn't identify themselves until the light turned green and then they would walk a few steps ahead and call back to the person that the light is green. So they would help, that would count for helping, but it was almost, if I can infer what they may have been thinking about, as if they were giving people the message, "Hey, I'll help you. I don't like this situation. I'm a little afraid here. I'm going to help you across the street, but this is as far as our relationship goes."

In 1992, *Weekend Edition Sunday* went to the Cathedral of Saint John the Divine in New York City to interview the head organist, DOROTHY PAPADAKOS. That was at the beginning of a four-year project to restore the cathedral's magnificent organ, a project that did not go according to plan. Three years later, Liane Hansen checked back with the young, energetic organist who in the first interview, on June 28, 1992, had shown her the cockpit, where she plays the keys, pumps the pedals, and pulls out the stops on the organ, which has two nicknames.

Papadakos: One is "The Beast" and the other one is "Scarlet."

Hansen: Why?

Papadakos: Well, right now the organ is eighty-two years old and it's really misbehaving, and "Miss Scarlet" is just very unpredictable.

Hansen: She's getting old.

Papadakos: She's getting very old. So we're going to give her a face-lift, a few nips and tucks, and it's going to take about four years to do it. But we're going to restore her to her former glory.

Hansen: Tell us about her former glory. What is she?

Papadakos: This organ is the greatest American classic organ in the United States. It's the finest of its style. It was Aeolian-Skinner's greatest opus, and it's an orchestral organ. It's a romantic organ. It has 118 stops. Those are all the different sounds I can make. And 143 ranks, 8,035 pipes. So it's not the largest organ, by any means. It's only the fifth largest here in town, but it's the best because of the perfection of the sounds. Also, the cathedral has an acoustic environment of eight full seconds. So you release a chord and you hear it linger and diminish for eight seconds, and that's great.

Hansen: How difficult is that for you, though?

Papadakos: You have to get used to it. The state trumpets are two football fields away from me.

Hansen: Tell us what those are.

Papadakos: The state trumpets are one of the loudest stops in the world, and they're mounted on the back wall just underneath the rose window, and they're made out of silver and tin, and they take a full second for me to hear the sound because it has to travel six hundred feet up the nave. They're extraordinary. You have to pull out two stops to make them work, to be really sure you want them on because they're so loud. They're under fifty inches of wind pressure, which is an enormous amount of wind. Isn't that wild?

Then, in September 1995, Dorothy Papadakos called back to say the organ's condition was critical.

Papadakos: In the beginning of the summer, the organ was actually in better shape than when we did the story with you because we had done a lot of restoration work. The state trumpets were back. And what we were about to embark on was repairing the wind reservoirs, which are really the lungs of the organ. They were leaking all over the place so we had set aside a couple of them to be restored over the summer. Then, in July, we had this horrible, horrible heat wave that hit the whole East Coast, and it hit 102 degrees for a couple of days in Manhattan, and my organ chambers on the north and south sides both heated up to 97 degrees. It got very steamy up there. One day, I had to turn on the organ for a state funeral. We had an African president who died, and we had this funeral. I turned on the organ, and we heard this huge boom. I thought, Oh, my God. Now what? It sounded like there was a lot of air flying around up there. So my curator went up and he came back down, and he said, "Well, we lost the choir reservoir, but I think you can do the service," you know? So I played for two hours on the stuff going on up there, and we went up into the north case after the service only to find that a whole bunch of the reservoirs had blown themselves apart, and you couldn't even put your hand to touch the wind lines because they were so hot because the motor was overheating, trying to compensate for all the lost air. So we had to shut the thing down, and I lost all the high-pressure reservoirs. I lost all the loud stuff on the organ, basically — the bombarde, the tuba, a whole bunch of the pedals, and the entire choir division.

Hansen: This sounds like an Arnold Schwarzenegger movie.
Papadakos: Yes.

Hansen: You get up to the bench, you turn the key, and the car blew up.

Papadakos: "*Hasta la vista,* baby." I mean, it was terrible. I couldn't believe it. I mean, literally, Liane, you know, it was so hot up there that the wood of the reservoirs expanded and all this eighty-five-year-old leather and glue cracked and dried and just literally when the air shot into the reservoirs, it just sheared the leather off the sides. I mean, it literally just tore itself apart. It's unbelievable.

Hansen: You're taking this very well, or not?

Papadakos: I left town. I'm on the beach. I can't deal with it. I can't. The cathedral sent out an emergency appeal to all my organ donors. You know, Liane, the organ donors have been incredible. I have close to eight hundred people who've given about 150,000 dollars now in the past two years. And it's just incredible. So we wrote to all of them. So the money's starting to pour in. It is reparable, that's the good news. I mean, it is fixable. It's a 6.5-million-dollar organ. You know, it's a treasure; it's a masterpiece. So it is fixable. It's just a question of getting the funds to do it so that we can hire the manpower to get these things back in action.

Affter earning a place in the *Guinness Book of Records,* JOEY DUHAMEL told Noah Adams about his accomplishment. Neither his feat nor giving the interview was easy. Duhamel calls square dances in Louisiana, and one September weekend at a dance in West Monroe, he called and sang and yodeled for thirty straight hours with five-minute breaks every hour, surpassing the previous endurance record by four hours. He was still recovering when he spoke by telephone with Adams. September 25, 1995

Duhamel: I'm still having a little problem with my voice. But other than that, it's fine. I caught up on my sleep, I think. So I'm OK. It didn't really affect me other than I had a sore throat after I got through.

Adams: When did it end for you?

Duhamel: We started at 8:01 Friday night, and I officially ended at 2:02 Sunday morning.

Adams: Sunday morning?

Duhamel: Right.

Adams: How did you feel then?

Duhamel: Good, except for the throat and my tongue. My tongue had moved so much it was even hurting. See, I yodel. I'm a yodeler. And I do a lot of yodeling with my square-dance calling, and I lost my yodel after the first ten hours. I just couldn't. I tied the record at 10:03. The old record was twenty-six hours and two minutes. It was set by a guy in England. This was a Guinness record. We had originally scheduled to go thirty hours, which would have been 2:01 Sunday morning, and by 10:15 I was ready to quit.

Adams: I would bet.

Duhamel: I had broken the record, and my dancers urged me to go on. So I did. And I made it. I quit doing my singing. Square dancing has got a lot of singing in it, and I quit doing the singing. I just did the calls and the songs and the heck with the rest of it.

Adams: What sort of response was there? When you finally did sit down, what was it like?

Duhamel: The biggest thing was when I tied the record. I was looking at my watch when I did it, and as I was calling I threw it in there. I said, "We just tied the record." Then at 10:04, I said, "You know, I broke the record." And they just shouted and hollered. Then when I finished that song, it was time for me to take my five-minute break. And I had a lot of people come up on the stage and hug me and shake hands and they were all real happy about it.

Adams: Did anybody suggest that you could have done some serious damage to your vocal cords by trying this?

Duhamel: Yeah. I had talked about that with people several times.

Adams: You weren't listening, though, were you?

Duhamel: No. I thought about it for a couple of years, and I talked to my club about it and they were behind me.

Adams: Mr. Duhamel, could I trouble you for just about ten seconds to hear the way you call a square dance?

Duhamel: Sure. I'll tell you what I'll do. I'll put a record on my turntable, and I'll let you listen to the music, and I'll kind of call into the phone for you. You've got to remember my voice is not up to par. "Circle to the left . . . So I sing me to sleep after the lovin' with a song I just wrote yesterday . . . Do an allemande left your corner . . . Turn the partner right . . . Allemande left . . . Weave the ring . . . You're all I wanted . . . You're all I hoped for . . . Swing and promenade . . . After the lovin', I'm still in love with you."

Adams: That's great.

Duhamel: How 'bout that?

MICK GANNON, who works for the Traffic Sign Division in Santa Cruz, California, is an amateur bass player and a collector of jazz memorabilia, particularly photographs. His missionary enthusiasm for jazz made him eager to oblige when the University of California at Santa Cruz asked to borrow some of his photographs for Black History Month. Gannon told the planners of an exhibit at the library to take their pick, "Just be careful to bring them back in good condition." They selected thirty-five photographs, many of them autographed. Then Mr. Gannon told Linda Wertheimer about his visit to see his collection. May 1, 1995

Gannon: I walked around a corner, and I saw a collage of cut-up pictures, and I thought to myself, God, those look like my pictures, but I said, No, that really couldn't be. Then I got a little closer, and I thought, I think that's what it is, and as I was standing there looking, there was this most magnificent black couple that were standing there, a large, large black gentleman, and he said, "Excuse me." He said, "Do you know who any of these people are?" So then I started naming off names like John Coltrane, Charlie Parker, Duke Ellington, Billie Holiday, Benny Webster, Coleman Hawkins, and he said, "That's really amazing." He said, "How do you know who all of these people are?" I said, "Well, you know, these are my pictures." "Well, these are beautiful pictures," he said, "but you should have a label on it somewhere so that everybody could know who they are. There's a lot of people who don't know who these people are." I said, "Well, you may not believe it, but all of these photographs were signed, and I think maybe they've folded the signatures underneath." I was hoping that they had. His wife went up and she looked real close, and said, "I hate to tell you this, but I think these photographs have been cut." That's how I found out. I actually got kind of sick and I didn't talk to anybody. I just left.

Wertheimer: You just left?

Gannon: I left, and then a number of days later, I called the individual that had been to my home, and I said, "What have you done to my pictures?" I said, "One of my favorites was Ray Brown, the great jazz bass player, because I am also a bassist." "Well," he said, "actually, don't worry about that. I can get you another copy of a picture of Ray Brown," and I realized this guy I was talking to had no soul whatsoever. I said, "Hell, I can get another picture of Ray Brown, and I can get it signed, but you're missing the whole point. How are you going to get me another picture of Charlie Parker," which is one of the most sought-after pictures.

Wertheimer: Autographed?

Gannon: Yes. It's worth about three thousand dollars minimum. I said, "Because I haven't seen Charlie in a while," and of course I was being sarcastic because he's been dead since about 1955, and Sarah Vaughan just recently died just a number of months ago. Miles Davis, of course, is dead. Billie Holiday is dead.

Wertheimer: There's nothing you can do about it.

Gannon: No. I'm speechless, I'm dumbfounded.

Wertheimer: Can you imagine any kind of restitution that would make sense to you?

Gannon: Yes. Money. I hate to say that, but that's the only thing. But I've had so many calls from people who have wanted to help. I just talked with a photographer who says that he thinks that he took maybe some of these pictures originally and he's going to do what he can to replace what I've lost.

Wertheimer: I guess it's a sort of a hard thing to do, but I wonder, when you think back over the collection that was and look at the places on the wall where they no longer hang, I wonder which of the ones you miss the most?

Gannon: The one that was given to me by Charlie Parker. I was just a kid. I think it was about 1953 that he gave it to me, and it said, "To Mick, Don't give up your day job, ha ha, Charlie Parker." So I always loved that one, and one from about 1958. I had gone to the Oakland Coliseum and there was this most magnificent black gentleman on the stage playing saxophone like I had never heard before. I was fortunate to talk with him backstage, and I told him I marveled at what he did and it was really beautiful, and he said, "Well, let me give you a picture," and he wrote on the picture something to the effect of "Keep practicing and someday you'll be up on this stage with me," and he signed it "The Hawk," Coleman Hawkins. I guess I miss them all is what it amounts to.

The folk wisdom that lightning does not strike twice in the same place would seem to offer little solace to those who have been in that place when it hit once. From the fifth annual Lightning Strike and Electric Shock Victims International Convention held in Gettysburg, Pennsylvania, HAROLD DEAL related his experience to Liane Hansen. Mr. Deal, of Greenwood, South Carolina, survived a lightning bolt in 1969. June 18, 1995

Deal: I was struck July 26. I had driven in my driveway in my truck, got out of the truck. In between the third and fourth step walking toward my house, lightning struck me in my driveway, throwing me over a six-foot redwood fence fifty feet away, up against the neighbors' house. I didn't know what had happened, but I felt like my head was back between my shoulders, being sucked down between my shoulder blades. And the inside of me, I felt as though a pincushion inside was sticking outward, and it was just like I had walked into a real soft, white cotton ball. I couldn't see anything. It wasn't blinding from brightness, but everything was just that real soft, white look.

Hansen: Have you had any lasting effects from the strike?

Deal: Yes, very much so. I never get cold since I was struck. I've got pictures showing me out in forty-four-degree-below-zero weather. That morning, the chill index at home was fifty-four below, and I had a T-shirt on and a pair of bib overalls on, working outside for approximately between five, five and a half hours, and my skin don't even turn red.

Hansen: And you don't feel a thing?

Deal: No.

Hansen: Are you insensitive to heat as well?

Deal: No. Heat bothers me. When it's eighty degrees, average people feel comfortable, and at eighty-degree weather, it feels to me like it's well over a hundred degrees.

Hansen: Oh, and no medical explanation as yet for this for you?

Deal: No. There hasn't been any at all.

Hansen: Do you worry about being hit again?

Deal: No. I just feel that night that I got out of the truck and walked, it was meant for that flash of lightning to hit that exact spot. And what it amounted to, in my mind, I was in the way of it. It's like, by trade, I'm an electrician. People thought that was an extreme oddity, an electrician struck by lightning. I like to tell them I could have been a diesel mechanic or whatever, it wouldn't have made any difference at all.

A treasure of French wine was sunk off the Atlantic coast of France at an undisclosed location in order to increase its value. The French wine producer who hid the ten thousand bottles of Pouilly Fumé under water plans to salvage the lot in 1999 and claimed that aging the wine there will give it a fuller flavor. The producer said that German buyers had already reserved six thousand bottles at a cost — thirty-three dollars a bottle — three times the normal price. HUGH JOHNSON, a wine analyst and author of *The World Atlas of Wine*, told Bob Edwards that while submerging wine may affect its value, it is unlikely to affect its taste. August 9, 1995

Johnson: I think it's going to do exactly the same as putting it in a fridge, quite honestly. The only difference is that it's in a colder place.

Edwards: So you'd expect it to taste cooler, but otherwise just the same.

Johnson: Yes. I'd expect it to mature more slowly. Now, they make a comparison with wines that used to be sent overseas in ships to mature. Well, they were in exactly opposite circumstances because they were sent through the Tropics, so they were hot and they had the constant motion of the ship, so they were given a good hot shaking. Whereas this wine is just going to be dumped on the bottom of the sea, where it will be cold and still. So it would have no relation to the old way of maturing wine at all. Quite the reverse.

Edwards: Now, there have been wines retrieved from shipwrecks.

Johnson: I've tasted some champagne that was at the bottom of the St. Lawrence River for about fifty years, and unfortunately it tasted of the bottom of the St. Lawrence River.

Edwards: So what is the philosophy or the science behind this technique?

Johnson: The science is quite simply that if you keep something very cool and very stable, maturation will just take a very long time. Slow maturation sometimes ends up with a finer drink at the end of it all. But whether that's measurably finer is hard to say, and whether it's worth two or three times as much I think is quite easy to say.

Edwards: Well, these wine producers have sold most of their ten thousand bottles, and at quite a premium.

Johnson: Yes. Quite a premium.

Edwards: So is it just a publicity stunt to get people like us talking about it?

Johnson: Deep down, really, at the bottom of the sea, it is a publicity stunt, and I'm quite surprised at the premium they charge for it, too.

For a stretch of 1995, art and life competed at mutual imitation on ABC daytime television. The News Division broadcast some live coverage of the murder trial of O. J. Simpson, preempting the soap operas, which ABC continued to produce. During breaks in the trial coverage, a service called *Soapline* would come on the air, informing viewers of what they had missed on such programs as *General Hospital:* "Lucy swore she would never, ever experiment on cute, little, fuzzy bunnies. And Sonny has a tough question to answer . . ." Linda Wertheimer asked the executive producer of *Soapline*, LINDA GOTTLIEB, about the thinking behind such a program. January 25, 1995

Gottlieb: The idea is to keep viewers loyal and to show them that we understand how they feel. The analogy that I have drawn is to say that it's like an airplane captain: when you're in turbulent air and nobody tells you what's going on, you get really annoyed. If the pilot comes on, and says, "We know you're experiencing some turbulence, here's what's going on," you understand what's going on. We're not happy to have our schedule interrupted. We're with the viewers. We want to get back on as soon as possible.

Wertheimer: Another thing I noticed was that you're in hot competition here with Peter Jennings for the time. When the trial stops, he immediately shifts into analysis and recap and so on. How do you get that time away from the head honcho here?

Gottlieb: Because it is worked out with News. Peter is on as long as Peter wants to be on for recap, but the minute he is wrapping up, if we have any time at all, like in a midbreak or station identification break, we'll come on for ten or fifteen seconds to tell people the latest update, and it really changes minute by minute.

Wertheimer: What I guess is the most amazing thing about this is the notion that the soaps roll on while no one sees them.

Gottlieb: Well, they have to because you never know when news is through. If they didn't roll on, you would have no programming.

You can't come into blank air. They say that they "roll in the mud," which means that they're rolling even though they're not shown on the air, and then whenever news is over and throws to daytime, we're ready.

Wertheimer: So you just rejoin.

Gottlieb: We rejoin. Now, in the past that just happened with a little slide saying, "Will rejoin in progress." This has been an attempt to have a human face there, filling them in and updating them on what they have missed.

Wertheimer: But just think of all of those scenes, all of that anguish that is just never going to be seen.

Gottlieb: The shows that are fully preempted will be seen the next day. *One Life to Live* yesterday was preempted for the whole network, and *All My Children* is preempted for the full network today. Those shows will just be seen a day later. The whole schedule pushes up. So you don't lose the anguish, you just see it a day later.

T here is a kind of foreign correspondent who transcends the business of reporting the potentially historic events of the capital to which he is posted, and by virtue of his insights and observations becomes an institution, an interpreter of one society for the benefit and understanding of another. T. R. REID, the *Washington Post* Tokyo bureau chief, became such an institution for listeners to *Morning Edition*. Among many other things, he told them about sumo wrestling, Japanese baseball, and a men's handbag fetish (*handu bagu*, he called it). When Reid decided to move back to Denver to write a book, Alex Chadwick called Reid on his last day on the job. A Japanese colleague at the office said that Mr. Reid was out at "a drinking occasion" and passed on the telephone number where Reid and friends were marking his farewell. August 29, 1995

Chadwick: I just want to say that around here you get more mail than Santa Claus, and our listeners are going to miss your regular reports from Japan.

Reid: You know, I really have to say there have been a lot of nice things about Japan for us. It made our whole family closer because if you're far away from home you need your family. We made a lot of wonderful friends here. I really think we just became better Americans. Alex, you remember that old bumper sticker, AMERICA, LOVE IT OR LEAVE IT?

Chadwick: Yes.

Reid: In my case I think it's AMERICA, LEAVE IT AND LOVE IT MORE because by living overseas I think all of us really got a much greater feel for the genius of our country, the way we've assembled people and races and creeds from all over the world and really made a shot at building a democratic society. I know it's not perfect, but it's so much better than what everyone else has done. So that was great. But one of the greatest things about Japan for me was the listeners of NPR. I'm telling you, Alex, your listeners are awesome people. They send me letters, they send me faxes, they send me audiotapes, they send me videotapes, books, pictures, magazines. Do you remember when we talked about how you order a pizza here and it comes with seaweed and squid on top? Remember that?

Chadwick: Yes.

Reid: So a woman in Maryland sends me some homemade peanut brittle because she feels my kids are eating too much weird food. I've had at least two dozen Americans who have just, like, dropped in to my office in Tokyo, said they heard me on the radio and wanted to come in and say hello. I mean, these are wonderful people. And then, you know, the hosts of NPR have been marvelous to me, charming, interesting, lovely to talk to. I mean Bob Edwards, but you, too, and the producers of *Morning Edition* have been great to me, but I have to say I have one major gripe about your producers.

Chadwick: Now, what's that, Tom?

Reid: Well, you know, during my time here, I have produced three books and your producers have never given me any time on your air to promote my books, and if I had the chance, you know, I would be shameless about this.

Chadwick: You would? What would you say?

Reid: Well, I would say, for example, my most recent book is the famous literary blockbuster *Ski Japan.* This is the only — the definitive — English guidebook to skiing in Japan. It's 350 pages long, and I know it's definitive because it's the only one. And you know, Alex, a newspaper here in Tokyo allowed me to review my own book.

Chadwick: Really.

Reid: My own ski book, yeah. It's the best review any of my books ever got, and I don't write the headline, but the headline of this review absolutely captured the tenor of my review. You know what it said?

Chadwick: No.

Reid: It said, "Definitive text rivals *War and Peace,*" which is fundamentally what I wrote about my own book.

Chadwick: People have gotten used to you telling stories about Japan that are memorable in a lot of ways that standard news coverage is not. That is, you find stories that are a little unusual. Why is that? Why is it that these things attract your attention?

Reid: Twenty-three years ago I made this really stupid decision to start learning Japanese. It's a very, very hard language, and I put twenty-three years into it, and, doggone it, I'm going to use it. So I watch TV, I listen to the radio, I tour around Japan visiting my friends, I read magazines like crazy, and I pick up all this stuff that, you know, you probably couldn't get if you hadn't wasted twenty-three years of your life learning this language.

Chadwick: With all the time you've spent learning Japanese and learning about Japan, why leave now? Why kind of walk away from that? All the Japanese you know isn't going to do you much good in Denver, I don't think.

Reid: We're Americans, you know? My youngest kid really had forgotten America. As I said on this show, she thought McDonald's was a Japanese restaurant, and it's time to get our kids home and get them back to the wonder of our own country, as I said. It's so great. Japan has been wonderful for us, but it's not America, so we want to get home.

Chadwick: Is there anything else you want to say, Tom?

Reid: There's one thing I need to say, Alex, but rather than do it in my kind of accented Japanese, I have recruited this group. We talked about it on this show, the best pop group in the world, Dreams Come True. This is a Japanese pop band. If their records were released in America, they'd be a huge hit, and I have managed to get them to come on this show and say my final word to the listeners of NPR.

Dreams Come True: [*in unison*] *Sayonara.*